You Only Live Once

Katie Price is one of the UK's top celebrities. She was formerly the glamour model Jordan and is now a best-selling author, successful business woman and star of her own reality TV show. Katie is a Patron of Vision Charity and currently lives in Surrey with her three children.

Praise for Katie Price

'Riveting, honest and heart-warming' *Woman*

'A revealing romp that you'll find hard to put down' *Star Magazine*

'With Jordan's honest, no nonsense attitude evident on every page, this is a truly compelling read . . . this latest look at her life makes for seriously juicy reading' *heat*

'A real page-turner' *OK!*

'Compulsive reading' *More*

'Katie is a Cinderella for modern times' *Glamour*

Katie Price

You Only Live Once

arrow books

Published by Arrow Books in 2011

2 4 6 8 10 9 7 5 3 1

This book is a work of non-fiction based on the life, experiences and
recollections of Katie Price. In some cases names of people, places, dates,
sequences or the detail of events may have been changed. The author has
stated to the publishers that, except in such minor respects not affecting the
substantial accuracy of the work, the contents of this book are true.

First published in Great Britain in 2010 by
Century
Random House, 20 Vauxhall Bridge Road,
London SW1V 2SA

www.rbooks.co.uk

Addresses for companies within The Random House Group Limited can be
found at: www.randomhouse.co.uk/offices.htm

The Random House Group Limited Reg. No. 954009

A CIP catalogue record for this book
is available from the British Library

ISBN 9780099525455

The Random House Group Limited supports The Forest Stewardship
Council (FSC), the leading international forest certification organisation.
All our titles that are printed on Greenpeace approved FSC certified paper
carry the FSC logo. Our paper procurement policy can be found at:
www.rbooks.co.uk/environment

Mixed Sources
Product group from well-managed
forests and other controlled sources
www.fsc.org Cert no. TT-COC-002139
© 1996 Forest Stewardship Council
FSC

Typeset by SX Composing DTP, Rayleigh, Essex, SS6 7XF
Printed and bound in Great Britain by
CPI Bookmarque Ltd, Croydon, CR0 4TD

I dedicate this book firstly to my ex-husband Peter Andre for helping create two of the most amazing people in my life: Junior and Princess! I also thank him for taking me on a wonderful journey of self-discovery – I've turned from the cocooned chrysalis into the butterfly that I am today! Peter, you have made me a stronger person and I hope you find the happiness you have always been searching for.

To my beloved husband Alex Reid, who has stuck by me through my torment and darkest hours and respects me for my individuality as I do his. I also thank my new family for their support and understanding.

To the most amazing three heartbeats in the world who bring me love, smiles and the inspiration to provide the best life I can for them. Harvey, Junior and Princess, you are my life.

I also dedicate this book to the most amazing family in the whole wide world: my mum, Paul, Daniel and Sophie – thank you for being there and believing in me always. Mum, I couldn't have wished for a better mum than you; you are my rock. I love you so much.

People and relationships are not always as they seem, but thankfully I now surround myself with true friends and I know what is real and what's not and you can't buy that! So I also dedicate this to my close and long-time friends Gary and Phil. We have been through so much and you really have stuck by me; you're with me until the day I die! Jane and Derek Pountney and Neil Tause, well, what can I say, you have known me since I was fifteen and are still the most supportive and loyal friends I could ever have. Melodie, you're a very loyal, hands-on friend who has been there for me any time, day or night. Clare (Atkinson), you have been there for me forever, and there are no words to describe our friendship other than real and true. Michelle Heaton, you know what I think of our friendship. We have been there for each other with our ups and downs and I trust you always. To my other friends Andrew, Polly, Lara, Emma, Nick and Royston – our friendship goes on.

Maggie Hanbury, Rebecca Farnworth and Random House, without you I would never have been able to do my books – thank you.

I'd also like to thank my amazing work team; I've found the best!

Finally, I dedicate this book to all my fans. You are the real stars for supporting me, being there and sticking up for me. Fans are like stars: you don't have to see them to know they're there – thank you!

Katie Price, August 2010

CONTENTS

CHAPTER ONE

TOO MUCH IN LOVE

'He was my life; I was so in love with him . . .'

This book isn't about me slating my ex-husband, Peter Andre. I've nothing bad to say about him; he is the father of my children and he's always going to be in my life because of that. I had the best years of my life with him when we were first together. The Pete I knew was a lovely, warm, funny, kind man who was a brilliant dad. He was my soul-mate, my lover, my best friend. In him I thought I had found the man I would spend the rest of my life with. But the fairy tale ended publicly on Monday, 11 May 2009 when he walked out on me. Though, the truth is, things between us had ended a long time before that.

And now this is my chance to set the record straight. So many hurtful lies have been written about me in the press, especially in the wake of my marriage break-up. Some people seem to think I'm a bitch, a slapper, some kind of monster. But I'm just a woman trying to get on with my life after a painful divorce and be the best mum possible to my three children. And along the way, I've been lucky enough to meet a fantastic new guy and fall in love again . . .

* * *

When I met Peter Andre on *I'm a Celebrity . . . Get Me Out of Here!* in 2004, I fell head over heels in love with him. It was absolutely love at first sight. In fact, as soon as he was voted off the show, I asked him to marry me! Impulsive, yes, but I knew he was the one, the man I had been waiting for all my life. I couldn't imagine being with any other man. I wanted him with my whole heart, body and soul. And he felt the same about me. Ours was a whirlwind, intense, all-consuming passion. We moved in together as soon as Pete flew to the UK after the show as we wanted to be with each other all the time.

Straight away Pete had to accept my son Harvey, from my relationship with the footballer Dwight Yorke, which he did completely. But our family life was always going to be different from many other people's because of Harvey's condition. Harvey was born with a rare disorder called Septo-optic Dysplasia which means he is visually impaired and his pituitary gland doesn't function. He also suffers from Diabetes Insipidus which means he can't control his water intake, and without medication would be contstantly thirsty. He is deficient in all the hormones the body needs to function healthily and has to take medication five times a day. As Harvey gets older he may have to have additional medication to help him go into puberty. He is also on the autistic spectrum.

Within a year I was pregnant with Junior, my first child with Pete. We couldn't have been happier. Not only were we living together, we were also working together as I had signed up with Pete's management company. I was worried that if I signed up with another management he and I would hardly see each other as our work commitments might clash. This way our diaries would be co-ordinated. In fact, that was to prove both a blessing and a curse. While at first it was great spending so much time together, a few years into our marriage it became much too claustrophobic. We lived in each other's pocket. We needed space from each other, all couples do; I know that now.

Also, practically from the moment Pete and I got together we began being filmed for what would become the first of our many reality TV series: *When Jordan Met Peter*. Filming for reality shows was to become a huge part of our life together. At times it was fun. But it also became a pressure, something that put a real strain on our marriage. It seemed that everything we did ended up being filmed – from our wedding, to the minutes leading up to the births of Junior and Princess. The reality shows captured the good times and the bad, and we had agreed to do them, but as the years went by, I sometimes felt as if nothing was private in our marriage, that we had nothing left for ourselves and that our lives revolved purely around making the reality show.

Looking back, I would definitely say that one of the things that contributed to our marriage breaking up was the intense pressure that filming a reality series involves. Of course, we weren't filmed all the time, but when we were it was full on and intense and took over our lives. I'm not sure if any relationship could have survived that.

And as a couple, while we were lucky enough to be so in love and to have such gorgeous children as well as enjoying wealth and success, we had more than our share of problems. After Junior was born, I suffered from crippling post-natal depression. It took me over two years to recover from it and it really tested our relationship to the limit. I was even suffering from it when we got married in September 2005, and it ruined my wedding day. I withdrew into a depression where I felt I couldn't confide in anyone, not even Pete, as I felt so ashamed. I felt I was a failure as a mother and that I had let down Junior by not bonding with him – feelings that other women who've battled post-natal depression will understand only too well, I'm sure. And because I felt so low emotionally my sex drive was zero, which put even more pressure on my marriage as I couldn't explain why I didn't want to make love and I'm sure Pete felt rejected. I was struggling to put on a brave face but inside I was a wreck. One night I felt I couldn't carry on any longer feeling so weighed down with depression. I got into my car in the middle of the night and drove away with no clear idea of where I was going. I ended up pulling into the car park of Harvey's nursery. For a few desperate, confused minutes I seriously considered driving into a brick wall; at least then I wouldn't feel like this any more, it would all be over. Somehow, by thinking of the children and of Pete, I managed to pull myself together. Back home I finally confided in Pete and my mum about how I felt. And after that I started a course of treatment: therapy and anti-depressants. It wasn't a magic cure, it took time, but eventually I did get through it.

There was also Harvey's horrific accident on New Year's Eve 2006, when he suffered a serious burn injury. We were getting ready for a party and we think that one of the guests accidentally left the stairgate open and so Harvey was able to go upstairs without anyone knowing. Usually all the doors upstairs would have been locked as well, including the door to my bathroom, but because we had guests staying for the party, some-one must have left the door unlocked because they weren't used to being as safety-conscious and Pete and I. At that time Harvey had an absolute obsession with water. Every night, just before I ran the bath for him and Junior, Harvey liked to run the cold tap and flick the water with his hands. So on New Year's Eve, once

Harvey discovered my bathroom door was unlocked, he must have gone in there intending to play with the cold water. But instead of turning the cold tap on, he turned on the hot. I can only imagine that he couldn't reach the water with his hands when he leaned over the bath and so he got into it, not realising that by now the water was boiling hot. And then as the scalding water hit his right leg he must have panicked and stood there, frozen in shock, while the water burned his leg. Somehow, in spite of the excruciating pain, he must have dragged himself out of the bathroom and on to my bed. The moment I discovered my son screaming in agony from his injury will remain with me for ever.

His burn was so severe – running from the top of his thigh all the way down his leg to the top of his foot – that the doctors would usually have treated it by giving him a skin graft. However, Harvey's existing medical condition made the whole situation even worse. He had suffered severe shock from the burn, which in turn caused him to have breathing difficulties, and it was then too risky to give him a general anaesthetic. The doctors explained that instead they were going to have to scrub his burn, to stop infection and to encourage new skin to grow, and that this would be an agonising experience for him. For the next month my poor son had to endure fifteen minutes of unbelievable pain every single day. He could only be given the morphine dose suitable for a five-year-old, as that's how old he was at the time, but because of his condition he weighed the same as a twelve-year-old, which meant the medication had little effect on him.

I remember telling Harvey that the doctors were going to help his leg get better, but I knew he didn't understand. And when the doctors began scrubbing at his leg, Harvey let out a piercing scream and continued screaming throughout the treatment. I have never heard screams like it. Harvey was struggling desperately to get away from the doctors and the pain, and it took four people to hold him down. I think I must have blanked out much of this time from my mind because it was so traumatic, but I can still remember the horror in Harvey's face as he looked at me as if to say, *Mummy, help me, please! Why are you letting them do this terrible thing to me, Mummy?* Watching Harvey endure that pain was the worst thing I have ever had to experience in my life.

Harvey was in hospital for several months and had to have a further two years of physio. Thankfully his leg is fine now but I can hardly begin to describe how devastating it was, knowing that my son was enduring so much pain and that there was nothing I could do to help him. All you want to do as a mother is to protect your children. Then, just as Harvey was recovering from his injury, Pete contracted meningitis in April 2007 and ended up in hospital while I was heavily pregnant with Princess.

When I gave birth to our daughter, Princess, in June 2007 I really hoped that the bad times were behind us.

We seemed to have everything we had ever wanted. We loved each other to bits, we had three beautiful kids, a fantastic house, work was looking good. But we hit another rocky patch just after Princess was born. I had been incredibly fearful of getting post-natal depression again; I think any woman would be. And so I had worked out with the doctors and Pete that I needed to be given plenty of space after the birth so that I could bond properly with Princess. That meant that I shouldn't have too many visitors and that we definitely shouldn't have anyone to stay at our house. Unfortunately Pete's dad became ill at this time and his parents had to come and stay with us. While naturally I was sympathetic about Pete's dad, it was a very difficult time for me because I felt so vulnerable after the birth. I was physically weak from the Caesarean, and even though there were no signs of post-natal depression this time , I was still anxious that it might return, especially if I wasn't given that precious bonding time. I felt scared and emotional and needed Pete by my side and for us to be left alone with the baby. However, it didn't turn out like that, and Pete's parents did need to come and stay with us. I know that Pete was in a very difficult position, concerned about his dad and about me, but I couldn't help feeling as if he was putting me second. He might not have meant to, but that's how I felt. It was just how he had made me feel when Junior was born.

After his parents left, when thankfully his dad was well on the road to recovery, Pete and I ended up having a terrible row – one of the worst of our marriage. But somehow we got through that and Pete said that he did want our marriage to work, that he did love me. I believed him when he said he wanted to make our marriage work, because that's what I wanted, more than anything, and so I tried to forget about the row. It felt as if we'd had so many things to cope with as a couple. In fact, we'd sometimes say that surely we'd been through all the bad things that could possibly happen in a marriage, more than most couples have to endure in a lifetime! We hoped that from then on we could just enjoy the rest of our lives together.

Looking back, those were famous last words, weren't they? But for a while Pete and I did seem to put our difficulties behind us, and if you'd have told me then that in two years' time he would have left me and our marriage would be over, I would not have believed you. Not me and Pete. We were unbreakable, weren't we?

CHAPTER TWO

LIGHTS, CAMERA, PANIC!

After the birth of Princess I actually had a decent amount of time off work, in contrast to when I had Junior. Then, I had rushed back to work and recorded a fitness DVD within three months of giving birth. I'm sure this must have contributed to the post-natal depression. As well as trying to get fit again, I also dieted and it was too much for me, both physically and emotionally. I'd become dangerously anaemic during my pregnancy with Junior and had lost far more blood than was normal during the Caesarean. I should have rested for longer after the birth. Also, poor Harvey had ended up in hospital for several weeks – and all this during the run-up to my wedding to Pete. It had been a very difficult time. But after Princess was born, I did take time off work which, to my surprise, I absolutely loved. I am really driven and love filling my day with work. Yes, my name is Katie Price and I am a workaholic! But back then I just chilled for four months, and bonded with Princess, and felt close to Junior, Harvey and Pete. It was such a happy time and I felt blessed to have my family.

My first major work commitment, after maternity leave, was for Pete and me to record our own chat show for ITV2, to be called *Katie and Peter: Unleashed*. When the idea was initially suggested to us, I was all for it. It sounded like a great opportunity for us to try our hand at something else, and I love a challenge. Straight away I thought of all the cheeky questions I would like to ask the guests – you know me, I like to push it! And I wanted our show to be different from everyone else's.

By October 2007 I was so used to being on television. I had filmed several series of the reality show with Pete; I'd appeared on *I'm a Celebrity . . . Get Me Out of Here!* and long before I'd met Pete I'd filmed several documentaries about my life for the BBC; plus I had been interviewed many, many times on TV. So all in all I was feeling pretty confident about doing the show. After all, how hard could it be to sit in front of a camera and ask questions? When you watch chat-show hosts in action they make it look so easy, so effortless, so relaxed, don't they? As if it is a piece of cake. I was about to discover that it was anything but . . .

The idea was to make *Katie and Peter: Unleashed* part reality show – with footage of Pete and me behind the scenes in the run-up to the show – and part chat show, with guests and sketches. As it drew closer to transmission the nerves kicked in and I started to realise that presenting a show and interviewing guests was very different from recording a reality show and being interviewed. And while I don't mind pressure and love being given new challenges, I felt under-prepared. After all, I'd had no previous experience of presenting or being a chat-show host.

At least we were given the chance to record a rehearsal show in front of a live audience. But even in rehearsal my confidence deserted me. To be honest, I was shitting myself! Our guests included the actress Claire King, who was lovely, thank goodness, and very easy to interview. Instantly I felt Pete was a much better presenter than I was; he seemed so much more relaxed and at ease, both when he chatted to the guests and when he did pieces to camera. He was a natural in front of the camera, whereas I had to work at it a bit more. I had done my research and prepared the questions I wanted to ask the guests. That wasn't the problem. What bothered me was when the director started talking in my earpiece while I was doing the interview, firing instructions like 'Ask them this question' or 'Get them to wrap it up now'. It was only what you would expect the director to do, but it was so hard having that going on in one ear while looking as if I was listening to my guest at the same time. As for trying to wrap up the guest, you can't suddenly stop them mid-sentence; you have to make the conversation flow. And then there was the autocue . . . Let me be the first to admit it: I become a robot when I'm reading it, I know. I lose all expression in my voice and in my face, I just can't help it. I really cringed when I watched myself back. But in my own defence, I had absolutely no training.

Anyway in spite of me being a robot and struggling to cope with the old talkback (that's the term for the director talking into an earpiece), the rehearsal show went well. But then it was the real deal and the six-week roller-coaster started. The show was based round having three guests, and from day one finding those guests was a problem. The production team had drawn up a massive list of possible guests, but they kept getting turned down. The feedback the team got was that many potential guests, a lot of them big names, had the idea that our show would be tacky and that it wasn't the kind of thing they wanted to appear on. Pete and I had been guests on Jonathan Ross's show earlier in the year. We had put him on the spot and asked him there and then if he would be willing to come on ours. He tried to wriggle out of it on air, but when I pointed out that we had come on his and it was only fair that he came on ours, he agreed. Well, he never did. And I think that was really out of order, Wossy! I reckon he was scared of what questions I would ask him because, yes, I would have come up with some proper cheeky ones for him. Well, why not? A lot of his material is very near the mark.

We started off with some good names, including Nicole Scherzinger from the Pussy Cat Dolls who was launching her solo career and Jack Shepherd from *Corrie*. I thought I did OK but Nicole apparently didn't get the format and the critics weren't especially kind. But then they never are. The audience liked it, though, and so did the viewers. That's what mattered.

The show was fun . . . different. There were silly challenges between Pete and me, for instance, like guessing which model had had a boob job (of course, I won that!), which allowed us to banter with each other. Parts of the show were outrageous, and Pete and I made a good team, I think. But as the weeks went by it got harder and harder to book what I would call big names, though there were some exceptions, including Rupert Everett, Jermaine Jackson, Craig David and Boy George. Each week as it drew closer to transmission there would be a mad panic when the production team still hadn't managed to book any guests. Some weeks we were so desperate it would be, like, 'Fuck, who can we get on the show?' and so we ended up with a lot of guests who had been on reality shows, and some of our friends – including Michelle Scott-Heaton, as she was then, and her husband Andy. And while it was great interviewing people we knew and liked, it would have been good to interview some people we *didn't* know. But perhaps I can understand why people were wary about coming on the show because I can be cheeky, and loud-mouthed, and they probably weren't used to that from other interviewers. Still, we didn't let it get to us. The show had to go on and all that. I'd just think 'Bollocks to you guys!' about the potential guests who turned us down. They didn't know what they were missing! An interview with the Pricey was bound to be an experience.

I'll admit, though, that there were some aspects of the show I really wasn't too happy about. OK, I'll just come right out and say it: I thought some of the items were in bad taste. For example, when we had the mud-wrestling couple. I didn't like it, it was too near the mark and I didn't want to have it on the show. When I saw the sketch in rehearsal, I actually said to the producer that I wasn't sure if I wanted that in, but they went ahead anyway and we did get stick for it. It felt as if Pete and I had no control, we were just there to front the chat show and had no real say in its format, and even though I understand that the production team were under pressure, I would have liked to have been more involved in the decision-making.

And then there was my look for the show. I wasn't allowed to wear anything revealing, so there was no cleavage, no legs on display. I had to wear trousers and high-collared shirts or else knee-length dresses . . . almost frumpy, and so not me. I mean, *perlease!* Everyone knows what my signature look is and it certainly isn't that. And it's not as if I would have turned up for the show in a bikini. But there you go; I had to go along with what I was told.

No way do I regret doing the show, though. It was

what it was, and now I feel I've been there and done a chat show. I would just be more cautious about doing it again, and wouldn't rush in, but I'd never say never. It certainly doesn't compare with my appearance on the Eurovision show in 2005. That is still my all-time top regret. I really don't have many regrets but that still tops the list. That is in my own personal hall of shame. And as for the pink rubber cat suit with the diamanté belt . . . let's not even go there, shall we?

There were lots of positives about doing the chat show. It was brilliant working with Pete, and we did spark off each other well. I've often said that we were like a battery in the way we worked as a couple – he was positive and I was negative. It was just the wrong concept for us. The behind-the-scenes parts didn't really fit and weren't how we usually filmed our reality show. They felt too staged and set up. But the interviews were fun. It was a good experience appearing in front of a live audience, and interviewing guests was good for my confidence. I did learn from the experience. I know the next time I do anything like that, I will make sure I am more in control.

And I loved getting back into work. We rented an apartment just opposite the studios because we would stay up in London one night a week. Princess was with us most of the time and sometimes we'd have the nanny with us too, so we could go out. You'd have thought that because we had the apartment and the kids were being looked after we'd have gone out partying, but we didn't.

We'd just go out for dinner at a restaurant near the studios. I didn't mind. I was just happy to be with Pete and then back home with the kids.

CHAPTER THREE

UNDER THE KNIFE

Once we'd finished the TV show there was only one thing on my mind: getting my boobs redone in LA. I had been all set to have my fourth boob job the year before, when Pete and I were in the middle of recording our charity album, *A Whole New World*. By then my implants were over nine years old, and I hated my boobs as they'd become saggy after having two kids. Even though all the surgeons I saw told me to wait until I'd finished having children, I knew I would have to get them done sooner. However, literally two days before I was due to have the op, I discovered I was pregnant with Princess. The op was off.

But that didn't mean I couldn't plan it. So when I was out in LA in the spring of 2007 and was around seven months pregnant, I booked myself in to see Dr Garth

Fisher, the cosmetic surgeon I had seen on the TV reality show *Extreme Makeover*, and whose work had really impressed me. He was also the surgeon Hugh Hefner, owner of the *Playboy* magazine empire, had recommended to me when I'd asked him for his advice. I'd posed for *American Playboy* in 2002 and had got on well with Hugh. As he's seen a fair few boobs in his time, and knows what looks good, I trusted his judgement.

'I want my boobs reduced . . . to be more pert and uplifted,' I told Garth. 'I like the stuck-on, fake look. I'm not a natural sort of girl.'

He took on board all my ideas but told me that he wouldn't do the procedure until six months after I'd had Princess. I was a bit gutted because as far as I know you only have to wait three months in England. But even though I wanted this boob job so badly, I decided that I would be patient and take his advice and wait the six months and booked myself in for December 2007. And, just so you know, this wasn't me acting on a whim, simply because I fancied new boobs – when you have cosmetic surgery, you have to accept that there will be a time when you need it redoing. It's as simple as that. My boobs had passed their sell-by date. They needed an upgrade.

There has been so much rubbish written in the press about me and my body – like how I must suffer from body dysmorphia, the condition where people hate their own bodies and want to change them, or that I am addicted to plastic surgery. And do you know what? It is complete bollocks. I'm *not* addicted to surgery, I've just been open about what surgery I've had done – and then the press exaggerates it to make it seem as though I am addicted! I sometimes feel as if I can't win with the press. I've admitted to having surgery and using Botox and fillers, and they still go on and on about it. Yet if you deny it or pretend you haven't, they still try and out you. Journalists write that I'm so fake. Well, hello! I *admit* that I'm fake. So what?

I had my first boob job when I was eighteen because I wanted bigger boobs, simple as that. I didn't do it to please any man, I did it for myself. I didn't hate my body, I just thought I would look better with bigger boobs. I had naturally been a 32B/C which is probably a reasonable size for most women, but I was making my living as a glamour model and felt that I didn't look as sexy or womanly as the other glamour girls. And I had felt unhappy with my boobs long before I became a glamour model.

To this day, I have not one single regret about having the surgery. My only regret is that I didn't have one boob job which took me to the size I wanted to be straight away, because as soon as I had the first op, I realised I would have to have another – the new boobs just weren't big enough. So, a year later I had another boob job, taking me to a 32D. I liked the size but I wanted to change the shape and, a year after that, had my third op which probably took me to a size 32DD. So, yes, three boob jobs in just over three years – not something I would have wanted ideally, but I finally got the boobs I wanted and they brought me a great deal of work and helped make me famous, so respect to the boobs!

And I don't care about what other people say, I do what I think is right for me. I don't judge other people for the choices they make. My boobs needed doing so I got them done. I'm not killing myself. I'd rather have an anaesthetic, with the risks that can carry, than smoke. Yet lots of people smoke, knowing full well how bad it is for them. I know I'm not ugly but if there's any room for improvement, I'll do it. I've been given one life, and if I want to make the most of my body while I'm here then I will. I had lipo-suction once, but what a waste of time and money that was! It was extremely painful and didn't even make any difference. I've had my lips done, too, but that wasn't permanent and I took the piss out of myself for doing it as I knew they ended up looking like a duck's bill! I called myself Daffy Duck. You can get permanent work done on your lips but I wouldn't. And I'd never have a face lift. I've see how horrific that can look, and if you ruin your face there's nothing you can do about it. I don't want a face that looks like a stretched cat's face. I've seen a lot of those in LA and it's scary . . . And however line-free and taut the skin is after a face lift, there's always the giveaway of that saggy rooster neck. So, no thanks, believe it or not I do want to age gracefully, and I accept that wrinkles are part of that. But while there are such things as Botox and fillers that can improve the way you look, then why not use them? I don't see any harm in that.

Anyway, back to December 2007. Back then I didn't get nervous about surgery. I knew there were risks to having any operation and it wasn't something to be taken lightly, but as far as I'm concerned, surgery happens every single day and you could just as easily die in a car crash, right? My opinion is different now after my experiences some six months later when I had to have more surgery, but back then it all seemed very straightforward to me – my boobs needed doing so that was that. And once I'd had a third child, they really, really needed redoing. End of.

Garth knew exactly what I wanted my boobs to look like, but you can't exactly choose what size you are going to be and say to the surgeon, 'Right, make me into a 32D,' because you don't know how the implants are going to fit in with your existing breast tissue. I knew I was going to end up with a different scar after this surgery, called a keyhole or anchor scar which goes round the nipple and straight underneath, instead of the scars I had from my other ops, which had just been underneath the breasts. But as I don't do topless modelling any more, the scars weren't really an issue for me. I was just relieved that he wasn't going to take the nipple off, which I had thought they did during the op and which gave even me, with all my experience of surgery, a bit of a weird feeling. I mean, it grossed me out!

I had only planned to get my boobs redone but as Garth is such a good plastic surgeon, me being me, I thought I would ask him if there was anything else he could do to improve my appearance. So as I stood in front of him in my underwear, I said, 'If you could change anything about me, what would it be?' And he replied, 'Your nose.' Well, I had never had a problem with my nose. I thought it was quite distinctive – I think the expression is that I had a Roman nose. In fact, the surgeon who did my first-ever boob job had also said that he could improve my nose, but I had never been bothered about it before. But then I thought, 'If I can make it perfect, why not?' And I'll be under the anaesthetic anyway, so it's like killing two birds with one stone. It wasn't a major procedure, he didn't have to break my nose or anything, just shave a bit of bone from the arch – making my distinctive nose more pretty and feminine, a cute ski-jump nose.

I had also decided to get the veneers redone on my teeth. I'd had the existing ones for years and they were starting to wobble a bit. I needed to be in LA for eight days to get my teeth done as that's how long it takes, as it involves several trips to the dentist, and I thought that would give me more than enough time to have the boob and nose job too, recover, and do a bit of shopping. I couldn't wait to be back home and showing off my new look!

Pete came with me to the hospital as I went into surgery. He really didn't like me having surgery – a feeling that was to intensify six months later – but he did understand in this instance that my boobs needed redoing. I was the one being light-hearted and joking, and he was the one being more serious and intense, telling me how much he loved me. Of course, I told him I loved him too, but I was also excited about finally having the op, knowing that afterwards I would have my new boobs. And, yes, I know that this is going to sound weird but I was actually looking forward to having an anaesthetic. I loved having them . . . or at least back then I did. I've different feelings entirely now after an experience in August 2008, but that comes later.

People used to ask me why I liked anaesthetics, as if there was some deeper psychological meaning behind my attitude to them. Was it because I couldn't handle reality? That it was the only time I could let my guard down and be fully myself, able to show vulnerability? Or was it just that I liked the sensation. Yep, it's the last one. I loved being put to sleep, loved the dreamy sensation of going under. Who knows why? I certainly don't like the experience of being in hospital, I just associate hospitals with pain and want to get out and back to normal as soon as possible.

I wasn't feeling so jokey when I came round six hours after the op. I felt terrible. My nose was really uncomfortable in the cast. It was itching like crazy and I couldn't breathe out of it as it was packed with gauze. I had a gross taste of flesh and blood in my mouth that made me want to retch. As for my boobs, they were extremely sore but I can deal with the pain if the result is going to be good. But when I looked down at them, I was really shocked. 'Oh my God!' I said to Pete. 'Look at the massive gap between them!' Straight away I was not happy and knew I would have to get them done again. I know people will think I was exaggerating, but I so wasn't! Fake boobs don't usually fall to the sides when you lie down, like natural ones do. But these fake ones did. You could have parked a bloody car in the gap! I was gutted.

There had been a delay of a few days before I could have my boob job, which threw my schedule, and because we had been away longer than we had planned, Pete had to fly home then to see the kids and so my sister flew out to be with me. I really missed the kids. Princess was only six months old and I had never spent this long away from her before. I spoke to Junior and Harvey every day but I really wanted to be home with my family, but all my other appointments had been put back because of the delay to my boob job.

A few days after my op I returned to the dentist's to have my new veneers put on. Yet again I had to have an anaesthetic, which I knew wasn't ideal as I'd just had one, but my teeth had to be done. I didn't realise anything was wrong immediately after I'd had the new veneers, probably because I was so drugged up. But the following morning – ouch! It felt as if someone was putting ice on the front four teeth on the right side of my mouth. So I was on painkillers for my boobs *and* for my teeth, and generally feeling very sorry for myself.

'Only one thing for it,' I said to my sister Sophie. 'Some beauty treatments and some retail therapy.'

First up was the hair. I wanted a change . . . a dramatic change. I'd been blonde throughout my pregnancy with Princess and in the months afterwards, but now I wanted to go dark, really dark. Black, in fact, an intense blue-black. And that's exactly what I did – and I loved it. Next I had some filler put in my lips. It only lasts six weeks so I thought, 'What the hell?' Oh, and I had all my Botox done too – I have it injected into my forehead and round my eyes. I have it done every four months and I love not having wrinkles. One of the celeb mags printed some rubbish about me worrying that I had gone too far with the Botox and that I was concerned that I couldn't move my face at all. I'm like, yes! Job done. Why do you think I spend all that money on it? That's how I want to look!

Retail therapy next. I was still weak from all the surgery and so when Sophie and I hit the shops, I wasn't with it. I admit, I looked a mess. I was wearing really comfy clothes – tracksuit bottoms, a big jumper and my UGGs – and I had my nose cast on. It probably wasn't my best look but . . . oh my God! You should have seen how the shop assistants in the designer stores looked down on me as soon as I walked in. They seemed to be wondering how someone who looked like me could possibly afford to buy anything there. They were so snotty, it was a proper *Pretty Woman* scenario – you know, when Julia Roberts goes into one of the stores in Rodeo Drive, still in her hooker gear, and the assistants are so rude to her? So in Dior I picked up a bikini while one of these snotty assistants was hovering nearby, clearly terrified that I might try and steal it, and she said, 'They come up very small.'

'I'm just looking,' I replied, not liking her attitude.

'It is very expensive as well,' she replied. And straight away a gremlin started up in my belly and I said, 'I don't care, I can buy what I like, money isn't an issue.' But she repeated how expensive the bikinis were. I was well pissed off! I said to Sophie, 'I feel like telling her that I can buy every fucking handbag in this shop if I want!' Then Sophie picked up a Louis Vuitton bag and the assistant exclaimed, 'Excuse me, that's my own bag!' She obviously thought we were going to nick it because she had us down for some kind of lowlife.

Then we wandered into Louis Vuitton and I ended up buying a grey monogrammed scarf and a bag, and the bill came to something like $4,500. And as I was paying the assistants were busily scrutinising my card as if I'd nicked it or as if it was fake. 'It is going to work, you know, why are you looking at it like that?' I said. And all the time I was thinking, 'What is your fucking problem!' Because they really were looking at me, as if to say, 'The likes of you couldn't possibly afford this.' And they were hanging on to the goods until the transaction had gone through, as if they were scared that I was going to run out of the store with them without paying. So bollocks to them! How dare they look down on their customers like that?

I actually went back to the store the day before we flew home. This time I looked good. The nose cast was off, I'd had my hair done and I was wearing make-up. And you should have seen the difference in the way those assistants treated me, practically falling over themselves to serve me. It was all: 'Hello, madam, how can we help you today?' It really pissed me off.

Anyway, I had the nose cast on for eight days and didn't get papped once, mainly because I was staying at the Beverly Wilshire and there's an underground car park you can drive straight out of without being seen. I was glad. I really didn't want to get photographed looking shit. Having the stitches out of my nose was definitely not a laugh – I didn't know if they were pulling a stitch out or one of the hairs. And then it was time to get the stitches taken out of my boobs – ouch again! I thought I would pass out. Never again, I said to myself, no more surgery. I do not want to put myself through this experience again. Enough is enough. But, you know what? You can never say never. It was still nagging away at me that the new boobs were too wide apart so I went back to see Garth. He was convinced that they would settle but I wasn't happy. However, by then I just wanted to get back home and was so pleased when I flew back on 23 December, after being in LA two weeks instead of eight days.

I knew I looked really different. My cheeks were still

swollen from the veneers, my hair was black, I wore massive dark glasses. And I had covered up – no way was I going to show any cleavage as I was still so sore. I had a big horrible sports bra on, a baggy jumper, and had wrapped my new Louis Vuitton scarf round me, to cover my chest. I was in agony on the flight home but couldn't relax as I knew I'd be photographed at the other end. I had to put make-up on and make an effort. Sure enough, I got papped at the airport, but the funny thing was that nobody picked up on the fact that I'd had a nose job. All the celeb mags and tabloids were going on about my new image, and speculating that I'd had something done to my face and lips, but they didn't spot the nose job. How ridiculous was that!

I couldn't wait to get home and see the kids – I'd really missed them and all I wanted to do was give them a big cuddle – but as I was so sore from the surgery I couldn't pick them up. And then it was straight into Christmas and the full-on family experience that I love so much. Everyone really liked my dark hair and my new nose, including Pete. They all said that I hadn't actually needed my nose doing, which was true, but I liked the new version. The real problem was with my teeth which were still absolutely killing me. I could only eat using the left side of my mouth and couldn't have cold drinks at all as it was so painful. Worst of all, I didn't like my teeth as I thought they looked too small, so I knew I'd have to get them redone as well as my boobs. Honestly, after all I'd been through!

CHAPTER FOUR

DOWN UNDER

At the end of December, Pete, the kids and I flew out to Australia. It was a chance to catch up with Pete's family who lived on the Gold Coast there. I knew how much Pete missed them and was so glad he would have the opportunity to spend this time with them. We were going to be out there for a month – the first week would be a holiday, and then we'd have three weeks or so filming our reality show.

It's always difficult taking Harvey to an environment he isn't familiar with. Because he is on the autistic spectrum routine is extremely important to him. He has to have everything done in the exact order he expects and constantly has to have everything explained to him – and I mean everything, even down to me saying something like 'Harvey, I'm going to switch the light on now' – or he can get very upset. If he has a temper tantrum he can throw himself around and lash out, and because he is such a tall, strong little boy it can be hard to calm him down. He has hurt me and my mum in the past when he has become upset – in fact, on one occasion my mum ended up with a black eye – but of course he doesn't do it deliberately. But there was no question that Harvey wouldn't come with us to Australia. As far as I'm concerned, he's part of the family and does everything the other children do, however much of a challenge it can be taking him somewhere new. That's just life with Harvey. He was five and a half then and was actually the best behaved of the children on the flight. He loves going on planes, and always wants to have 'hot chips' as he calls them, and so long as he could watch *Barney*, his favourite DVD, he was happy.

It was good to spend time with Pete's parents again especially as I hadn't seen them since I'd had Princess and Pete's dad had been unwell. By then, thankfully, the negative feelings I'd had because of the post-natal depression about other people being close to my children had long gone. Pete's mum helped out by feeding Princess, and often held her, and I didn't have any problem with that at all. Instead I loved the attention she gave Princess, I was so proud of my baby daughter. And sometimes, when I went out shopping with Pete, we would take Junior and leave Princess with his mum.

In fact, we had a brilliant time staying with his family who are so hospitable. We ate lovely meals, played cards, and chatted. I got to spend time with Pete's sister, Debbie, who had just had a baby boy, and it was nice to have that connection with another new mum. All in all it was very chilled out. His parents lived in a beautiful house with a lovely pool, which Harvey especially loved as back then he liked nothing more than floating in water and pointing out the 'blue rectangle swimming pool' as he called it. I couldn't fully relax as I'm always worrying that Harvey might break something – back home he's broken quite a few TVs in his time. And, sure enough, he ended up breaking a table, but he didn't mean to. Harvey is Harvey. People have to accept him for who he is.

It's sad remembering that time now. Since Pete and I split up, I haven't spoken to or seen his parents. Nor have I had any contact with his sister who I had grown close to, or his brothers. I suppose that's what happens when most couples divorce, but one day I hope we can be in touch again.

After our week of chilling out we were joined by the film crew. I would have liked us to have had longer together as a family – a week on our own just didn't seem enough. I knew that I had committed myself to make the reality series and on the whole I loved making it, and was something I had chosen to do but sometimes I wished that Pete and I could have a holiday without the cameras being there. It was a feeling which was to grow stronger over time. We needed more space as a couple and as a family, but we weren't getting it. And what was also starting to bug me slightly was that when I watched the shows, I always seemed to come across as the bad guy. I suppose that's down to the fact that I am always myself on film and if I'm in a bad mood I show it. In contrast, if Pete was in a bad mood he would forget about it once the camera was on him. I used to have a go at him about it and we would bicker, but that's just what we were like then. Lots of bickering, lots of loving.

But we did get to do some amazing things when we were out in Australia, which were filmed for the reality show. We went to the Great Barrier Reef, which is beautiful, and went snorkelling; and we got to go to Sea World before it opened to the public, which was a real treat. It was especially sweet seeing Harvey with the dolphins. They say that dolphins have an affinity with kids with disabilities and there was something really special about seeing Harvey with them. I really felt as if he was making so much progress. I know that I came across as a bit of a moaner in that episode, but I am wary around water ever since I had a panic attack as a teenager while I was swimming. I had been a very good swimmer and swam for my county. I would train three times a week and all I remember about the panic attack was that one moment I was swimming then suddenly I felt as if I was being dragged underwater and was going to drown. I was powerless to do anything. The lifeguard had to dive in and rescue me. My legs were numb and it felt as if they were paralysed. You don't forget something like that and as a result I now find it really frightening to be out of my depth or underwater.

I also have a real problem with the cold. I swear I'm not being a diva, I actually experience a burning sensation if I get too cold. As a result, when I put on the wetsuit and got into the water, which may have felt warm to everyone else but felt freezing to me, I just couldn't enjoy the experience of swimming with the dolphins. I was too busy thinking, 'Get me out of here!' And when Pete and I got to go in one of the massive aquariums and saw all the tropical fish, I was rigid with cold and anxious about being underwater. All the fish in all the colours of the rainbow weren't going to change that! Everyone who knows me understands that I have a problem with cold. At home I'm constantly turning the thermostat up and driving everyone else mad as they are roasting hot. It's like a never-ending battle where they turn the thermostat down and I whack it up again.

We also got to re-visit the location of *I'm a Celebrity . . . Get Me Out of Here!* where we'd met four years earlier. We couldn't go into the camp as another series was being filmed, but we got to walk along the bridge that leads to it and went down some of the tracks. It was quite emotional going back there. So much had happened to us as a couple since then, but this was where our relationship had started. Just being back there brought back so many memories of meeting Pete for the first time: how I had fallen so deeply in love with him, being desperate to be with him, knowing he was the one for me. I didn't want to show how deeply I felt as we were being filmed. That was one of the times when I wanted five minutes on my own with Pete, without the camera on us. I would have liked to tell him then how I felt about him and how much I still loved him. It would have been a really special, private moment, just for us. But it didn't happen. Then again, if we hadn't had the camera crew with us we probably wouldn't have been allowed to go there anyway, so I suppose it works both ways. Of course, I had no idea that in a little under two years I would be back, appearing in *I'm a Celebrity . . . Get Me Out of Here!* on my own, a broken marriage behind me . . .

There were so many positive things about that trip, but when I looked back at the episodes filmed in Australia it did feel to me as if a big deal had been made of one particular row Pete and I had. It was at the opening of his night club in Cairns, and it was the same old story of how Pete didn't like me to have a drink because he thought I became a different person then and he couldn't trust me. I've talked about it before in my other autobiographies, and four years on it was still an issue between us. He was worried that I would get drunk and end up cheating on him. I think he was maybe remembering his own past when he went out clubbing. 'I know what drunk girls are like, Kate,' he would tell me, 'I know how easy they are.'

'That must be the kinds of girls you went with, Pete,

because I'm not like that, never have been, never will be,' I would tell him, but it never seemed to sink in. And so on this particular night, Pete was off talking to guests at the club and I was hanging out with his brother Danny and his wife, having a few drinks and a bit of a dance . . . just having a good time basically. I wasn't being lairy or loud or flirting with anyone, I was behaving like every other clubber there. Anyway, it was getting late and the club was due to close and I said to Pete, 'Oh, no! Why not leave it open?' I didn't want to go home yet, as I was enjoying myself. We didn't have many nights out together like that. Well, Pete didn't like the way I sounded, he thought I was drunk, and instantly got the hump with me, coming out with the same old comments about how I was a different person when I'd had a drink, and how he didn't like that person.

The following day I flew back to the Gold Coast with his family and Pete stayed on another night because he was still angry with me. I knew he'd come after us the following day, so it really wasn't a big deal, but the episode makes it look as if it was a huge drama and how I might be making plans to fly to the UK on my own with the kids . . . when all the time I knew Pete would be joining us. As it was the only row we had when we were out there it seems a shame it was highlighted like that. Of course, the director then wanted to film us making up – they wanted the drama, I suppose. Pete was back to being charming and said on camera that 'our love was stronger than any argument'. And he apologised to me, though I took my time accepting it.

I decided that from then on I wouldn't have a drink when I went out with Pete. Yes, it would probably mean that I wouldn't have quite such a good time, because a drink does relax you and put you in the mood to enjoy yourself, but it would save the endless same old arguments that wore me down. But, looking back now, I think I was already starting to feel as if I could never have any fun. I'm not saying I wanted to go out and get pissed, I just wanted it not to be such an issue if I had a couple of drinks and a bit of a laugh.

*   *   *

'Oh my God! I don't believe this!' I exclaimed, completely stunned, as I was confronted with the headlines in the *News of the World*: 'Jordan Exposed'; 'Perfect Mum? What a joke'. It was the beginning of February 2008 and our former nanny had gone to the press. They had then run a story making out that Pete and I were bad parents. I couldn't even bring myself to read the lies; I knew they would upset me too much – as they would any loving mother. We'd had no warning that such a story was coming out; the paper hadn't given us any chance to reply to the made-up allegations, and usually they would over such a big story as this. Straight away we called our lawyers. We knew that we could disprove every single one of the paper's allegations.

But the fact that we knew the story was all lies didn't

make me feel any better. People believe what they read in the paper and I hated thinking that they would believe we were bad parents. Every time I went out with the kids after that, I would feel that people were watching me and judging me as a mum. That they were wondering if I was just being nice to the kids as I was in public and that back home it would be a different story. And that was incredibly hurtful because I am a good mother. The kids are the most important people in my life and I would do anything for them. And I know Pete felt the same way. Of all the things in my life, I am most proud of my children. I love all three of them to bits and I am so protective of them that knowing that such vile lies had been written about me as a mother cut me deeply.

I felt completely betrayed by our former nanny. She had been part of our family, she had looked after my children, I'd trusted her completely . . . and she had turned round and gone to the papers. I have had so many bad stories written about me in the past which have been blatant lies and never sued the paper, but this time it was different. No way was I going to sit back and let the paper get away with printing such vicious, hurtful lies about Pete and me and our family. The only good thing was that we received lots of support from our fans who clearly didn't believe a word of the story. Nor did any of the other papers pick up on it. People could see what kind of parents Pete and I were from our TV show; could see how much we loved our children. And because of Harvey's condition we have a lot of contact with doctors and Social Services who would have been the first to notice if anything dodgy was going on, which of course it wasn't.

I'll never know what motivated our former nanny to go to the papers in the first place. I can only assume it was for the money, but what a terrible thing to do to a family you had known so well and been so close to.

Five months later we were proved right when the *News of the World* settled out of court, retracted all comments made in the article, admitted that the allegations were false and said they regretted that they had been published. We were paid substantial damages. It was a great moment; I felt that the record had been set straight and our names had been cleared. We gave half the damages to the NSPCC and the Vision Charity, and the other half was put into a trust fund for Junior, Princess and Harvey.

But back to February 2008. I had *Pushed to the Limit*, my new autobiography, to promote. The book launch was on Valentine's Day. I had been keeping a low profile since my return from Australia and hadn't been out much, so the paps hadn't got any recent shots of me. I knew the press would be interested now because it would be the first chance they'd had to photograph me with my reduced boobs and new nose, and I wanted to put on a show for them. You know me, I don't do understated. So I dressed up as a vampy Wonder Woman, wearing white hotpants, a sequined corset, and white cape. I was accompanied by four hunky guys dressed as Clark Kent, with ticker-tape raining down on us. I always like to make an entrance. And something else made an entrance too – as I held up my arms in a pose, a cheeky nipple popped out! Which, of course, the photographers captured. But the wardrobe malfunction didn't ruin my day. And, no, it wasn't planned.

Later, I was thrilled when *Pushed to the Limit* went to number one in the bestsellers list. I had been anxious about it. It was the third volume of autobiography I had written and it dealt with some tough and emotional issues, in particular my battle with post-natal depression and the strain this had put on my marriage. But I hoped it would help other women who'd suffered in the same way to realise that they weren't alone. That they could get help and get through it, just as I had.

I then went on a nationwide book tour and did a number of signings. As always it was great meeting my fans. A special highlight for me was when I met a mum whose son had the same condition as Harvey. As well as meeting my fans on tour, I get a lot of letters and messages from fans on my website. Some of them have really tragic stories to tell about their experiences of looking after a disabled child, and they say that I inspire them and have helped them with the problems they face. I feel quite overwhelmed when people say that, but I suppose it's because I'm in the public eye and have always been open about what it's like being a mum to Harvey, and how much I love him. I've never tried to hide him away. I don't ask for sympathy. People can see that whatever life has thrown at me, I have coped with it and got on with it. And they can also see that I've come from nothing and have made something of myself.

CHAPTER FIVE

HARVEY

In November 2007 I stared in disbelief at the picture of my lovely son which *Heat* magazine had made into a sticker with a slogan reading, 'Help, Harvey wants to eat me!' The magazine was openly mocking Harvey for his weight, which was caused by his medical condition. It seemed the lowest of the low to blatantly mock my disabled son. Take the piss out of me, but never my child. That is crossing a line that should not be crossed. How could anyone think that a sticker like that was funny? I was deeply shocked and upset.

I think *Heat* must have realised pretty quickly that they had made a terrible error of judgement as even before we got the Press Complaints Commission involved and threatened to take the magazine to court, they apologised unreservedly and made a donation to the Vision Charity, of which I am a patron, which raises money for blind and visually impaired children. Apparently the magazine's internet forums had been flooded with complaints from readers about the Harvey sticker, and the Press Complaints Commission also received a large number of complaints about it.

A month later I agreed to do an interview on *GMTV* with Phillip Schofield and Fern Britton and to take Harvey with me. I was so proud of how much progress Harvey had made. I didn't want to show him off and make him perform in some cringe-inducing way; I just wanted people to see how much he had come on. I've done so many TV interviews but this was the one I was most nervous about because I was not completely in control . . . I can't say it was an easy experience! Harvey was very well behaved while we were on air, apart from throwing his stick and Phil having to retrieve it from behind the sofa. It was getting him there which was the problem. He had a tantrum in the car about putting his shoes on. He always likes taking them off in the car and is never keen on putting them back on. As we walked along the corridor to the studio, he sat down at one point and refused to move. And since he weighed around eight stone then, he was a force to be reckoned with! But I'm so glad we did the interview, for the sake of all those other mums who are struggling to bring up a disabled child.

Phil asked me why I wanted to come on *GMTV* with Harvey and I replied that my reality series could never really show just how hard life with Harvey can be as it has to be edited, while this appearance was live. Harvey can only ever be himself and I knew the viewers would get a better understanding of what that meant from a live interview. I also told Phil that I wanted to show that you shouldn't be ashamed of having a disabled child; that to me living with Harvey is normal. I love him as I love all my children; he is so special to me and I wouldn't change him. Above all, I wanted to prove that doctors aren't always right.

When Harvey was born we were told he would never see and that he would hardly be able to do anything. His prospects seemed really bleak. But I refused to believe that and, helped by my mum and by Harvey's specialist teachers, worked hard to provide him with the stimulation he needed to develop. And the older Harvey has become, got the more he has developed and the richer his life has become. For a start, although he is visually impaired, he can see, especially out of his left eye, and possibly sees a lot more than we realise. He recognises family and friends when they come into a room, and if, for instance, I walk in and ask him what colour t-shirt I am wearing, he will be able to tell me. On his regular car journey to school he knows all the landmarks.

He is also getting on really well at school. Harvey attends a specialised school for the blind and they are fantastic. We go and watch all the children at sports days and concerts, which makes me really proud. He now knows all his colours and shapes. He can hold a pen and draw, and write the letter 'H' for his name, and if you show him the alphabet he knows all the letters and numbers. He works on touch-screen computers and still puts me to shame with his ability to use the computer, even though I keep saying that I must get more computer-literate! He can switch on the TV and DVD player when he wants to watch something, and he will look through his DVD collection and be able to choose which one he wants to watch. He loves counting and showing off what he knows. When, for example, I make his toast for breakfast and cut it into squares, he will look at it on the plate and say, '1,2,3,4 squares, good counting,' to himself before eating it.

He has music therapy at school, which he loves. Music is really important to him. He particularly enjoys playing on his keyboard. He has also become much more active, which has helped control his weight. He goes horse riding, swimming, and uses the trampoline. He loves running on the treadmill, at school and at home, and particularly likes the assault course they have set up at school. He still has a wheelchair but wants to go in it less and less, preferring to walk, which is a brilliant development.

When he was younger he had a real issue with eating and only wanted things that felt hard to the touch, like toast or chicken in breadcrumbs, and it was a constant battle to get him to eat healthily. But now he eats anything and always has healthy food. The downside is that I think he might have Prader-Willi Syndrome, which makes a sufferer eat compulsively. He doesn't know when he's full, and could easily carry on eating. For instance, if you were to put a loaf of bread or a chocolate cake in front of him – not that I would! – he'd eat it all.

The older he's got, the more affectionate he's become. There was a time when he didn't seem to want to be cuddled or hugged, and would give you a hug only if you asked. But now he's really affectionate. He's grown so tall and heavy that I can't lift him any more, and when he sits on my lap to have a cuddle he practically smothers me! He loves me cuddling him when I say goodnight to him, and especially likes me to massage his head and shoulders when he's about to go to sleep. He still likes massage cream being rubbed on his leg where he suffered the burn injury, even though it has completely healed. The doctors were really pleased with the outcome and Harvey doesn't need to go back to the hospital for any more checks for that.

Harvey will say, 'Mummy nails, itchy scratchy,' to get me to massage his leg. He's also obsessed with my boobs and loves pointing at them and saying, 'Boobies! One! Two!' You've got to smile . . . I try to involve him as much as possible in all aspects of family life, so for instance when I cook a roast dinner, Harvey likes to help. I'll chop up the carrots and he will put them in the saucepan. He's got a certain chair he likes to sit on at the table. We call it the King chair.

For months after suffering the burn Harvey was terrified of having a bath. I would have to run the cold tap and let him check it was cold before he would get in. Throughout his bath I would have to leave the cold tap running, so he would know there was nothing to be afraid of. But fortunately he has got over that fear; it helped that during the summer of 2008 we spent a lot of time in Cyprus and Harvey loved swimming in the pool there. Now he is obsessed with cold water! I will run him a warm bath, and he likes me to fill a bottle with cold water and then pour it over him while he giggles! He especially loves having a bath in my bathroom. If I put my bubble bath in he will lie back in complete contentment. I sometimes think he would live in the water all day if he could!

As he has Septo-optic Dysplasia, along with his visual impairment he is deficient in all the hormones the body needs to function healthily. He also has cortisol deficiency, which affects his stress responses and makes it harder for him to fight off illness and cope with shock. He has to take medication five times a day, to make his hormone levels normal, and an injection of growth hormones. He has regular hospital check-ups to ensure his medication levels are right. His cortisol deficiency is extremely serious because if he gets ill or has an accident, he needs an extra cortisol injection straight away. Without it, he could potentially have a fit and die. This was one of the reasons why his burn injury was so serious. I can remember begging the paramedics to give him the injection when they arrived to take him to hospital because I feared he could die without it. Even when he was given it, he still had breathing difficulties.

Whenever we go away we always have to prepare in advance, with Great Ormond Street making contact with the nearest hospital to where we'll be staying so they know exactly what to do if Harvey does become unwell. He's only partly potty trained; in the day, you do have to keep asking him if he needs to go to the loo. At night he still wears nappies.

Harvey is also on the autistic spectrum which affects his behaviour. It is this possibly more than his medical condition which is the biggest challenge. He is obsessed with his own routine and cannot cope with anything that happens to disrupt it. And by that I mean he can kick off into a massive tantrum, where he will throw himself back, lash out, and potentially hurt himself and anyone else who is near him. Everything, and I mean everything, has to be done in the order he expects, and we have all developed a particular way of talking to Harvey that's unique to him. It's like Harvey language. Whenever you want him to do something he will say, 'And then?' and you will have to outline each of the things that is going to happen, in precisely the right order. He likes to know the whole scenario of whatever you do. We have a board that we go through at night, which Harvey goes through with us so he knows what he will be doing the next day and where he is going.

For example, he loves Cheerios and likes having them

without any milk in a particular bottle of Princess's, and he likes you saying half the words with him. So I will say, 'Harvey, do you want some Chee . . .?'

And he will reply '. . . rios.'

And I will say, 'In a . . .'

And he will reply, 'In a b . . .'

And I will have to say, '. . . ottle with a white lid.' Sometimes I will speed him up by saying it all but he'll still come back with 'And then?' He always wants to know what's happening next. There is always an 'And then?' with Harvey.

I wouldn't have him any other way. When he is happy he is so fantastic and loving, but his disabilities, especially his autism, mean that to some extent our lives have to revolve round him. For instance, you have to warn him about what you're going to do every step of the way. If you walk into a room and switch the lights on without warning, he'll fling himself back and create a scene. But if you say, 'Harvey, do you want the lights off?' he'll stop having a tantrum and say, 'Yes,' so then you have to turn the lights off and say, 'Lights on?' and he'll say, 'Yes,' and you can switch them on again. You can never rush things around Harvey; everything has to be done at his speed. If he does lash out in temper he has been known to break things, especially TVs. If he doesn't like what's on, he gets angry and he will throw the television and break it. He's very strong. Afterwards he'll say, 'Oh, broken,' not understanding the connection. We have got through quite a few tellies! Now his flat-screen TV has to be mounted on the wall, safely out of reach.

He gets obsessions with different things, too. At the moment he has one about undoing the Velcro on his shoes. And now he's becoming more independent, he doesn't want anyone to do it up for him. When you're running late it can be frustrating, but you really can't rush him. He wants to be the one in control. Everything has to be done in the order he expects. It's part of his autism. We have all had to learn strategies and techniques on how best to cope with Harvey's behaviour. My mum, one of his teachers from his special school and the special needs nannies we employ have all been on a course run by the Autistic Association. Now we have a series of cards with pictures on them that we can show Harvey, so he will know exactly what is going to happen next.

If we're about to get in the car, he will wait for the doors to be unlocked and then he has to open his first. That's the way it has to be. When we're in the car and we go under a bridge he will always say, 'Over your head, turn around, look over.' If we come to a roundabout he will say, 'There's a circle roundabout.' He constantly talks like this in the car and you have to give him your full attention, which is sometimes very tough on Princess and Junior. Plus he only ever wants to listen to Usher and if you put anything else on he goes mad! I mean, I like Usher, but I wouldn't mind listening to something else! When we play music and stories in the car, he sings along and mimics the voices and sounds.

My mum plays a big part in Harvey's life – I don't know how I would manage without her. One of the many things she does is to take him to and from school each day, with a driver, and it is a bit like a military operation where Harvey expects everything to be done in the precise order he is expecting. He knows the exact point in the journey when he's allowed to have his apple. He recognises the landmarks on the journey, and knows when they reach the M25. He can get very upset if they have to change routes for any reason. He'll say to my mum, 'Harvey got dressed today', and then she has to list every single item of clothing that he has put on, and if she forgets any he will almost certainly have a tantrum.

When they arrive at the school, Harvey mentions the three speed bumps they go over and then they always have to park by the yellow bin. If someone is in the way, they will have to wait until they move. Mark, the driver, then has to ask Harvey if he can turn the engine off and there is a particular order Harvey expects things to be done in – even down to my mum waiting for Harvey to unclick her seatbelt! And it's not over until they have walked him into school, the way he expects, along the yellow path. Once they have arrived at his classroom, he will say, ''Bye, Nanny, go in black car,' close the door, and then my mum is free to go.

It sounds like hard work, and it is, but I suppose we have all got used to it being normal now. It is very difficult coping with Harvey when he has a major tantrum, and it's only going to get harder as the doctors predict that he will grow to be very tall, quite possibly six foot four. So as well as keeping him in the routine that makes him feel happy and secure, we also try and teach him to control his temper with a range of strategies. Sometimes you can get him to calm down by telling him that he can't do something he likes. So, for example, that might mean he won't be allowed to play with his train track, one of his favourite toys, and that can be effective. He will say sorry and calm down. But sometimes he goes beyond the stage where you can reason with him and has to be left to come out of the tantrum by himself. Our main concern is to help him through it, by making sure he doesn't hurt himself and keeping him safe and secure.

We've had to teach him about different emotions so that he can recognise these moods in himself and in other people. And he has definitely become more aware of his emotions. At his school there's a chill-out room. If he's feeling agitated for any reason, he can take himself off there, and return to the classroom when he's feeling calmer.

He always has been very sensitive to noise and still is, though there has been a slight improvement. Nonetheless you still have to warn him when you are about to shut the stairgate. It doesn't matter where he is in the house, he will still hear the 'click' of the gate shutting and lose his temper. At Christmas he hates the sound of presents being ripped open. And while he has become much more affectionate, he doesn't like being around large groups of people. He is perfectly happy playing on his own.

His Septo-optic Dysplasia can also affect his behaviour if his medication is out of balance. If he is slightly unwell, we have to weigh up whether to give him more cortisol and constantly ask ourselves whether that is affecting his behaviour. There are so many things to consider with Harvey. But when his health is fine, and he's naughty, well . . . he's just being a typical naughty boy and you can't make special allowances. For example, he's got several keyboards and one day he asked me for his blue one. 'Harvey find it,' I told him. But he said, 'No, Mummy find it.' And when I said that I didn't know where it was, he began making the moaning sound which is usually the signal that he is getting angry and is about to kick off. But I was firm and said again, 'Harvey find it.' And he went off and found it. I think he knew where it was all along, he just wanted me to get it!

He can also be quite cheeky. On one occasion I was putting him to bed and he said, 'Cuddles in bed.'

'In a minute,' I replied, as Princess had just called out to me. Harvey started moaning, so I left him to calm down on his own. The next thing I knew he had unzipped the large bag of colourful plastic balls which he has in his room, and had thrown them over the balcony so they had rolled all over the hall. When I asked him what he was doing he ran back into his room, knowing perfectly well that he'd done something wrong. But actually, although I told him not to do it again, I didn't mind him doing it as it was more cheeky than naughty, and showed the fun side to his character.

I love Harvey so much. To me he's unique because of his condition and I can honestly say that I wouldn't want him to be any different. But having a child with special needs can make family life a challenge. Harvey does need one-to-one attention and that can be difficult when you've got other children because they need your attention as well. If we're in the car together and I talk to Junior or Princess, Harvey will start to get agitated because he wants to know that he has all my attention. He'll always want to do the 'And then?' game or get you to finish his words. My mum could see that I needed to be able to have some time with Junior and Princess, so I could do some activities with them, and so she organised for Harvey to go to a respite centre at the YMCA on Saturday mornings, along with other children with special needs. Initially, I was resistant to this. I would always say, 'We're a family, and we should do things together.' But the problem is, if we go out as a family, it always becomes all about Harvey and that isn't always fair on Princess and Junior. Once the respite care was arranged, it meant I could take them riding at the weekend. As for taking all three children out together on my own, that just isn't possible. For instance, on Christmas Eve 2007 I wanted to go to the supermarket to pick up some last-minute shopping, and thought I would be able to manage them all. But by the time I got there, they were all playing up. At that stage I couldn't always rely on Harvey to walk, so I had to have the wheelchair with me as back-up and thought, 'How the hell am I going to push a wheelchair and a trolley? I was going to insist Harvey walked, and promise him a cake as a reward, but then I thought, 'I just don't think I can do it. Harvey is so unpredictable. He could be in a good mood getting into the car, but then I could ask him to put his shoes back on, which he doesn't like, and he'll have a tantrum, and I'll be stuffed, and I won't even be able to get him out of the car!' So I ended up forgetting the supermarket trip.

Being a working mum, I sometimes have to take the children with me to work. A business meeting with a large retailer in 2008, when I had to take Harvey along with me, is one which stuck in my mind. Harvey had an important hospital appointment later in the day which I wanted to attend with him, so he had to come with me. This was an important meeting for me, and the retailers had a lot of products to show me. My mum was there too, but I still felt as if I was split in half, trying to make sure that Harvey was OK while also having to give the retailers my attention. At times that became quite stressful. But then, I could also see the funny side as well. Harvey is always the centre of attention, and that day was no exception. The company had arranged lunch for us, complete with chocolate cake for dessert.

As soon as Harvey spotted the cake he started singing 'Happy Birthday' to himself, ending up with 'Hip-hip-hooray!' He always does this whenever he sees a cake, it doesn't matter where he is or who is with him. And while he did that, the business conversation ground to a halt. It was Harvey time. At moments like that, you just have to smile.

Harvey has to be supervised all the time. Even if he is playing on his own in the playroom, someone is always checking that he is OK. In fact, we've got cameras throughout the house so we can always monitor Harvey, Princess and Junior. We can never leave Harvey alone with the other two just in case he lashes out at them. Because of his size he could really hurt them, though of course he wouldn't mean to as he loves both of them.

He has become much more used to Junior and Princess now, and he was much more accepting of Princess when she was a baby. I think he found Junior's arrival hard to deal with as there was suddenly this new baby, making all this noise, which Harvey hated and didn't understand, and drinking out of his bottles! Junior and Princess understand that Harvey has to be treated differently from other children, especially Junior. For instance, Harvey will ask Junior if he can have a particular toy, and Junior will hand it to him and then say, 'Say, Thank you, Junior,' and Harvey will say it. Harvey loves Princess and always gives her a kiss when he sees her, and he doesn't do that to everyone. He never likes to share his food with anyone but he will always share his Cheerios with her. He's also getting on better with Junior nowadays, though Junior is still quite wary of him, I guess because he can remember Harvey lashing out. Princess, even though she is so little, knows that you have to treat Harvey differently from other children. She gently strokes his head, and kisses him, and says 'Ahhh' and gives him a cuddle, though sometimes he will push her away which is why we need to be so careful and never leave her or Junior alone with him.

But Harvey can also be the most happy little boy: playing on his keyboard, floating around for ages in 'the blue rectangle swimming pool', singing 'Happy Birthday' every time he has cake. That's Harvey and I wouldn't have him any other way.

I don't know what the future holds for him. I do know that he will most likely always live with me because he needs constant supervision, but I am not worried about the future. No one expected Harvey to make the progress he has, but he's come on so far and his life now is full of variety. That's all I want for him – to live a full, happy and active life, and to know that he is loved.

CHAPTER SIX

PINK UP MY PONY

By 2008 I had built up a pretty impressive business empire. There were my autobiographies, my novels, my children's books, my reality TV shows, my two perfumes, my lingerie, my bedlinen, and my range of hair products . . . and I was itching to try my hand at something else. As you know, riding is my passion and a lifelong hobby, and that gave me the idea for my next business venture. I had long thought that riding equipment – from clothes to tack – could do with a lot more glamour and sparkle. You only seemed to be able to get clothes in muted greens, blues or brown, and they were so dowdy and unfashionable. It was dull, dull, dull, and so not me! I saw a gap in the market for equipment and clothes that were feminine, girlie and, yes, PINK! I had always handled any business ventures through my management company in the past. I'd come up with suggestions for various products, and they had arranged it all for me. But as riding was my passion I wanted to see if I could set up my own company to bring out equestrian equipment.

I mentioned my new idea to Diana Colbert, who is my book publicist and shares my love of riding. Whenever we went on book tours together we would spend hours chatting about horses, no doubt boring everyone else! I saw my idea for an equestrian range as a bit of an experiment; I didn't have any great expectations and imagined it would take ages to set up anyway. Diana just happened to know Cath Hart, who has a background in retail and would be an ideal partner as she would have all the contacts and would know about product development. Diana drew up a business plan and the three of us met up and decided to form our own company: KP Equestrian.

What every company needs, of course, is a logo, something to make them stand out and be easily identifiable. I wanted to have hearts and a crown, like my tattoo plus my initials. Cath came up with the idea of having the horse's bit, holding the design together, and we had a banner at the bottom, which I thought I could adapt for use with any other products I brought out. In this case it would say 'KP Equestrian' but I was already thinking of bringing out a baby range called 'KP Baby'. I think we were all pretty inspired as we knew there was nothing on the equestrian market that was as glamorous and fun as our products.

When we met up again a few months later Cath brought along a book of drawings of possible designs, along with fabric samples. I was really impressed with everything and thought, 'Bloody hell! This could actually happen.'

We approached Derby House, the main mail order company for equestrian equipment. We didn't want to retail from shops, we just wanted to start small and see how it took off with Derby House as our exclusive retailer. Our first products were t-shirts, tracksuits and shorts, so you didn't have to be into riding to wear them, all of which had the striking KP Equestrian logo on them. And there was various equestrian equipment, all pinked up, including horse rugs, bandages, headcollars and leading rope. My mission to turn the riding world pink had started but I was prepared to use other colours as well – so long as they weren't dull and frumpy ones.

I had done a signing for my children's pony books at a Derby House stand at one of the horse shows, so they had seen for themselves how popular these events could be and how much support I have from my fans. When we had a meeting with Derby House where we presented our ideas, they were very impressed. The next stage was to get samples of the clothes made up, which we did, and Derby House loved the result and placed an order. KP Equestrian was good to go! It had only taken six months from seeing the first drawings to the products being available. Quite an achievement for our little company, I thought.

The big launch was in September 2008. I've said before how much I love coming up with ideas for launches and this was no exception. I've always understood that it's a two-way relationship with the press when it comes to launches. If you want the paper to print a picture of you promoting something, you have got to give them something in return. This time I gave them Katie Price meets riding Barbie! It was glamour and glitz and pink all the way. Some people might say that glamour is wrong for the horse world, but I can't please everyone. I am a glamour girl. I like to put my own spin on things, and to stand out. So I tied my hot-pink KP Equestrian t-shirt round my waist to flash some flesh, wore a pair of matching shorts, plus long socks and heels. We created a set that looked as if it was straight out of Barbie world, with fake flowers, fake grass and a white picket fence, complete with an adorable little white pony. She even had pink hoofs to match my pink heels! I wore dark smoky eye shadow and my hair in pigtails, and pouted for the camera. I wanted to be the complete opposite of what most people would imagine a rider to look like, and I think I pulled it off. The press got what they wanted, and I got to promote my range.

It was an instant success. The online orders poured in and our products flew off the shelves. Derby House couldn't believe how successful it was. They received their biggest orders ever for KP Equestrian. I was thrilled! This had been my hobby and now it had been turned into a successful business. It had also been a bit of a dream, and I'd never imagined it would take off like it has.

From there we went on to do a range of children's clothes, more women's clothes, men's clothes, accessories including wellies and bags, more horse equipment – including pink hoof polish! But the clothes and equipment weren't all pink. We also went for other bright colours, such as turquoise, blue and purple, that were fun and fashionable.

I was so proud that we had created our own business from scratch, and that it was to do with riding which I am so passionate about. It just shows that if you've got a dream and a passion for something you can turn it into a business, so long as you do your research and know your market.

Later on in the year I bought a horse box which had been customised especially for me – in other words, it had been pinked up to the max! Outside it was hot Barbie pink, with my KP Equestrian logo; inside, the personalised leather sofas and cushions had been specially dyed to match the exterior. It can sleep four. There is a top-of-the-range kitchen and bathroom, and of course plenty of space for the horses, along with air con to keep them cool. I think I made quite a statement when I drove it to various shows!

CHAPTER SEVEN

UNDER PRESSURE

Although Pete and I spent so much time together working, recording the reality shows, it increasingly came to feel as if we never had any quality time on our own. I loved filming but it did take over our lives, and sometimes it took the fun out of mine. I know I had chosen to make the TV series and I had been well paid for it so I'm not asking for sympathy, I'm just describing what my life became and what impact it had on my marriage. We spent so much time filming that it put pressure on my relationship with Pete.

I would get stressed because we were filming so much and because I didn't feel completely relaxed with the crew in my house. I often felt as if the film crew treated our house as if it was a film set rather than a family home. I realise that they most likely felt under pressure themselves to get the right footage, but to my mind there were better ways of achieving that. And the problem was that because the filming stressed me out, I would then end up arguing with Pete.

Now that I have my own production company, making my own TV reality show series, I know that filming doesn't have to be so full on. Even when we've got a busy schedule nowadays it's more relaxed and I don't get so stressed because I am more in control and I'm working with a crew who I have chosen and who I like.

But when I was with Pete, I came to dread hearing the doorbell go in the morning, signalling the arrival of the film crew. Often they would be accompanied by our manager Claire or her assistant Nicola, there to ensure we got the filming done. I had always felt that there was no point in the crew filming Pete and me for hours at a time. To me it seemed like a waste of time and energy. They were never going to get the best out of me that way as it is draining having a camera on you all the time, however used to filming you are. I would always say, 'Why don't you just film for three hours when we've got energy and we're on form, and then stop?' But there always seemed to be pressure on us to film more footage. I still don't understand why as now I've got my production company, I'm never filmed all day. When I want to stop, we stop, and there has never been a problem with not having enough footage.

As our reality show had become such a huge hit on

ITV, I was feeling more and more that I wanted to be involved in the production process. I wanted to become a partner in CAN TV which our management had set up to make the reality shows. I felt I should be able to be part of the production company and share more in the success which Pete and I had helped bring to it with our popular reality show. I felt increasingly frustrated about the lack of control I felt I had over filming.

I felt as if I was always being told what to do, what to film, when to film and it seemed nearly all the fun things we wanted to do would end up being filmed for the show. For instance, there was my surprise thirtieth birthday party in 2008, where our manager arranged for my family and friends to spend the weekend at a five-star spa hotel. I had absolutely no idea what had been planned. I had wanted to throw a thirtieth birthday party at a London hotel. I had even got as far as booking the venue and was about to send out the invitations when I happened to watch a TV show where the reporters went undercover to expose bad hotels – and there was the one I had booked on-screen! The cleaners were shown wiping toilet seats with the same cloths they used for the sinks and the cups. And to cap it all, there were rats! No, thanks! I cancelled the booking and decided I would rather have a small party with my family and friends. I had only just got back from a trip to LA to have my veneers redone and prior to that there had been our big trip to Australia. I just wanted to chill. But then Pete told me that a surprise had been planned and all I had to do was pack my swimwear and outdoor clothes. He wouldn't let on where we were going. As we were in our garden, I noticed a helicopter flying over. I was about to comment crossly, 'Why the hell can't the paps leave us alone?' when, to my amazement, it began its descent and landed on our lawn. I think it made Junior's day!

'What's going on?' I exclaimed.

'Surprise!' came the reply from Pete. And I thought, 'How brilliant that he's planned something special for my birthday. I wonder where he's taking me? This is so exciting and romantic!'

As we flew off in the helicopter I kept asking him where we were going but he wouldn't let on. When we approached what looked like a stately home in the distance, I almost thought it was Highclere Castle where we had got married but instead it was a luxury hotel. 'That's so sweet,' I thought, 'Pete is taken me on a mini-break. It will be so good to spend some time together, just the two of us.' Then, after we had landed and were making our way towards the entrance to the grand hotel, my family and a group of my closest friends came round the side and called out, 'Surprise!' And I was thrilled that everyone was here to help me celebrate. I actually said, 'This is the best surprise I could have had for my birthday!' It meant so much to me that my friends and family were all there. 'I'm such a lucky girl,' I thought.

But then I was handed an itinerary, setting out all the details of the activities that were planned and telling me where I had to be at what time, and I realised the whole event was going to be filmed. 'Fucking hell!' I thought. 'This isn't a birthday treat, this is just work.'

Yes, it turned out to be a fun-filled day, with archery and clay-pigeon shooting and beauty treatments, and it culminated in a lovely dinner, but it was all done to a timetable with the cameras rolling. I didn't want my family and friends to be filmed. Because they're not used to it, they weren't really themselves and were all slightly on edge. The whole day didn't feel as relaxing as it could have done.

I did get a chance to relax away from the cameras at one stage and have a massage. Afterwards I was chatting to my mum in the shower. We knew we had to get ready for dinner at a certain time. 'Don't stress about it,' I told my mum. 'It's my birthday, it doesn't really matter what time we get there.' But then Nicola came in to hurry us up. 'Mate,' she said, 'you've got to go and get ready for dinner. We're running late. Gary's waiting to do your make-up.' But I didn't want to rush, so I said, 'Let my friends get theirs done, it really doesn't bother me.' I wanted to go natural; I didn't want to get dressed up.

I would have preferred to put on my comfy PJs but instead I had to get changed into a long evening dress and be fully made up as they wanted to film the build-up of me getting ready. And I was moaned at for being late, which didn't put me in the best of moods! At the dinner everyone was drinking but I felt I couldn't because Pete would get the hump with me. And that was a perfect time when I fancied a drink because it was supposed to be a celebration with my family and friends. I do appreciate the fact that so much thought and planning had gone into my surprise party. The dining room had been beautifully decorated with flowers; wonderful cakes had been made for me, including one with a figure of me on it, and I can remember thanking Claire and telling her I had enjoyed the surprise more than I had anything for a long time. It's just a shame that it had to be filmed. It would have meant so much more to me if it had been a private celebration.

Meanwhile, throughout that weekend, Pete was making comments about our sex life and how he wasn't getting any, which really put my back up. Moaning about the lack of sex, especially on camera so the whole world knows, is one sure-fire way to make sure you don't get any! Claire and Nicola had also arranged a selection of sex toys in our bedroom and been filmed doing so, which hardly made me want to rip off my kit and get down to it. Sometimes it felt as if there was absolutely nothing left to the imagination, that everyone knew exactly what Pete and I could get up to in our bedroom. Well, that night, I'm going to leave to your imagination . . . Actually I don't think anything happened.

As well as the pressure to film the reality show, I came to feel that I had allowed our management too much involvement in my private life. I felt that they knew everything about my life and my marriage because I had confided in them and because they spent so much time with us while we filmed the reality show. I had signed up with a management company who pride themselves on being very hands-on with their clients, and at first I was absolutely fine with that. After all, I had chosen to sign up with them because they represented Pete and I wanted our diaries to be co-ordinated. I quickly became very good friends with Claire and came to count her as one of my closest friends, someone I confided in and trusted. I also became good friends with her assistant Nicola. During the early days of my relationship with Pete, I was so deeply in love with him that I could think of little else. I was totally taken up with being a mum to Harvey and my feelings for Pete. Then I fell pregnant with Junior and suffered from crippling post-natal depression which it took me nearly two years to fully recover from. By then the pattern was set, and our management were very involved in our lives.

I came to realise that there seemed to be no separation any more between my work life and my private life. It became a little claustrophobic because Claire was my manager and I also counted her as a very good friend – and they always say don't mix friends with business, don't they? I would sometimes ask myself if Claire and I would be friends if she didn't manage me because we really did get on so well. I always thought we would, but I was to be proved wrong on that score as you will find out later . . . I think, looking back, that I made a mistake by being so open with our management. If Pete and I rowed, as sadly we came to do more and more in our marriage he would immediately get on the phone to Claire to let her know, and then she would call me to see if we could patch things up. And I would frequently end up phoning her as well, asking her to talk to Pete and calm him down. Claire knew him so well that she was especially good at talking him round if we'd argued.

'We're like family,' Neville Hendricks, Claire's fiancé and business partner, was fond of saying. 'And we look after our family.' But I already had my own family and my children; I didn't need another one. I've always been someone who likes being surrounded by people, but I was increasingly to feel that Pete and I were always with other people and that we never had any quality time on our own.

And even when Pete and me were on our own, the sad thing was that we hardly ever went out together as a couple. Back then because Pete rarely drank – years earlier he'd had a severe panic attack – he didn't like going out anywhere where people were drinking so we'd have friends over for dinner or barbecues, or chill out watching films. Sometimes I felt I was getting old before my time. I thought about my friends' lives and they all seemed to go out way more than I did, both with their partners or on nights out with their girlfriends. Even my mum and dad seemed to go out more than I did! I come from a very sociable family where my mum and dad often have dinner parties and are probably out most weekends with their friends and I expected to have that kind of social life myself – it was how I was brought up. But it certainly wasn't what my married life was like. I loved Pete so much, don't get me wrong, but after a few years together, when you're working with someone as much as we did, you need a break, a change of scene. Occasionally I'd go out clubbing in London with my girlfriends but this was always a huge issue for Pete because of his fear that I would get drunk and cheat on him.

I admit that when I went clubbing with the girls I would have a few drinks, and because I was such a lightweight with alcohol it really wouldn't take much to get me drunk. And then I would drive my girlfriends mad as I'd be the one who wanted to stay out all night. As nights with the girls were such rare events for me, I wanted to make the most of each one as I didn't know when I'd next be able to go out. And I would want to club hop – to pack in as much fun as I could. In fact, my girlfriends would tell me it was an hour later than it really was, to try and get me out of the club, otherwise I would have been there until it closed! But cheat on Pete? Never in a million years. All I wanted to do was get glammed up, let my hair down, hit the dancefloor with my girlfriends and have a laugh.

But that night out would cost me far more than a hangover and would inevitably lead to a row with Pete. Two days after my night out there would almost certainly be pictures of me in the tabloids. Of course, they would never choose ones where I looked good, they would always go for ones where I looked bleary-eyed, so they could print some crap about how I was out of control, and pissed, when most likely I was just blinking because of the flashes going off in my face. Pete would see the pictures and say, 'Look at the state of you! I thought you said you weren't that drunk?' And then he would be really angry and wound up about it.

If there were ever any well-known men in any of the clubs I went to, the press would make out that I had been chatting them up, when I probably hadn't even said as much as hello to them. And that would piss Pete off as well.

I got to the stage where it didn't seem worth the stress and aggro it caused to go out. But I think that did eventually bring me down. I was in a rut. I loved Pete and the kids, loved being part of a family – it's all I've ever wanted – but I needed something else in my life. I needed to do something just for me. I felt I needed a hobby, something separate from work.

CHAPTER EIGHT

GROWING APART

Back in 2008 I felt as if all I ever did was work and then come home and there was never any down time, never any way I could switch off. I'd started up my KP Equestrian range and that was going well so I decided that I wanted to ride more and challenge myself by learning dressage. It seemed the obvious choice. I have always loved riding. Horses are my escape and my passion. I'd been riding since I was seven so it wasn't as if it was this new thing that just came out of the blue. I already owned several horses, two of which were on loan to friends, but I was hardly riding at all, apart from the odd hack. And I did want to push myself. I wanted a fresh challenge. Learning jumping didn't appeal to me as I thought it looked too dangerous, but I liked the look of dressage. It's a highly specialised sport where the rider has to make the horse perform a number of precision moves by using their hands, legs, and the position of their body. It is occasionally called horse ballet. It looks beautiful and elegant but it is really hard!

Once I've decided what I want to do, I don't hang about. So next I had to get a dressage horse. The horses I already had were not trained in dressage. So I flicked through *Horse and Hound* and saw what looked like the ideal one for me advertised. Not only did it sound impressive but it also happened to be black and that is my all-time favourite colour in a horse. The only problem was that it was in Glasgow and my hectic schedule meant that I didn't have time to fly up and see it. So I called the owner and said, 'You're going to think I'm mad but I want your horse and I can't come and see it, so can I send a vet round to give him his five-stage vetting? [That's like a horse MOT.] And then I can decide whether to buy it or not.' The horse passed its inspection and I called the owner again and asked if she would drive it down to me. I transferred the money into her account and was now the proud owner of a horse I'd never seen. Yes, I admit that was impulsive. It was a fifteen-grand impulse buy! People think you need to spend a lot more than that on a dressage horse, but I think that's crap, because this one, who I called Jordan's Glamour Girl, went on to teach me a lot.

So the horse arrived, and as soon as I got on her she began rearing. This was not a promising start. The owner said that she didn't usually do that. Typical, I thought. I've gone and bought a dud horse. Why didn't I see her before I spent the money? But then the owner got on and I saw that the problem was with me, not the horse, because she had her trotting and cantering round the ring and the horse looked stunning. So I tried again but I couldn't even get her to walk, let alone trot! And when I gave her the signal to walk on she began doing all this fancy footwork. Because the horse was so finely tuned to dressage instructions, I couldn't ride her as I would usually; I had to learn the dressage moves first.

But instead of learning dressage then, I was so busy with work that I ended up loaning Jordan's Glamour Girl to one of my best friends, as she then was, Michelle Baker, another keen rider. And I paid for the horse's upkeep. I knew Michelle from my glamour modelling days when she was still Michelle Clack. I couldn't keep Jordan's Glamour Girl at my house as my stables weren't yet ready and such a highly trained horse needed to be exercised regularly otherwise her fitness would suffer.

Several months later I realised I was back to square one with my riding ambitions. I was the owner of yet another horse and yet again someone else was riding it! I really would have to find a dressage instructor. Dressage is not something you can teach yourself. So while we were busy promoting *Pushed to the Limit*, I asked Diana to help find me one in my area.

Diana did her research and found Andrew Gould. He is one of the leading dressage riders in the country as well as being a dressage instructor and trainer. He also happens to be young and good-looking, and when Diana showed me the information on him and I saw pictures of him, we both said, 'Oh, Pete's not going to like this.' At that time Pete seemed quite down. He had put on weight and wasn't working out. I think it was also tied up with how frustrated he felt about not having an album deal and that while I was busy working on so many different projects; all he really had was the reality show. It didn't matter to me that he had put on weight. I loved him however he looked, and always thought he looked good. The fact remains, I didn't choose Andrew as my instructor because of his looks – I couldn't have cared less what he looked like. He could have looked like Shrek for all the difference it made to me. I just wanted to learn dressage!

Diana had given me the telephone number of his stables and I called up and spoke to Andrew's wife Polly about the possibility of learning dressage with Andrew and keeping my horse at their stables. As we chatted we got on really well. I thought, 'Excellent. Maybe we could be friends with this couple. It would be so good to know another young couple with children, especially one that shares my love of riding.'

When I first went to Priory Dressage – Polly and Andrew's training livery stables – it was a Saturday sometime in March 2008 and the place was buzzing with riders and horses. I watched at the outdoor school and was blown away by seeing all the absolutely stunning horses and fantastic riders. I thought, 'I would love to be able to ride like that. But, bloody hell, there's no way I'm riding in public yet because I can't even get my horse to trot!' Andrew and Polly seemed like such a nice couple, both down-to-earth, both really friendly. I moved Jordan's Glamour Girl to their stables so that Andrew could train her up and I started having lessons.

At first I was nervous. I am a very good rider but dressage is such a specialised sport that getting on a finely trained dressage horse made me feel like a novice. But it didn't take long for me pick it up. Very soon I was connecting with my horse and learning how to get her to make the dressage moves. I got a real buzz from learning and started having lessons every day first thing in the morning, before any of my work commitments.

I decided I wanted to enter some dressage shows and compete. I always need a goal to work towards. Taking up dressage gave me such a good feeling, and I loved being around the horses and the stables. People who love riding will totally understand where I'm coming from – though I guess it's like any hobby which you enjoy. For me, going to the stables was about switching off; it was somewhere I wasn't going to be filmed or photographed. It was my escape and riding made me feel so happy. At last I was starting to feel that I did have some space away from work.

At first Pete seemed fine about me riding so much. After all, he was spending practically every day in the studio working on his music – something which I fully supported, as I knew how important his music was to him and how much he longed to bring out another album. And he knew how much I had always loved horses and riding. When he first met me, for instance, I'd just bought a house in a small village in the Sussex countryside and had stables built there for my horses. When we later moved to Ockley, in Surrey, the main reason I bought that house was because it had stables, school and a field for my horses. But then Pete met Andrew and everything changed. He had met Polly and Andrew briefly when they both came round to the house once before we went off to a horse show, and even in that brief meeting, which was filmed for our reality series, I got a bad vibe from Pete, but thought maybe I was imagining it.

I admit we were both jealous in our marriage. When we first got together we were so into each other, we were in each other's pocket 24/7 and that was how we both wanted it to be. And so a few years down the line when our relationship had grown more comfortable, as all relationships do after a time, when one of us wanted to do something different, without the other person involved, it would feel odd. The fact is that riding was something I had always done, it wasn't something new. But jealousy is a poison, a cancer, and once it starts growing out of control, it can destroy everything . . .

* * *

I had been learning dressage for nearly three months and to give myself a challenge, had entered a competition at

Hickstead on 11 June. It was my first one and it felt like a big deal for me, especially given that I could hardly ride Jordan's Glamour Girl when I first got her and now we were working so well together. It was made more nerve-racking for me because it was being filmed for our reality show and the paps turned up in force to photograph me as well, so I felt under added pressure. As I got ready to go on I anxiously scanned the stand, looking for Pete. My mum, brother, sister and a couple of my friends had come to support me and Pete had promised to come along as well, but there was no sign of him. I felt disappointed that he wasn't there. It might have been only a small competition, but it was my first and so was particularly important to me. In the end he turned up after I'd finished competing because he'd got lost on the way. I couldn't help thinking that everyone else who was close to me had managed to arrive on time.

I came sixth out of a class of twenty-three in the competition, which I didn't feel was at all bad given that I was so new to the sport. Afterwards the show director of Dressage at Hickstead, Dane Rawlins, told *Horse and Hound* that he was impressed by my performance, commenting: 'She did a bloody good job. She didn't hype it. She got a good round of applause. She just wanted to do it properly. Everyone was quietly impressed. She was very pleasant and friendly to everyone and has set her sights firmly on improving. She got the lines right and got to grips with it well. She's good news for the sport, as everyone likes a touch of glamour.' I was thrilled to receive such positive feed-back. As Dane Rawlins had trained riders to Olympic level, he would know a good rider when he saw one.

Now I was riding again I didn't feel I needed to go out clubbing for a release. When I was with the horses, I loved it so much that it took my mind off everything else and gave me the freedom I craved. But the thing about riding is that it is all-consuming – being around horses, riding itself, being with other riders who understand your passion for horses, being out in the fresh air all day – it takes up a lot of time. I could go off riding feeling stressed or down, but by the time I'd ridden for a few hours all that stress and tension would have vanished. I would feel fantastic, exhilarated. Anyone out there who is interested in horses will know that you can happily spend all day at stables just because you love being with horses and everything that goes with them. Whenever my fame comes to an end, as it is bound to one day, my dream is to have a house where I can have stables and fields and then I will spend all day outside with the horses, along with my kids. That would be my idea of heaven.

Just as there are football widows there's the phe-nomenon of horse widowers – men who find that their wives and partners get so involved with their passion for riding that they spend hours away from home, getting up early when usually nothing except work will get them out of bed, and riding all weekend. I so wanted Pete to understand my passion for riding and to share it, but I'm afraid we were getting on so badly that this wasn't the case.

I would say, 'Why don't you come along and watch me ride?' I was desperate to involve him.

'You don't really want me to,' would be his reply.

'I've just said you could!' I'd exclaim.

And he would come back with, 'So why are you saying it with an attitude?'

I felt I could not win. Whatever I said was wrong. We had always had a passionate relationship where we bickered and argued with each other as you can see on our reality shows. That's just the way we were. But our arguments were getting worse, more destructive, and really threatening our marriage.

Meanwhile riding was playing an important part in my life. I was making such good progress with Jordan's Glamour Girl that I decided I wanted a better horse. She was great but she was never going to make it to Grand Prix (the highest) level in dressage because she had a problem with her suspensory ligaments. Pete had bought me a horse for my thirtieth birthday, a gorgeous chestnut called Dan. He was really young so would be ideal for training. I kept him at Andrew's stables, but after only a few weeks one of his riders had a fall from Dan after he bolted and Andrew said he didn't think the horse would be suitable for me. He suggested I sent him to a stables in Holland to be trained and later sold. That left me itching to get another horse.

There was a big horse sale coming up in July in

Holland and I decided to go there with Andrew and Polly and their other clients to see if I could buy one. I was also taking Diana, Michelle Clack, my mum, dad, my sister, Gary, Phil and Jamela. I asked Pete to come as well but he had plans to go to Cyprus. The trip was hardly a big secret; it had been in my schedule for ages. However, Pete and I were getting on so badly by then it was really starting to get to me. All I wanted was to pursue my hobby and buy some decent horses. I was getting such a good buzz from riding. Pete had his studio at home; that was his thing. I wanted something for myself. Over in Holland I bought a horse and even named him Andre.

I thought about buying Pete a horse too and asked him if he would have riding lessons so that he could share my passion. I wanted the whole family to ride; Harvey has riding lessons at his school and loves it, Junior has riding lessons and loves it too, especially since I've bought him a pony of his own, and I want Princess to get into riding as well. Then we can all go out on hacks together and I can take them to shows. I had this dream of us all going off to shows in my huge pink horse box and staying in it, imagining some really fun family times. But that never happened when I was with Pete.

I kept trying to get Pete to see what a great couple Polly and Andrew were, and how our two families could be friends. But he just wasn't having it, and if ever he did see them I would sense a bad atmosphere and probably act differently because I was so tense. Polly and Andrew are an outgoing couple who have always socialised with their clients. Whenever they asked Pete and me over or out anywhere, I always felt I had to make excuses. Pretty soon they cottoned on that Pete seemed to have had a problem with them and commented, 'Pete doesn't like us, does he?'

I hated the fact that Pete and I weren't getting on. I even thought about moving my horses to a different stable and looked into it, but the fact was there was no one else nearby who was suitable and anyway Andrew was one of the best trainers around. Also, I thought why the hell should I?

But, ironically, at the same time I was also happy because I loved the feeling of freedom which riding gave me as well as the challenge of learning dressage. I had always wanted to compete from when I was a little girl but my mum could never afford to buy me a good pony; we had to have one on loan. He was called Star, and had reached the grand old age of eighteen. Whenever I took part in any pony shows he was always the ugliest and hairiest pony there, although it didn't matter to me because I loved him! So now I could afford a decent horse, I felt I could really pursue my dream. I would come home on such a high, wanting to talk to Pete about what I'd achieved, but he just didn't seem to want to know. I kept asking Pete to the yard to watch me ride but if he did come he never seemed that interested. He would be on his phone and look as if he'd rather be elsewhere. I felt uncomfortable and tense because of all the arguments. I wanted him to understand my passion for riding and to enjoy it with me, but he was always focussed on other things.

I knew that Pete was low because we weren't getting on, as was I. He was also desperate to get his music career going again and really wanted to be famous for his music again, but didn't yet have an album deal. I thought he definitely deserved one because he was so talented. My mum would often tell him that he would be brilliant in a West End musical so why didn't he go for that? I thought the same. But he would just reply, 'I'm waiting to see what Claire gets for me.'

I wanted to support him but because he was giving me such grief over my riding we weren't getting on. It was a vicious circle that neither of us could seem to break. He would say, 'Why are you being so defensive?' but I wasn't. I'd tell him again and again during this time that I loved him, that I wanted us to work out, and I really did.

During this time when we weren't getting on Pete would quite often go over to his house in Cyprus and inside I would think sadly, 'This so isn't what I want from my marriage. What happened to the guy I was in love with . . . the guy I married?' And then I'd think, 'This is all fucked up, this all because we're filming too much. Why can't we disappear from it all, take a break?'

But it didn't happen. And the more we argued and were filming, the worse it got. Pete was better at making an effort in front of the camera than I was. If I felt moody and unhappy then that's how I was when I was filmed, and that put still more strain on our marriage. However, things weren't bad between us all the time. Some days we'd get on brilliantly, but then it would turn bad the next. And I think it became a pattern and then the good days grew fewer, as the bad times took over.

Because we weren't getting on I didn't want to have sex with Pete and that became yet another problem area between us. Every night I would get into bed and dread him getting in next to me and bringing up the subject. I would feel myself tense up, not wanting him to mention the lack of sex and how he wanted it. Our bedroom was now another battle ground. But what woman wants to have sex when they're rowing with their partner? If a man's giving you a hard time, it's the very last thing you feel like doing. Plus I was still on anti-depressants – admittedly a very small dose, but my sex drive was lowered because of them. At the same time I really loved Pete and wanted to cuddle up with him, to be close to him, I just didn't want sex. I didn't want any other man. I did still fancy him and I loved him so much. But at the same time I'd hate him for the way he was going on at me.

Maybe if we could have had a quickie to clear the air that might have helped break the deadlock. As I commented to my hairdresser once on my TV show, 'Isn't it nice to have a quickie sometimes and not something that lasts forty-five minutes?'

I've heard an expression which nails our situation

perfectly back then – that men need to have sex to feel loved and women need to feel loved to have sex. And there were many times when neither of us felt loved.

What made the situation between Pete and me even harder was that around this time the press was full of stories that we weren't getting on and were about to split up. None of the reasons the press reported were the right ones, but it was an added pressure. It was clear that someone we knew was selling stories. Whoever it was was telling a fragment of the truth, embroidering it, and then selling the story to the magazines.

I felt very unhappy during this time and deeply sad. I hated Pete and me not getting on. I felt that we had so much going for us as a couple. We loved each other, we had our brilliant kids, our lifestyle, our work . . . why couldn't we make our marriage work? So I suggested that we have marriage counselling. We had problems and needed help. We seemed to have lost all perspective and our marriage was falling apart as a result. We both agreed to have counselling as we thought that would help our marriage. So I asked the therapist I had seen when I was suffering from post-natal depression to recommend someone suitable. We started seeing a therapist once a week. I was willing to try anything to save my marriage. I was sure that this was just another bad patch and that we would get through it. My constant hope was that things would work out between Pete and me.

In July 2008 we moved to a new house in Surrey. I

hoped that it would be a fresh start for us after all the things that had gone wrong in the old one. It felt as if that house in Ockley had brought us nothing but bad luck as a family. There had been Harvey's horrific accident, Pete's meningitis, and a further terrifying accident when a mirror fell on Harvey and broke his nose. We had both come to feel that the house was jinxed for us in some way. The new one seemed perfect for us as a family. It had plenty of room with seven bedrooms, a spacious living room and a gym. It was set in 1.5 acres and had an indoor swimming pool which all the children loved, but especially Harvey. I really liked the modern design of the house. It had an open feel, with plenty of light flooding in, and the large kitchen was the focal point, which suited us all. It even had a sweeping marble staircase into the hall which was great for posing on though of course it had to be made secure with stairgates. There was, however, one big drawback: the paps could park right outside our gates, whereas our old house was on a private road and they couldn't get close. With this new house, every time you drove through the gates you ran a good chance of being photographed. This was something that was to become a real problem.

CHAPTER NINE

HAVE I GONE TOO FAR?

Ever since I'd had my breast reduction in December 2007, I'd known I would have to have further surgery on my breasts. I went to see several surgeons in the UK and they all agreed that the gap between my boobs was far too wide. When I lay down they fell to the sides and you could see the breastbone in the middle and see where my boobs should have been. So it wasn't me going off on one, there was a real problem. I was so frustrated! I had looked forward to getting new boobs back in December but now I had to have yet another op. I hated to think about what my poor body had been through in the past seven years – what with having three children and all the surgery.

In April 2008 I flew out to LA to get my veneers redone – these were the ones that had been causing me

The family tucking into lunch.

Happier times. Me, Pete and the kids at Disneyland.

Pete and Harvey.

Me and Junior
meet our favourite
characters.

On holiday with the in-laws.

Katie and Peter stateside.

Us in New York.

The famous sign – beam me up!

April 2009,
the London Marathon.

Running in aid of
the Vision Charity.

so much pain because of the bonding glue. Talk about suffering to be beautiful! During that visit I went to see Garth Fisher again. He agreed that I needed another breast op. This was the way he described it to me. Imagine what would happen if you put a small pillow into a large pillow case – it would have a lot of room to move around in. I'd had big implants and Garth had replaced them with smaller ones but he hadn't taken away enough skin, so the implants had too much room to move around in. 'I can't do any of the shoots for my underwear lying down,' I told him, 'my boobs just roll to the side and look really ugly.' After what I'd been through to get them and the money I'd spent on them, I wanted a good result! I was relieved that Garth agreed with me. I didn't want him to think that I was some kind of freak who liked being put under the knife for the sake of it. And although I wasn't happy with the first boob job he'd performed, I knew he was a really good surgeon and trusted him to put things right.

I had been worried about what the scars might look like as I'd had to have an anchor scar where they cut around the nipple and vertically down the breast and underneath it, but Garth is very good at stitching and the scars were already fading, even though the ones underneath my boobs were quite long.

'I want bullets!' I reminded him. 'Pert bullets! I want the best tits in the UK!' I'm sure most women would want a more natural look, but not me.

I flew back to LA on 4 August 2008 with the film crew

of our reality show. I'd agreed they could film me just before I went into the operating theatre. Not many people admit to having surgery like I do. I don't have to tell anyone anything about what I've had done, but I have chosen to be open about it because I want to share what I go through. And I've been open about it from my first-ever boob job all those years ago, which was why I didn't mind being filmed as I got ready for surgery. But as for what goes on during the op . . . that is between me and the surgeon.

Pete came with me as he wanted to record some tracks for his album in LA. Things were still very difficult between us, though I hoped that being away together might help. But it was tough because it was getting closer to September and we had already said that we would renew our wedding vows then. I had wanted to do this for a long time, ever since I had recovered from the post-natal depression that had wrecked my wedding day and put such a strain on our marriage, and Pete had wanted to as well. Although we had only been married for three years, we both felt that we had been through so many problems as a couple we wanted to celebrate our love again. But by now we were arguing so much that I really didn't think I wanted to go through with it. 'Maybe,' I told myself, 'things will be OK again by then . . .' It's what I hoped. However tough things were between us, back then in 2008 I didn't want my marriage to end. I still thought we would pull through.

* * *

As time is always so tight in my schedule I also wanted to get some dental work done while I was in LA. Because the plane was delayed I had to go straight to the dentist, without any time to recover from the flight, and the film crew came along too and filmed me being given the anaesthetic. As usual I was saying how much I loved the sensation of going under and asked the anaesthetist to give me the anaesthetic as slowly as possible, so I could enjoy every second. I said to the dentist, 'Do you think I'm mad?'

And he joked back, 'Totally!'

But by the end of the week, I certainly wasn't saying that. And after what happened next I can honestly say that I've had enough of anaesthetics to last me a lifetime . . .

I was also filmed just after I came round from the op. A month or so later as they were putting the episode together Claire showed me the footage and obviously I vetoed much of it. The footage showed me looking really dazed, talking gibberish, and was actually very disturbing.

They didn't use those clips but they did include several of me seeming out of it, and one of me being walked to the toilet by Pete and the nurse. I thought it was rather upsetting when I saw the complete episode. I felt disturbed seeing myself in that state, and I know it really upset Pete. I've seen Harvey have an anaesthetic and I know how distressing it is seeing someone you love lose consciousness and then having that anxious wait until they come round.

The following day I was booked in to have my boob job. I wasn't nervous as this would be the fifth time I'd had surgery on my breasts. I thought it would be a routine op where the problem would be put right and I would finally get the pert boobs I wanted. In my mind it was all very straightforward. I'd have the op, take a few days to recover, and then enjoy LA. Because I was being filmed just before the op, I messed around and squished my boobs together and said, 'Goodbye, my lovers!' I was just having fun because the director wanted me to say something about my boobs. I joked that I was going to come out Plastic Woman. I had also decided to have a small op on my belly button. I'd had whooping cough as a baby and had ended up with an outie as a result. I wanted an innie and, as I was having the boob job, thought I may as well get that done at the same time. But here's a tip . . . don't bother! It cost eighteen hundred dollars and a few months later it ended up looking exactly the same.

It was a five-hour operation and seemed to go well. At first I felt OK after the surgery. I was in recovery for a few hours, I think, and then I was taken to an after-care clinic. It's all very different from the good old NHS where you stay in a hospital and are seen by your doctors. In LA it seemed that once you'd had the op, you wouldn't see your doctor again. Instead you'd be in a clinic, taken care of by nurses. All the time you are very aware that you are paying for everything – from your food to your medication. Because Pete was working on his album, my good friend Jamela – well, she was a good friend back then, though that changed after Pete left me – spent a lot of time with me in the clinic. Two days after the op I went to the salon at the Beverly Wilshire hotel to get my hair extensions put in again. I had booked the appointment ages ago as I'd thought I would be fine by then and, as I was only in LA for a week, I knew I had to get them done as quickly as possible. I hadn't checked out of the clinic, this was just a trip out for the day. But on the morning of the hair appointment I wasn't feeling at all good. I was exhausted and still felt knocked out from the anaesthetic, and my boobs were really sore. Also, my right arm felt numb, like a dead arm, and I couldn't lift it. I had told the nurses at the clinic and they had been injecting me with painkillers. The drugs knocked me out but didn't help my arm. It wasn't that it hurt, just that I couldn't seem to feel it. All I wanted to do was lie down and rest. And on top of feeling so rough, I was being filmed. After major surgery it's hard enough to recover, never mind when you've got a camera in your face.

I wanted to say, 'Fuck the show, I really can't deal with this,' but I didn't. And so the cameras were still on me and I know I came across as having the hump and being moody, but I felt really shit. Pete came to see me while I was getting my hair done and was all excited about recording tracks for his album, but I just felt so out of it I couldn't talk, even though I was pleased for him.

He thought I was angry with him, but I wasn't. I was in such pain that of course I wasn't myself.

As soon as I'd had my hair done I went straight back to the clinic. When I mentioned the fact that my arm was feeling numb again, the nurses gave me more painkillers which knocked me out. I was already on painkillers to ease the pain of the surgery and couldn't seem to think clearly. I was trying to text friends back home but as soon as I'd had the painkillers my head would feel so heavy I couldn't carry on.

The following day I thought I would surely be OK to go out for a bit of retail therapy. It was a mistake. I was in Juicy Couture buying clothes, along with Jamela and Nicola and the film crew. Outside the store the paps were pressed up against the glass, jostling to get a shot of me. Suddenly I felt really unwell. 'I've got to go back to the clinic,' I told Nicola. I didn't want to let on to the paps that I was feeling ill so I put on an act and forced myself to smile. But as soon as I got in the car with its tinted windows, I collapsed back into the seat. I was in absolute agony from the surgery and my arm was still numb. I could hardly move it at all. It was freaking me out.

Back at the clinic I again told the nurses about my arm. 'Look, I can't move it,' I told them as I lay on the bed. And this time they could clearly see that there was a problem and phoned Garth. It was around eight in the evening by the time he arrived. It was such a relief to see him. He examined me but couldn't see any reason why there should be a problem with my arm. He told me that he would have to operate again so he could take a look at what was going on inside. Instantly my heart sank. This would be my third anaesthetic in less than a week and I knew that wasn't good. What's more, Garth wanted to operate right away.

I was on so many painkillers by then and in such pain that my memory of that time is quite hazy, but I can vaguely remember getting into Garth's car and being driven to his clinic. It was closed and he had to open up. It was weird as I saw no one else in the building except for us. I had called Pete and he was on his way. I felt very vulnerable and wanted him with me. He arrived just as they were about to give me the anaesthetic. I wasn't joking around and laughing this time. I was really scared.

I was out for three hours while Garth investigated the cause of my numb arm. He couldn't see that there was any reason why my arm was numb. It was most likely because of the position I was lying in for the breast surgery. My arm had had to be stretched out above my head for five hours. He was certain that the feeling in it would return very soon, that it wasn't serious. It was a relief to hear that, but meanwhile my arm was still numb, and I was still on painkillers and feeling out of it, and now I had a third anaesthetic to recover from.

That was probably enough for anybody to deal with, but I had also decided to have surgery on my prolapsed womb. I have a tilted womb which makes you more susceptible to having a prolapse. Having a natural birth with Harvey and him weighing in at over eight pounds hadn't helped. And even though I had Caesareans with Junior and Princess, just being pregnant puts a great strain on the womb. Garth had recommended a gynaecologist who saw me and said it was a straightforward procedure to fix the prolapse and only took forty-five minutes. I wasn't having a designer vagina. Medically this was something I needed to have done or I would need a hysterectomy eventually.

This time I didn't let them film me going into surgery, but I did allow them to film the doctor explaining that this was an operation carried out for medical reasons. After the op I was back at the clinic once more. Through the haze of the anaesthetic I remember thinking optimistically that I was now sorted from head to foot – I had new boobs, a new belly button, and I was fixed down below. I didn't need anything else except my Botox and fillers, which I'd have done just before I flew home.

But instead my situation went from bad to worse. I was now in excruciating agony from all the surgery. And the more pain I was in, the more painkillers I was given, which made me feel completely out of it. I lost all track of time, the days merging into each other in a blur of pain. My memory of this time is full of blanks. Jamela told me that she would be talking to me one minute and the next I would have fallen asleep. I would text friends but my messages would be complete rubbish. At one point I asked my mum how a pregnant friend of mine was doing. 'She told you she lost the baby the other day,' Mum said in surprise. And I had no memory of it. I cried because I felt awful for my friend all over again, and I felt frightened because I couldn't remember something so important.

I had already said that there was no way I could be filmed as I was in such agony. Fortunately I didn't have to argue about it. Nicola agreed. In fact, I think she was shocked by my fragile state. I know I had chosen to have surgery, so I'm not asking for sympathy, but the breast op had been to correct something that had gone wrong and I'd had no idea that the other surgery would leave me in such pain. I know that everyone close to me hated seeing me like this and was desperately worried about me. And I was scared.

After this last op I was bedridden. My arm hurt, my boobs hurt, I was so sore down below that I even couldn't sit down. It was the worst pain I had ever experienced in my life – yes, even worse than child-birth. I actually thought I was going to die. I had a catheter because of the surgery and the nurse said they were going to take it out to see if I could go to the loo, but I couldn't. I was in agony. The amount of anaes-thetics and painkillers I'd been given had seriously affected my bowels and my waterworks. My stomach swelled up so much it looked like I was seven months pregnant. The nurses gave me suppositories and prune juice but nothing worked and when I tried to go it was agony. I would be on the loo for hours trying to poo out a tiny pebble. It was as bad as labour pains.

I got Jamela to take a picture of me down below so I could see what was wrong and it looked horrific – swollen and purple and blue. No wonder I couldn't go to the loo. The nurses couldn't give me any more painkillers to cope with the pain, so they said they would have to put in another catheter. I was crying and shouting out in pain as they did, but at the same time because of the painkillers I felt as if I was in a dream. Or rather a nightmare.

I must have gone to sleep again after that, but when I woke up I was in so much pain it was as if someone had lit a match and I was on fire down there. I was trying to shout out but no one was coming, and I was in such agony I couldn't even reach the bell to ring it. Somehow I managed to get my phone and call Pete. I was sobbing.

'Please come over, I need you . . . I'm in agony!' I think he was really shocked to hear how bad I sounded and, thank God, he rushed over to the clinic straight away. I didn't think I could take much more of this.

Some time later the gynaecologist came to examine me and said he could see no reason why I was in so much agony. It was supposed to be a straightforward operation but maybe I had put my body through too much with all the other anaesthetics and operations. They removed the catheter and I tried yet again to go to the loo, but I couldn't. But I couldn't bear the thought of having another catheter put in.

All I could do during this terrible time was hobble out

of bed in the morning and sit in a bath filled with salt water, to try and ease the pain in my stomach from the constipation and help with the healing. I couldn't even wash properly because of the stitches on my boobs. I went from being bubbly and excited about my trip to LA to being like a frail, helpless old lady. Jamela washed my back for me and shaved my legs and armpits. It doesn't matter what state I'm in, I still want that to be done. She stayed overnight with me at the clinic several times because I didn't want to be on my own.

One night it was arranged that Pete's songs would be played in a certain night club. I didn't want to ruin anyone's trip by asking them to stay with me, but I did feel especially alone and vulnerable that night. And I couldn't help feeling hurt that Pete would never go clubbing with me and yet now he was off clubbing with a group, including my friend Jamela.

Worst of all, Pete had to fly back home. By then we had been out in LA for seven days and one of us needed to be back with the children. Jamela stayed on with me after I offered to pay for her to stay at the Beverly Wilshire. I couldn't bear the thought of being out in LA on my own when I was feeling so very unwell. I was desperate to go home too but I couldn't because of the state I was in. And each day I was staying in the clinic was costing me a fortune. I think the whole trip must have ended up costing me some twenty grand, because, although I didn't have to pay for the second surgery on my boobs, I did have to pay for everything else, and meanwhile I was like a zombie, pumped full of drugs.

I was in that clinic for two long weeks. At one point in the second week I felt I was going stir crazy and suggested to Jamela that we went shopping and got a manicure. We dropped in to Kitson, one of my favourite shops on Robertson Boulevard, which sells designer clothes and accessories. As usual the paps tracked me down. Once again I didn't want them to know what surgery I'd had done so I put on an act that I was fine when really I was in agony and could hardly sit down for the manicure and pedicure. After that I just wanted to go back to the clinic where I knew I could get more painkillers.

But a few days later I was convinced that I could leave the clinic and that I would be all right. I still hadn't managed to do a poo, and after nearly two weeks, believe me, that is no laughing matter. The nurses gave me something which they said was guaranteed to make me go. I checked into a suite at the Beverly Wilshire, my favourite hotel, but only stayed there one night. I took the liquid but it didn't work and I spent three and a half hours on the loo. I was rolling around on the bed in agony, trying to relieve the pain of my bloated stomach, except I couldn't roll that much as it hurt my boobs. And I couldn't lie on my side because of my boobs, so I had to lie on my back. What a great way to spend your time in a five-star hotel. In the morning I had to return to the clinic as I couldn't cope with the pain on my own. During that nightmare time it felt as if someone had created a voodoo doll of me and was testing my endurance to see how much pain I could take. Well, not much more, I can tell you. I was at breaking point.

The day before I flew home, I managed to go to the clinic and get my Botox done. I was almost hysterical, laughing and crying, saying, 'I've had so much done, what's another needle!'

All I wanted to do then was to get home, see the kids, see Pete. I had missed them so much. It felt as if I had been away for ages. But I was still in pain and felt spaced out on the flight. I was picked up at the airport by my driver, and the director was in the car to film my arrival home. I felt overwhelmed by everything, as if I was on a different planet. I was extremely tearful, and at one point I cried and said, 'I think I'm going to have a panic attack, I really need to see a doctor.' I tried to make a joke of it, saying that I couldn't cry because of my false lashes, but I felt so low. The director had to stop filming. I looked out of the window, trying to calm myself, and saw a horse in a field, and even that made me feel anxious and weepy because I had agreed to perform a dressage piece at the Horse of the Year Show in eight weeks' time and just the thought of riding made me wince with pain. When you're in that much agony, you can't imagine ever being well again.

I felt like a little old lady as I got out of the car and hobbled into the house. It was wonderful to see the kids, but I also felt overwhelmed and cried again. I can remember crying as I saw Pete and saying, 'I just need you, I've missed you so much. I'm so pleased I'm home.' It was such a contrast being surrounded by my family after spending the best part of two weeks lying in a hospital bed.

I knew I had to see a doctor so the following day I phoned Brent Tanner, a surgeon I know, and practically begged him to see me. I think he could tell I was in a state as thankfully he agreed to a consultation that day. It was such a relief to see him and to talk through what had happened. He also arranged for a gynaecologist to examine me. I was very relieved when he said that everything looked fine and that the surgeon had done a good job. I think I might even have made a joke, asking, 'Will Pete be pleased? Is it nice and tight?' And he said yes. Not that I had any intention of testing that out for at least six weeks! That was how long I still needed to recover.

Brent checked out all the painkillers I'd been given, some of which were really strong. He said I probably wasn't taking them correctly and took me off all of them, giving me different medication and antibiotics instead and explaining exactly what I needed to take and when. I felt he was my saviour because he knew me and understood what I was talking about. I had thought the States would be a great place to get my prolapse done and had been told it was a straightforward procedure, but it had obviously been too much for my body to cope with so soon after the surgery on my breasts.

That whole experience shocked me. It was the most

horrific time of my life because I was in such pain and felt so out of control. I'm not saying it has put me off surgery for ever but I certainly don't need any more at the moment. I'll have my Botox and fillers and, probably, in a few years I'll need another boob job. That's because when you start having cosmetic surgery, there will inevitably come a time when it needs to be redone. But I'm in no rush and I've definitely gone off having anaesthetics.

I am so thankful that I didn't die and that my body pulled through. And I thank Brent Tanner most of all because from the moment I saw him and he sorted out my medication, I felt better. My arm was still a concern, though. I couldn't pick the kids up, or clench my fist, or even pick up a mug of tea. I saw a physio on the same day I saw Brent and he said that I had a frozen shoulder from where I had been lying in the same position for five hours during the op, and that the oxygen had not been able to get through to it. He told me I had to have treatment on it or it would get worse, and I definitely wouldn't be riding as I could put my shoulder out. So I arranged to have sessions with him, but it took a while to get back to normal. When I did a shoot a few weeks later, I couldn't put my arm on my hip. I had to pick it up with my other hand and put it there. Even after six months it felt numb and bruised. However, there was one good thing – I did love my new boobs. American bullets, I called them, and they were exactly what I wanted. Which was just as well, after everything I had been through to get them.

CHAPTER TEN

CAN WE MAKE IT WORK?

After my surgery, the next big event we had coming up was the renewal of our wedding vows. However, since we had been arguing so bitterly, it really didn't feel like the right time to do it. After our trip to America, there were still problems between us and I think I was hurt that Pete had flown home without me.

In the weeks leading up to September I felt as if I was being torn apart. I loved Pete and wanted to prove it to him by going through with the ceremony, but then at other times I hated him because he was giving me so much shit. 'It's the wrong time for us to be renewing our vows,' I told him, 'I want us to be happy doing it, not putting on an act for the cameras.' But the trouble was our reality show had been sold to ITV with the plan that Pete and I would be filmed renewing our vows. I had even talked about it with our marriage counsellor, saying that I did want to renew them but didn't want to film them.

But when I voiced my concerns to Claire she explained that we needed to go ahead with the filming; that it was one of the series highlights ITV were expecting and she had already booked the hotel where we would renew our vows and the safari that was to follow the ceremony. She said she was sure we could work something out to give Pete and me some space, so long as the vows were filmed. I felt that I didn't have a choice because the arrangements were all in place.

It would have meant so much more to me if Pete and I could have gone away on our own to renew our vows, without any cameras. Even though we weren't getting on I still didn't want our marriage to fail, I still wanted to be with him. We needed to keep something for ourselves. Most of all we needed to sort out the problems between us. But I felt I couldn't say no to the filming; the Katie and Peter Show had to go on.

It helped when we decided we wouldn't renew our wedding vows but would go for a love affirmation ceremony instead. We both thought that vows should be something you renewed after ten or twenty years of marriage, while we had only been married three years and were going through a difficult time. Our wedding had been a kind of Disney-style fairy tale, with the castle, the Cinderella horse-drawn carriage, my Swarovski crystal-encrusted pink dress, and the pink marquee. This ceremony was going to be in complete contrast. As Pete and I were getting on badly in the weeks before it, I left all the arrangements to Claire. But I did want things to be good between me and Pete again, and deep down hoped that the trip to South Africa would help heal things between us.

Even though this was going to be a low-key ceremony, I still wanted a beautiful dress. I had lost weight before my most recent boob job, but when I returned from the States after the surgery my belly was badly bloated. I had expected to have my new boobs and a small waist, I hadn't planned for a pot belly, but there you go, you never know what's going to happen. I paid a visit to one of my favourite boutiques in London: Doly. I love their dresses; they always fit perfectly, with plenty of glitz, and are right up my street. The one I fell in love with was white, with a crystal-encrusted bodice and full skirt which flared out from the hips. It showed off my back and just the right amount of cleavage. It was twelve grand but they let me have it for eight as I'm such a good customer. My wedding dress cost considerably more than that, but I preferred this one. It just shows, it's not down to how much money you spend.

Ironically we flew out to South Africa just as the press began speculating that we were going to split and, yes, things had been really tough between us but I genuinely did want us to pull through. We'd had problems before and had always got through them.

On the flight I made the decision that I wasn't going to

allow the cameras to film us exchanging our vows. I discussed it with Pete, 'I'm doing this for us, not for the cameras.' And he agreed with me. I didn't tell Claire at this point, but as soon as I had made this decision I felt so much better. I felt that if Pete and I could have this time to say the things we really felt – just to each other, with no one else there and no cameras recording everything – we just might be able to make the ceremony mean something for us and we really might be able to put all the bad things behind us.

We were staying at Thornybush Lodge, a five-star game lodge in the heart of the African bush, within a game reserve. I loved the setting. The animals were free to wander around and we would wake up to see groups of monkeys chattering in the trees outside our window. I kept imagining how much the kids would love it if they were with us and thought how next time I would love to bring them all out here on a family holiday – little knowing that there wouldn't be a next time for me and Pete . . .

I really wanted us both to enjoy our time there, but from the moment we arrived it seemed the cameras were always on us and it drove me fucking mad! I started resenting Claire and the film crew, felt they were intruding on what could have been a really special time for Pete and me.

The plan was to have the ceremony out in the bush, which would have been amazing. However, as is typical wherever I go, the weather was shit. Instead of blue skies and hot sun, it was chilly and raining. And it hadn't rained in that area since February! I swear, if I ever go skiing there will be no snow. So the ceremony had to be switched to the lodge grounds. Two thousand orchids had been flown in plus twelve crystal chandeliers and a team of twenty to prepare the location. Claire oversaw it all and, to give her credit, it really did look beautiful. But I felt all the effort was made more for the cameras and the show than for Pete and me.

As soon as we settled into the lodge, the director kept asking us what we were going to say in our vows. 'That's for us to know!' we'd joke back, but I knew I would have to come clean and let them know that I wasn't going to let them film us. Even when we met the minister to discuss the ceremony the cameras were on us, and the journalists from *OK!* were there too as we were going to a do a shoot for the magazine after the ceremony. I felt this didn't exactly give Pete and me the space to make the ceremony special to us. And I thought, 'Bollocks to this! I'm not doing this for the show or for a magazine, I'm doing this because I want to, because I love Pete. I don't care if I upset anyone. I'm going to say what I feel.' So I said to Claire, 'Can you turn the cameras off, please? I need to tell you something.' I waited until they were off then I launched into my speech. 'I have to be honest here . . . I'm not doing these vows for anyone else but me and Pete. And I don't want them to be filmed.'

Claire was dismayed. 'Oh, no! How are we going to

handle this?' She went on to say that ITV were expecting to have the vows on film.

'Our lives are an open book as it is!' I replied. 'Isn't it enough that you're filming the preparations? You can still film us walking down the aisle. Just not the vows. I want them to be personal. You get enough of us as it is. Our wedding was filmed, and the moments leading up to the births of Junior and Princess. For once I want to do something just for me and Pete. '

She tried to talk me round but I stayed firm. 'I'm putting my foot down and that's it. We'll talk about our feelings before and after. You can film us from a distance, but not the actual words.' It took a while and several phone calls but finally it was agreed that we would do it my way.

Now I started to feel more relaxed. Pete had already come up with the idea that we should leave our phones at home and it was the best thing we ever did. I advise anyone who is going on holiday to do the same. Because we didn't have our phones to distract us, Pete and I gelled again. It was as if someone had lifted a dark cloud from over us and we began to have a laugh again, like old times. Pete revealed that he felt the same love for me as he had when he first met me, and I felt the same about him. We really did love each other so much. Pete said on film that over the last five years I had become very bossy and demanding, but 'for all the stress she gives me, I love her more than ever'. And I simply said, 'I love you.'

'Is that it?' he asked.

And so I told him that he was my first, my last and my everything. And I really meant it. However, we didn't have much time on our own. We were with other people most of the time, even when we weren't being filmed.

On the day of the ceremony the skies were grey and overcast and it was chilly, but I was happy and looking forward to the day. Pete also had a smile on his face as we'd had sex the night before. It was the first time since my surgery in August as I'd had to wait six weeks after the operation.

I can't say it felt great. I had been in such agony after the surgery that my mind still remembered the pain even if my body was healed, so I couldn't exactly relax. However, it was good to get close to him again. In fact, we were getting close in every way and I couldn't help wondering what the fuck we'd been arguing about before. We loved each other and that was all that should matter.

Gary was with us to do my hair and make-up, and as he got to work on me on the day of the ceremony, and we sipped champagne, I was looking forward to the moment when I would tell Pete how I felt about him. I loved the white dress I'd chosen and the delicate diamanté tiara. In fact, I preferred the way I looked for this ceremony to how I did on my wedding day. Even though my pink Swarovski crystal-encrusted dress had cost an absolute fortune, it wasn't quite how I had wanted it, and my pink crystal tiara and massive hair pieces had weighed me down. Whereas in my white number, with my hair down, I felt sexy and classy. I had to wear my grey UGGs, though, as it was so cold.

Pete too looked better than he had for our wedding, wearing a stunning white suit. And this time he hadn't had Botox or hair extensions. I thought he looked gorgeous. I stood at the end of the aisle, which had been created outside with white urns and candles, and flowers woven on to the trees, and smiled at him.

Pete had chosen 'Love Is' by Vanessa Williams and Brian McKnight to be played as I walked up to join him. I felt as if it was a special moment as he took my hand. 'This is the beginning of a new day for you,' the minister told us as we exchanged the rings we'd made ourselves out of pieces of local leather we had both plaited. Sweet idea – but give me diamonds any day! The minister had this lovely idea of each of us lighting a candle then each of the candles lighting a bowl of methylated spirit, to symbolise our joined love which would hopefully burn for ever – the love, that is, not the fire. We were meant to take the bowl home and relight it on our anniversary, but the fire burned a bit too well and the bowl got so hot that it broke and burst into a fireball which had to be extinguished before it set the table on fire. Some people might have thought that was a bad sign, but if you spend your whole time worrying about things like that, you're not really living your life, are you? However, looking back, given what did happen to my marriage with Pete, it is a bit ironic, isn't it? Then finally the film crew left and we got the chance to say what we wanted to each other, just us, in front of the minister.

Then the cameras were back on as Pete and I walked arm in arm back down the aisle to the sound of 'If You Were Here Tonight' by Alexander O'Neal, and after that it was time for our wedding dinner. I wished it could have been just the two of us. It would have been so romantic to be outside, with the glow of the candles, the beautiful white flowers and the roaming deer. But Claire and Gary were there, the film crew were filming us, and then we had to do a photoshoot for *OK!* So beautiful as it looked, it ended up feeling like more work. I couldn't help feeling that Pete and I never seemed to be able to do anything on our own, without it being filmed or part of a photoshoot.

Later on we went on a brilliant safari and got up close to the animals; but yet again we were rarely on our own, except when we were in our hotel room, watching movies in bed. But I did feel that we were bonding again, that our marriage was back on track. And I think we both rediscovered our love for each other. We spent five great days in the bush and then went to Cape Town. It didn't feel like a second honeymoon because we were being filmed, but it still felt good.

In the back of my mind was the thought of my upcoming appearance at the Horse of the Year Show which was making me nervous – not just because of the performance itself but because of how Pete might react when I started riding again. Polly had filmed Andrew performing the dressage piece we were going to do, so that I could watch it while I was away and learn the routine. I only watched it when Pete wasn't around as I couldn't bear him to get wound up again and for us to argue, but he knew I had the film with me.

The South Africa trip definitely brought us closer. And it was a big test. I believe if you can love someone even though at times you hate them, then you've still got a relationship worth holding on to. If it had got to the point where we didn't care what we said to each other or what the other person did, then I think that would have been it. Sadly, this time of happiness together was to be short-lived.

CHAPTER ELEVEN

BACK TO BAD

As soon as we flew back from South Africa I had to rehearse intensively for my appearance at the Horse of the Year Show in early October. I only had two weeks to prepare when ideally I would have liked at least two months! But I hadn't been able to ride for over six weeks after my surgery, plus we'd had the South Africa trip. It was a lot of pressure because I had a dressage piece along with two other riders to learn from scratch. Admittedly I wasn't competing, as this was only a showcase, but it would still be a test of my riding abilities and I would be judged on it. Of course, I only had myself to blame as it had been my idea in the first place. We were doing a stand for my KP Equestrian range and a signing at the Horse of the Year Show and I had suggested that I perform a dressage showcase. I wanted to prove that I was a serious rider who was passionate about the sport. But now, as time was so tight, I was almost regretting my big mouth!

I chose the music for the piece, and included the track 'Mysterious Girl' as I wanted Pete to feel included. I even asked him if he wanted to come and sing live while I performed. The event was going to be live on SKY and I thought it would be a good opportunity for both of us to show off what we could do. I knew Pete was dying to perform his music live. OK, it was a song that he had sung many, many times over the years and he wanted to move away from it, but it was still a chance to sing live. And after our time away in South Africa, I thought this would be a great opportunity for us to work together, to show that we supported each other, and to hold on to that closeness that we'd rediscovered. But Pete didn't want to perform the song.

I don't think he realised what a huge event this was in the horse world – it was the biggest show of the year and so it was a big deal that I was going to perform there. To me this was like a dream come true – it's what every rider dreams of doing. It was one of those moments when you wish you could meet your teenage self and say, 'Just look what I'm doing now! Can you believe it?' I had to go to the stables every day, often twice a day, to practise my routine for hours at a time. Sometimes I would have to go in the evening because I was working during the day. I had to rehearse with Andrew and with another rider called Henry Boswell, who were both performing the showcase with me. Our timing had to be spot on – there was no margin for error. But while I was happy to be working on this routine and getting it as near-perfect as I could, back home it was a return to the tense atmosphere. I hated things becoming like this again when we had been getting on so well together.

I was feeling hurt and worn down by the constant rows, getting sick and tired of living like this. There was no fun or sparkle in my life. If it wasn't for my riding I don't know what I would have done. It was my one escape. The only chance I had to be me.

And the press were yet again saying that we were splitting up. They were full of stories saying that I was being cruel to Pete, mocking his music, putting him down . . . but that was all complete crap. We were still convinced that someone close to us was selling stories to the press, but we didn't know who. All these things piled on the pressure.

But I was given a boost when the organisers of the Horse of the Year Show told me that they had sold out of tickets for my showcase. Dressage rarely features in the press so I felt I was helping raise its profile and showing that it didn't matter what background you came from, you could still be a good rider. All my family and friends supported me whole-heartedly and were proud of me, but I was still getting that negative vibe from Pete.

I travelled up to Birmingham the night before the show with my very own support entourage of my mum, dad, sister, Gary, Phil, Michelle and Jamela. I'd wanted Pete to come up with us too, but he didn't. I don't know why.

Although he did drive up on his own the following day, I can't say the atmosphere was any better between us. Then it was time for my big moment: the showcase. Both Andrew and Henry are exceptionally talented and experienced riders, and I will most likely never reach anything like their standard, but I was determined to do my best. I did feel extremely nervous before I went out into the arena on Jordan's Glamour Girl. It was packed with some eight thousand people – not that I knew that then, I found out later – and there was a great sense of anticipation and excitement coming from the audience. It was the first time I had ever performed a dressage showcase and it was the first time for my horse as well. I had no idea how she would react in front of the crowds. Initially she played up a little and I had to really fight to get her under control. She is sixteen hands three inches which, take it from me, is big, but I managed and I think people respected me for that.

Our routine was five minutes long, which doesn't sound much but, believe me, feels like for ever when you're in front of thousands and are being filmed and going out on live TV. But it went well and I got great feedback from the crowd, who seemed to love it. I knew my performance wasn't perfect but I was still proud of it. I'd only been learning dressage for six months. To me, performing a showcase at the Horse of the Year Show felt like one of my biggest achievements ever. Though I don't just want to do showcases, I want to compete too. I know that I am never going to be a top dressage rider – I would have to dedicate my whole life to it, which I can't do, and I would be fooling myself if I thought I could ever be the best as there are some amazing riders out there who have been doing it most of their lives. So reports that I was going to be in the Olympic team were wildly exaggerated! But I do want to compete, just for myself, to see how much I can improve. And I can't wait for the day when Junior and Princess compete in horse shows – I will be the proudest mum there!

After the showcase I had lots of press interviews to do, not just with the tabloids but also the broadsheets, and the following day there was really positive coverage about the event. I had made all the nationals and the organisers were very pleased. So pleased that they asked me to perform in the finale on Sunday. Whether people liked me or not, I felt they should at least be pleased that I was bringing dressage to public attention because usually it is overlooked. I did come in for a bit of stick for wearing a glittery jacket and my full glamour girl make-up, but I wasn't competing so I felt I could. At least I was wearing dark colours. The organisers should count themselves lucky I didn't come out wearing pink! After the Horse of the Year I received lots of offers to do other showcases but I don't want to be seen by people in the horse world as someone who just performs show-cases. I want to compete alongside everyone else.

I had hoped that Pete would be pleased by my success. After my performance and interviews we all went to get something to eat. There was large group of my friends and family, plus Andrew and Polly and Henry and his girlfriend. This should have been a chance for us to celebrate together, but as Pete and I weren't getting on it put a downer on the occasion. It had been such a big achievement for me, and I'd got such a buzz from it, but as soon as I saw Pete looking so moody, I thought, 'Fuck, why can't we just celebrate my success?' I felt so angry.

I ended up turning to him and saying, 'You may as well go if you're just going to sit here and be negative.' I didn't want him to but he was bringing me down and ruining what should have been a fantastic experience. To me, appearing on Horse of the Year had been brilliant. I had loved it and felt on such a high. Why couldn't Pete get that? Unfortunately he took me at my word and ended up leaving. What the hell was happening to my marriage?

After he left I had to get on with the signing for my equestrian range. It was actually a relief that Pete wasn't around any more. I'm afraid more and more of my marriage had become like this. There were still good days but there were many bad days. All too often Pete and I would be having a go at each other. At one point I noticed that my dad and Nicola had left and wondered where they had gone but thought no more about it. The signing went well. As ever it was great meeting my fans.

Then I happened to check my phone and discovered a text from Pete that really worried me. He didn't sound like himself at all.

Then Mum told me that he had suffered a panic attack on the way home, and that my dad and Nicola had had to pick him up and drive him home as he was in such a bad state he wasn't able to drive himself. Pete had suffered from panic attacks in the past before I had met him, and when he was recovering from meningitis he had suffered from them again. I've suffered from them myself in the past and know how frightening and over-whelming they are. I felt terrible because I had told him to go. I'd had no idea that this was going to happen. I phoned Pete but he couldn't answer as he was still in such an emotional state. So I texted him to tell him that I was sorry about the attack, that I loved him and I wanted our marriage to work out. That was what I always said to him throughout this time. I just wanted him to realise how much we had going for us – we had a great life together, beautiful children, we lived in a big house, we were so lucky. We had everything we wanted, didn't we?

* * *

It was during the autumn of 2008 that I noticed a change in Pete, which all my friends and family commented on as well. He seemed to have a new air of confidence about him. By then he knew that he was going to record his album in LA in the New Year and was very focussed on that. He began working out regularly at a gym – we had already signed up to do the London Marathon the following April. He also started getting in contact with his old friends again, including some of the dancers he had worked with in the past, and would invite them over to the house. I was fine about having people over, but it was quite a change for him as he hadn't asked them over before. Then he started to go out a little more at night, which was very uncharacteristic of him. He even went clubbing once or twice and he'd always claimed he hated clubbing. It felt to me as if he was saying, 'It's my turn to be in the spotlight now, Kate, so step back.' And while I wanted him to do well with his music, I couldn't help feeling that he wasn't being very nice about it. He just wasn't being the Pete I knew – the one who was such a lovely, open and easy-going guy.

I was starting to feel by then that we had lost some of the spark between us. And it was so sad. I couldn't help feeling that we were growing apart and I hated it. I felt that we no longer had the closeness we'd always shared. I would know that when I came home after work and walked in the door, Pete wouldn't look pleased to see me and my heart would sink. You want to come back to a happy home, don't you? Not a miserable one.

But however bad things got between us, I never considered walking out on him – I really did want us to try and make it work. I would only have considered ending our marriage if he was unfaithful or if he walked out on me.

CHAPTER TWELVE

LA BLUES

In early November we flew to the Maldives for a week with Princess. Although things had been tense between us, we both wanted to put things right. As we knew that we had got on so well on our recent trip to South Africa, we hoped that this trip also would help. The press made out it was a last-minute bid to try and patch things up in our marriage, but I was still hopeful that things hadn't got nearly as bad as that.

We chose the same resort we'd been to on our honeymoon, which had such happy memories for us – the five-star Conrad Maldives Rangali Island – and stayed in the same villa. I love it out there; it really is as close to paradise as you can get. We were staying in a luxury waterside villa which you reach by a little wooden walkway, so you're surrounded by the calm, turquoise blue Indian Ocean as far as your eye can see and behind you is a beautiful white sand beach. I always feel I can relax out there.

Once again we didn't take our phones. Although that was good for our stay as it meant we didn't have any distractions, it wasn't so great when we were ten minutes away from Heathrow and Pete realised he hadn't got his passport with him and we couldn't call anyone to bring it to us! So we missed our flight.

But when we finally got there, a day late, it was brilliant. We completely relaxed, had some lovely times with Princess, ate good food, sunbathed, swam and had treatments. I'm surprised I wasn't rubbed away by the number of treatments I had! We also trained in the gym for the Marathon and it was good to do something together that wasn't about work or being filmed. Because Pete had been working out so regularly he was pleased that he was losing weight and toning up and I was pleased for him, though as I've said before I really didn't think he needed to. Back then I always thought he was gorgeous even if he didn't have a six-pack. I still felt quite wary about having sex, after the surgery, but we did. I felt as if we were getting close again, and we planned to come back the following November and bring all the kids with us. It seemed whenever we were away together and there were no cameras on us and no one else around, away from everything, we got on really well. Sadly, in just over six months I would be back in the Maldives, but this time on my own after Pete had left me . . .

Practically as soon as we returned home, there seemed to be tension between us again. Pete was spending more and more hours at the gym, and the rest of the time working on his music. I could see that our marriage was changing and not for the better. We were drifting apart. The press continued to write negative stories about our relationship. There was one saying that we didn't want to be together any more but realised that we couldn't break up as we were a business and a brand. It was unbelievable – I would only stay with someone for love. Fame and money are nothing to me compared to that.

The next big work commitment we had coming up was our trip to LA in January 2009 to film the latest series of our reality TV show – *Katie and Peter: Stateside.* By then I was so unhappy with the lack of control I had over filming and the fact that I played no part in the running of the production company. In fact, I hadn't wanted to sign the contract for the latest show. But I knew Pete would be devastated if he couldn't record his album in LA, he had been working so hard on his music and I didn't want him to lose out, so reluctantly I did end up signing it. I think I had stayed with our management CAN because Pete was with them and had known them for so long. I was worried about the impact on him and me if I ever left them, and that our diaries might not be co-ordinated then, which might cause further tension. But, increasingly, I had come to see that I did need to take action and make some changes to the way I was managed.

We were going to be out in LA for three months

filming the show and I had very mixed feelings about that. For a start it was going to be hard for me and Pete to sort out our problems because the cameras were going to be on us. 'Maybe a change of scene will help us,' I tried to convince myself. But it was no good, I was already apprehensive about the trip. Apart from the Maldives holiday, we'd been getting on so badly that the thought of being away from home, and from the support network of my family and friends, was stressing me out. In contrast, I think Pete was looking forward to the trip as he was going to be recording his album. And he knew that I would be away from Andrew.

There was so much we needed to plan first. My top priority was getting the right school for Harvey. He was so happy and doing so well at his school in the UK, I really wanted him to have an equally great experience in the States. We could have got him private tuition at home but I wanted him to go to school so he could socialise with other children. I knew that there would be so much he would like about America, from the flight over – because he absolutely loves planes – to swimming in the pool in the sunshine. I always used to worry about taking him somewhere different, but increasingly as he got older I felt excited about seeing how he would respond to a new school and hoped that he would make good progress there. My mum, who does so much for Harvey and me, was brilliant at researching American schools and found one which seemed perfect: the Junior Blind of America School.

It was very important to me that Harvey went to a school which didn't involve a lot of travelling, and that would really determine where we lived in LA. Of course, location was important for our work as well but to me Harvey was the most important factor. It was easier planning for Princess and Junior as we decided that they would go to nursery a couple of days a week and on the other days get involved in playing golf and tennis, the same activities that they do in the UK. And I wanted Princess to take up ballet and tap – if she wanted to. I've never been one of those pushy mums who want their kids to do activities all the time, but I do think it's good for them to try different things.

I was happy that Pete would finally be able to finish recording his album. Music has always been his passion and I wanted him to have a successful music career again. I also hoped that there would be further work opportunities for me in the States as well. Our management were coming out with us and staying for three months and Claire assured me that we would be doing lots of interviews and shoots with the celebrity mags to help raise our profile. She also said that she had contacted chat shows to try and get us on, and I was especially pleased when she told me that she had contacted Oprah and hoped to set up an interview for me where I would appear with Harvey and talk about what it was like being a mum to a disabled child.

I was especially keen to do the interview with Oprah as Pete had discovered some really despicable chat-room sites in the US which were commenting on our imminent arrival and writing vile racist abuse about Harvey and abuse about him being disabled – calling him among other things 'a disabled black c***' and 'monkey boy'. I was absolutely shocked to the core to think that anyone could be so cruel and vicious about an innocent child, and that made me even more determined to have Harvey with us in public and show everyone that he is a lovely little boy. Yes, he can be hard work but he's adorable when you get to know him. I'm not ashamed of him; in fact, I'm incredibly proud of him and everything he has achieved, and I'm not going to hide him away.

I certainly didn't think that I was going out to try and 'break' America, whatever some of the UK press made out. So many stars from this country have tried that and failed. Of course, deep down I would like to be successful out there. Who wouldn't? And I had all my existing business ventures and products which had sold very well in the UK, and was keen to see if I could make something of them in the States. I had even put together a portfolio detailing all my books and products, so that I could hand it out to the relevant people in business and the media in the US.

As our departure date grew closer I started to feel a bit more optimistic. Everything seemed to be falling into place. Our management said that they had found us an amazing house, Harvey's school was sorted, our nanny was coming out with us, along with my mum, to help settle Harvey into school. I hoped that we would all be able to enjoy the experience and get something out of it. I also hoped that Pete and I would be able to do some fun things together, like go to some film premieres and meet up with some of the celebrities that I know out there, including Paris Hilton and Carmen Electra. So I did go out with an open mind.

However, from the moment we arrived in LA things went wrong. The first problem was with the house we were staying at. Our management had rented us a huge Italian-style villa in Malibu. Although I had been to LA many times before I had tended to stay in the heart of Beverly Hills, which I love, and had not actually been to Malibu and so had no idea how far from Beverly Hills it was. It was an hour's drive. It was an amazing seven-bedroomed mansion with a gym, cinema and games room, swimming pool and incredible views, but I didn't want to spend all my time there. I couldn't help feeling stuck in the middle of nowhere.

But the house was just the tip of the iceberg! I hated my time out in Malibu. They were three of the worst months of my life. It was there that the filming really got to me. I had had enough of it. Pete was so taken up with his album that I hardly saw him, and when I did see him we argued because I was so stressed out by the constant filming.

I wanted to work and get the most out of my time in LA, but I ended up doing a lot less than I had expected in the three months we were there. Apart from filming our reality show we just did a couple of shoots for magazines over there and a shoot for *OK!*, plus some radio and TV interviews. I also appeared on a chat show in New York and on some TV show about plastic surgery. Nothing ever came of the idea that I should appear on *Oprah*. Claire tried to reassure me that I shouldn't worry. She'd arranged for the buggies and cribs from my planned baby range to be sent over from the UK together with my new perfume, perhaps to reassure me, and show me how much I had going on.

But, of course, when Pete left me, I lost the baby range and the perfume, and it took over a year for me to bring out my new ranges . . .

This lack of work and new opportunities really got to me. I have worked since the age of seventeen and am not used to sitting around doing nothing. And it wasn't as if we were on holiday, because the cameras were on us practically all the time it felt. The house in Malibu was supposed to be a home for Pete, me and the kids, but we would often find the camera crew wandering in without knocking, as if it was a film set. As I've already said, I didn't get on with them and was sick of being filmed. I think it's true to say that I had lost all trust in the crew. Whenever I knew they were trying to film me in the house, I would deliberately go a different way so they couldn't . . . which is one of the perks of staying in a mansion!

They always wanted to get my reaction to everything and I hated that, it seemed so fake to me. For example, if they had done up the house, and I hadn't seen it, they would want to catch me going, 'Oh my God! Look at that! Isn't it amazing?' But instead I'd just walk in and pretend nothing had changed, so they couldn't get their reaction shots. When I appeared on two TV shows in the States, the crew were waiting to film me afterwards and would say to me, 'What was it like?' And I knew they wanted me to gush about my feelings so I would reply, 'It was fine,' knowing full well that I hadn't given them what they wanted. But *I* wanted to say, 'Fuck off! You know what it was like because you've just filmed it!' I didn't click with that particular crew at all, which makes it very hard when you're filming a reality show.

And Claire would want to set up new activities to film with Pete and me and the kids, like suggesting that we should all play together in the pool as it would make a good scene. And I'd reply, 'No! I don't fucking want to get in the pool! This is supposed to be a reality show, I don't want to fake playing with my kids. It's the Katie and Peter Show not the Katie, Peter and Kids Show.' My view is that if the kids happen to be in a scene, then OK. I didn't want scenes to be engineered around them.

Because there were no work commitments to film us going to, apart from Pete in the recording studio, Claire would set up activities for us to do, such as going bowling or roller-blading, but to me that just seemed fake. I would never usually do those things, so why film them? And roller-blading was a nightmare because of the paps who followed us everywhere, trying to get their shots. It wasn't fun at all. I was more concerned with trying to breathe in than with learning to skate, as you would be if you had all these cameras clicking away at you, knowing that a shot of you looking dodgy could easily end up in a mag.

Oh, yes, and the weather was shit. It rained and was chilly! I was trapped in this bloody mansion, in the middle of nowhere, when we should have been out there enjoying ourselves. I had hoped that when we were in the States Pete and I would actually be able to spend some time together, go out and do some fun things. But we were hardly ever alone and we hardly went out. Practically the only time we got to be on our own was when we went running, in training for the Marathon. My only friends were the nannies – and thank God for them! They would tell my mum that they felt sorry for me, stuck out in Malibu, with nothing to do and Pete giving me a hard time.

I can count on one hand the number of times we went out, including the night when we both went to the Elton John Aids Foundation Oscars party. And not even that went smoothly as the dress I had chosen in London got stuck in customs and it was a rush to get another one for the event. There was a report in the press about some designer not wanting to lend me something to wear because I didn't have the right image for her. Well, bollocks to that. I didn't even ask to borrow one of her dresses because I hadn't ever heard of her! And anyway

I was lent a pair of £400,000 diamond earrings, which beats a borrowed dress any time. I can't exactly say it was a great night as Pete was watching me to make sure I didn't drink so I didn't even have a glass of champagne, even though everyone else was. And I only wanted one glass; I wasn't going to get caned!

The following day the British press made a big deal of how I was at the Oscars party with Victoria Beckham, and was there still this big feud between us, and did she snub me? Well, the truth is I didn't even attempt to say hello to her as I was busy talking to Simon Cowell and his then girlfriend Terri who were on my table, along with Richard Desmond. There were lots of other people I could have gone and said hello to, and just because I didn't, it didn't mean that we were having a feud. And anyway I wasn't trying to run around after the big stars. I'm not bothered about mixing with celebrities. I don't mix with any in England and I didn't in the States. I don't use people just to get publicity. I've got no problem with Victoria Beckham whatsoever. There, that's my last word on the subject!

Pete was completely taken up with recording his album, and while I understood his desire to finish it, especially since he was paying for it himself, I didn't want to go to the studio every single day. That's not to say that I wasn't supportive, and if we had still been together then I would certainly have gone on tour with him. But, to be honest, sitting in the studio hour after hour, hearing him go through the same lines over and over again, was boring! He would even play the tracks in the car. I had heard most of them, including 'Behind Closed Doors' and 'Call the Doctor', and was upset by the lyrics which all seemed to be so negative, about couples not understanding each other, someone feeling alone even in a relationship, and the relationship breaking up. 'I hope that's not what you think about our marriage?' I said to Pete. 'Because it's not very nice hearing it described like this. I feel really hurt, if you must know.'

He replied, 'Listen to the lyrics, they show how hurt I've been at times. But it's not just about us, it's about any relationship.'

I wasn't convinced. And, looking back, I can't help wondering if he was already planning to leave me.

When Pete wasn't in the studio we were bickering because of the pressure of filming. It was sheer misery. I didn't even have the escape of riding. I had just bought a horse and had her flown over to the States, but I really needed Andrew to come over and train her up for me because we weren't connecting properly. But, of course, I felt I couldn't ask him because of what Pete's reaction was likely to be. Instead I flew another trainer over, but she didn't know me or how I ride and every time she came to the stables the horse was fine. So now I was paying for a horse that I couldn't ride as well as I wanted.

The only good things were that my mum had done a fantastic job of finding such a brilliant school for Harvey

– he was settled in and making great progress – and Princess and Junior were happy.

And then Claire received a letter from my lawyer setting out the suggested new terms for the management contract between us. They were a lot less favourable than the ones she was used to and we were unable to reach an agreement. It was decided she would officially stop being my manager on 23 June 2009. Whatever was subsequently said in the press, I consider myself the one who ended our business relationship.

The atmosphere between all of us became even more tense and strained after that. There were arguments between me, Claire and Nicola, with Pete as piggy in the middle between us all. The rows were always about work. How I didn't want to be filmed all the time; that I wanted to spend more time with Pete; that I wanted to be part of the TV production company. I got even more sick of the filming and just wanted to return to the UK. I could see that this situation was damaging my marriage. I wanted Pete to be my husband, not to work with him all the time. It was so unhealthy.

As I've said before, I can't put on an act that everything is OK for the camera if I'm unhappy. If I'm in a bad mood, I will still be in a bad mood when we are filming. And later, when I watched our *Stateside* series – not that I wanted to as it just reminded me of how miserable I was – I can see that I come across as the bad guy nearly all the time, with Pete as good cop, me as bad. It comes across that Pete is perfect and I was a miserable cow and that he looked after the kids on his days off while I just went to get my hair and nails done. And it wasn't like that.

But there were several moments in the show when even Pete didn't come across so well, one of which was when we were supposed to be going roller-blading. The paps were all outside the store where we were renting the equipment, and it was raining, and I didn't want to go out and roller-blade with them all taking pictures as if I was some performing fucking dog! When I first started going to LA I thought the paps there were far more polite than the British ones, but all that had changed. By then they were just as ruthless about getting their shots. Or even more so, it seemed. I didn't want to be photographed every single time I left the house.

So Pete and I were holed up in the store with the young sales assistant and Nicola. I was just making small talk with the assistant to pass the time when Pete started trying to wind him up, making out he was some-one that he was not. I thought he was being pathetic. The guy was just doing his job; Pete didn't have to be like that.

Straight away things turned nasty when Pete said, really sarcastically, 'He doesn't know who you are.'

Like I fucking care if some sales assistant in the States knows who I am or not! I'm not so insecure in myself that I need to be recognised constantly. Funnily enough, though, I met that same guy again on the red carpet at the 2010 Oscars – and joked to him that I'd since got remarried!

I told Pete to stop being such a knob; said that he was 'an old fucking singer no one knows about'. Of course, the row kicked off big time after that.

'You're a miserable cow and living with you is miserable,' he retorted.

I just shrugged; I had heard him speak to me like this so many times, I was hardened to it. 'I'm the one who makes the money, so I'll have things my way,' I replied. That may have sounded harsh but I was sick of him sniping at me, and sick of the situation we were in.

'You're a psycho. I hope you're proud of yourself,' he exclaimed. 'You're a fucking idiot . . . a fucking arrogant bitch!'

We had always rowed and bickered in the past, but never as bitterly as this. I think things got so bad between us in LA that there was no coming back from it. We seemed to have lost all respect for each other and both said some truly terrible things. Then, as we were about to fly back, I was burning some rubbish in one of the fireplaces in the house and asked Pete if there was anything he wanted to put on the fire. 'Yes, you,' he replied. It was a joke but it wasn't funny. Later, on film, he said that he loved me, but I couldn't answer him. At that moment it really didn't feel like he did.

We never, ever should have gone out to America to film the show.

Out with Gary and Phil.

Me and my gorgeous sister Sophie.

The irresistible Price women!

Out on the town at an awards ceremony with Phil, Hannah, Melody, Laura and Michelle.

There's always time to strike a pose!

Paradise!
In the Maldives
with Princess
and Junior.

The infamous Ibiza holiday.
Shooting my calendar.

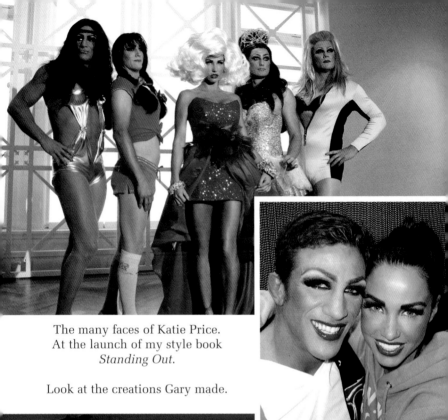

The many faces of Katie Price.
At the launch of my style book
Standing Out.

Look at the creations Gary made.

CHAPTER THIRTEEN

KATIE AND PETER: THE FINAL CHAPTER

But we didn't just have ourselves to think about any more because in March I found out I was pregnant. Even though our relationship was under such strain, I was thrilled and so was Pete. It wasn't that I hoped this baby would heal the problems in our marriage because I don't think you should ever have a child for that reason. I had just always wanted more children. Of course, I had no idea that in just over a month Pete would have walked out on me. I still thought we were going through a rough patch but would get through it. By now we'd been through so many rough patches but also so many good times that I thought that's just what marriage was like. In spite of our problems, I still felt that we were so close. It never crossed my mind that we could split up.

As soon as we were back in the UK I went to see Dr

Gibb, my obstetrician in London, to check that everything was OK with the baby by having a scan. I was probably around ten weeks by then and certainly had all the symptoms of pregnancy. I felt nauseous and bloated, with sore boobs. I always feel anxious about having scans because of the time I was nearly four months pregnant in 2006 and the doctor discovered during a scan that my baby had died. I was devastated and found it really hard to get over that miscarriage. That was what made going on to have Princess, the following year, all the more wonderful.

Pete came to the clinic with me. I lay back on the couch and waited while Dr Gibb rubbed the cold gel on my belly and then pressed the scanner against it. 'Please let my baby be all right,' I thought apprehensively, as Dr Gibb moved the scanner around, trying to locate the baby. I anxiously looked at the screen and then I saw the tiny outline. Surely that meant everything must be OK? But Dr Gibb was very concerned; he explained that he couldn't detect a heartbeat and said that I would have to come back for another scan in a few days. He also did a blood test. This didn't seem like good news and I had a horrible numb feeling inside as I prepared myself for the worst. I felt so upset.

But a few days later Dr Gibb called to say that the levels of HCG, a hormone created during the early stages of pregnancy, in my blood were still high, which indicated that the baby might be alive after all. I clung to this hope. But when I went in for another scan he said the words that I had been dreading: 'I'm so sorry, Katie, I can't find a heartbeat. I'm afraid the baby's died.'

Anyone who has ever had a miscarriage will know what a devastating feeling it is. You go from believing you are pregnant, carrying a new life, and being excited, to feeling an unbearable sense of loss where you feel numb and empty. I couldn't believe that this was happening to me again. I had the option of taking some tablets which would trigger a miscarriage over several days or else having an operation. I chose to have the operation. I needed the ordeal to be over with as soon as possible. Pete was upset when he came up to the clinic to be with me before the op. He wanted to know what was wrong with the baby and why it had died. He didn't seem to understand that we didn't know. How could anyone know?

I had the operation and was discharged that night. Physically I felt drained and sore, and emotionally I felt incredibly vulnerable. I just wanted to curl up in bed and mourn my lost baby. But I couldn't. I was taking part in the London Marathon at the weekend – just five days away. After the operation I was still bleeding and the very last thing I felt like doing was running a Marathon, which is probably one of the most physically demanding things you can put your body through. But I felt I couldn't let down the people who had sponsored me. I was doing this for Harvey and for the Vision Charity, which raises money for the benefit of blind, visually impaired and dyslexic children. I was also a patron of the charity, so it was really important to me personally. I would have done the Marathon had I still been pregnant because I had been training for it and by then my body was used to the demands of training. Lots of people do carry on running when they are pregnant, though of course if my doctor had advised me not to run it I wouldn't have.

The day after I'd had the operation I had to go to the press call for the Marathon. I felt really low emotionally and physically very uncomfortable. I was sore and bleeding and still having stomach cramps.

I felt very low and weepy for the rest of that week, not myself at all. But as I was shooting the photographs for my style book, I had to put on a brave face and carry on. Pete was really upset by the miscarriage as well, but I do think it's different for men. They're not the ones who have been carrying the baby and they will never know what it feels like when that baby dies. But I didn't feel as if Pete was being particularly sympathetic towards me, given that I had just had a miscarriage. I suppose it's easier for men to deal with as they are not coping with the physical and emotional after-effects.

By the time Sunday, 26 April arrived, I still felt low; all I could think was, 'Please let me get through this somehow,' which was such a shame as I had been looking forward to taking part and raising money for the charity. But Pete and I were still pleased to be taking part as we had done so much training together over the months. I was still bleeding from the op and worried about blood clots, but told myself that if I felt unwell or if I started bleeding more heavily I would pull out of the race. I knew it wasn't advisable to run the Marathon in that condition but I'm such a trouper and I really didn't want to let my sponsors or the charity down. And on top of feeling so emotional and physically quite weak, I had also damaged my knee in training which was going to make running even harder. But I did my best and put on an act that everything was OK.

The day itself was clear and sunny – perfect conditions for running. The atmosphere around the Marathon is incredible. There are so many people running to support different charities – many of them people who have lost loved ones to cancer and other diseases, and want to raise funds in their memory – so many spectators cheering the runners on. I was wearing a bright orange t-shirt with the Vision logo on it and also a picture of Harvey, and kept telling myself to focus on why I was running the race, though it wasn't easy. But we did get the most fantastic support from the crowd as we ran past and I really appreciated that.

I was running with Pete, my brother and sister, and Nick, the husband of my then friend Michelle, and they had promised to go at my speed. My sister ran ahead, but I don't blame her as she had trained hard and wanted to prove she could run the race in a good time. I couldn't run very fast. I kept imagining I was bleeding more heavily and felt really scared. I had to keep going to the loo to check, but thankfully it was OK. But Pete, my brother and Nick were a fantastic support. They stayed by my side for the whole race, even though there's no question that they could all have achieved very respectable times if not – especially my brother who has run several Marathons.

At eighteen miles my knee buckled under me and I had to get it bandaged up. The pain was excruciating. It was only sheer determination and will-power that helped me carry on. I managed to stagger – and stagger is the word – but at twenty-three miles, with the end so close, it gave way again. I was in tears of agony as I literally hobbled over the finishing line. It had taken me over seven hours but I had done it. I hadn't let my sponsors down and that was all that mattered to me. And as I suffered no ill effects from running the Marathon after having the miscarriage, I still feel I was right to do it.

We grabbed a McDonald's and then headed for home as we were all exhausted. As we were nearing the house I suddenly noticed a horse loose on the road. 'Oh my God!' I exclaimed. 'Stop the car, I have to try and rescue it! It will get hit by a car if we don't do something.' Instantly my dad stopped the car and got out, and somehow I managed to summon the energy to drag myself out as well.

I could barely walk as my knee was killing me but somehow I managed to limp after the horse and catch it. I'm certain we saved it from being hit by a car.

A few days later Pete, the kids and I flew to Cyprus for

a mini-break. Life had been so manic and emotional during the past weeks that we felt we needed some time on our own as a family. And for once we weren't being filmed. One day Pete and I went to the gym – I wanted to keep my fitness up. When we came out there were two girls standing there. Pete got talking to them while I walked over to the car. I could instantly sense that one of the girls must be an ex-girlfriend, just from Pete's body language and because I knew him so well. He didn't introduce me to them and I was furious. When he got in the car I said, 'How fucking dare you not introduce me, and stand there chatting in front of me? That is so disrespectful.' I could just imagine how he would have reacted if I'd done the same thing to him with one of my exes. I felt jealous and angry.

There was a bad atmosphere between us for the rest of the day. Then we went out to dinner and finally had a heart to heart about our relationship and where we thought it was going wrong. The bottom line was that, in spite of everything, we both really loved each other and wanted to make our marriage work. Pete said that he still had a problem with me going out on my own. It was all the usual things about him worrying that I would get drunk and end up flirting with another man or even being unfaithful. And the fact was that back then, because of the strain our marriage was under, I was jealous whenever Pete went out on *his* own. Because we spent so much time together working and so rarely went out on our own, when one of us wanted to, it made the other one feel insecure. So, for instance, if Pete wanted to go the cinema with his friends and not me, I would wonder why he didn't want to take me and would feel hurt. Looking back, I know that it is not healthy for a relationship to be with each other so much, but that's how it was for Pete and me.

He suggested that we should both agree that from then on we wouldn't go out on our own but only as a couple. My heart sank. What was wrong with me wanting to go out on my own? I was only having a laugh, going clubbing with my girlfriends, like so many other women did every single week without it being a huge issue for their husbands. This was supposed to be a marriage, not a prison sentence. But because I wanted my marriage to work, I agreed. I wasn't happy but I didn't want to be without Pete. The moment the words were out of my mouth, I regretted them. It wasn't a promise that deep down I believed I could keep or even wanted to keep because I still thought he was wrong to have a problem with me going out. But I did agree. I wanted things to be happy and calm between us, wanted us to get along. I hated it when we didn't. I tried to push it to the back of my mind. Little did I realise that this was the last family holiday we would ever have, but for some reason I packed up a lot of my things from the Cyprus house and brought them home with me.

Back in the UK I had a signing for KP Equestrian at the Badminton Horse Show on Friday, 8 May. Pete was going to stay out in Cyprus for a few more days but, because we had made this pact to do more things together, he said that he would come to the horse show with me. I was looking forward to us spending more time together and was pleased that he was going to be there to support me. I wanted him to come with me, as in the past when he'd come, or I had gone along to his club Pas, it had been the perfect opportunity for us to spend some quality time together, and have a night away in a hotel.

But then, unexpectedly, Pete changed his mind. He said he had things to do and would I mind if he didn't come? I was very disappointed; this was supposed to be our fresh start, where we made an effort to do things together. However, I didn't make a big deal of it and I went off to Bristol and did my signing alone. While I was at the show I bumped into Andrew and Polly who were there along with other friends. We all watched some dressage together and I made a joke to Gary and Diana, saying, 'Oh, you'd better not sit next to me, just in case we're photographed together!' Little knowing that later a photograph of me and another rider would trigger Pete to walk out on me.

After the show we all chatted about our plans for the evening, and we thought it would be good to meet up for dinner later. It was all very relaxed and laid-back, just the kind of dinner you have after you've been working all day, as I had been. We all got on so well – there were my business associates and friends Diana and Cath, my best friend Gary, a couple of riders that I knew – Spencer and Jay – and Andrew and Polly.

Then someone suggested we go on to a club. Instantly, I thought of the pact I had just made with Pete and replied, 'You go, but I can't come because of Pete.' But then I thought, 'How pathetic does it sound for a woman of nearly thirty-one not to feel able to go out with her friends?'

'But you're a grown-up!' Gary exclaimed. 'You're not doing anything wrong!' And he was backed up by everyone else round the table. I explained how I had made the pact with Pete and that we had agreed we wouldn't go out without each other. I could tell that my friends all thought the pact was a bad idea, and more than one person commented, 'What! Are you seriously never going to go out on your own again? It's normal to go out on your own sometimes!' And they were giving me a bit of stick about it. As they teased me I thought again that it was true, I wasn't doing anything wrong. I just wanted to socialise with my friends and business partners.

So I went to the club and carried on drinking and having a laugh, and that's all it was. Unfortunately there were also plenty of arseholes there with camera phones who took pictures of me. I know I'm a lightweight when it comes to alcohol and it really doesn't take much to get me drunk. And when I am drunk I suppose I can be a real exhibitionist, and I probably was being loud, dancing lots and possibly singing – I can't remember!

But the point is, that was it. I just had a few drinks and let my hair down. Big deal. I probably needed to after the trauma of the miscarriage. And it was also a belated celebration for having run the Marathon the previous Sunday. Everyone else I knew who had taken part in the race had gone out and had a drink to celebrate, whereas we had gone straight home because Pete didn't like me having one.

The following day I spoke to him on the phone and he asked how my night had been and I said fine. I didn't tell him I had gone out to a club with a group of friends which included Andrew and Polly, knowing that it was bound to trigger an argument. I suppose I hoped that Pete would never find out – and anyway, what was there to find out? I'd just gone out with my friends after work.

I drove back home and got ready for the British Soap Awards where Pete and I were going to be presenting an award. We were getting on fine, had the usual cheeky banter between us on-stage, and then went out to dinner at Nobu with Gary and Phil. Sadly it was to be the last dinner I ever had with Pete. We had a really good night together. If someone had told me that in just over twenty-four hours my marriage would be over, I would have thought they were completely mad.

Next day I drove back down to Badminton as I had seen a black horse I liked the look of at the show. I bought it. Back home everything seemed fine and Pete was pleased that I had managed to get the horse. But it was the calm before the storm. On Monday morning I got up early, keen to get to the stables and have my riding lesson. I was just about to leave when my mobile rang. It was Andrew. He sounded serious. 'Have you seen this morning's paper, Kate?' he asked. 'You're on the front of the *Sun*. It doesn't look good.'

With a sick feeling in my gut, I walked over to the kitchen table where the papers were still bundled up. I rummaged through them to get to the *Sun* and the sick feeling got worse. There I was, plastered across the front of it, in a shot taken in the Bristol night club, looking the worse for wear. I was flashing my cleavage and sitting next to Spencer Wilton, one of the riders I knew, who just happens to be gay but when did the papers ever let the truth get in the way of a good story? I knew Pete would go absolutely ballistic even though he had met Spencer before and knew he was gay. I couldn't face having the inevitable argument, so I quickly left the house and headed for the stables.

'Pete is going to go crazy when he sees the paper,' I told Andrew as soon I met up with him. I felt sick with apprehension at the thought of the rows starting up all over again. I just didn't think I could take any more, especially so soon after the miscarriage. I felt nervous, fearful of Pete's reaction, working myself up into a state as I wondered what he would do. But then I tried to pull myself together, telling myself to stay calm because I had done nothing wrong.

I was halfway through the riding lesson when my

phone rang. It was Pete, fury distorting his voice as he shouted. I knew that he was going to see his solicitor that day to sort out his record deal. And, sure enough, he added that he was going to ask about getting a divorce as well.

I had heard him say things like this so many times, but I knew that this time he meant it. I think deep down I had reached the end of the line with our marriage. So in the heat of the moment, instead of begging him not to jump to the wrong conclusion, I bit back with, 'Well, go and see your solicitor then! Divorce me!'

I know things had been really rocky between us, but I'd never dreamed that Pete would go this far and walk out on me. And, more to the point, walk out on me less than three weeks after I had lost our baby. I think I ended the call, I don't know. I was in complete shock.

'Come on, Kate, I'm sure he doesn't mean it,' Andrew said, looking pretty shocked himself.

'He means it,' I replied grimly, hardly able to believe what I was saying. 'It's over.'

I didn't cry. My marriage to the man I had thought was the love of my life was over, but I didn't cry. I know some people will take this to mean that I'm hard or unfeeling but it's not true. I had cried so many times during my marriage to Pete. I was still so shocked and reeling from what he had said, I felt fearful and sick. I had no idea what was going to happen next but I knew I had to be strong. That was all I kept telling myself.

I had vowed a long time before I even met Pete that I would never let a man break me again. I had sobbed, begged, pleaded with Dane Bowers to take me back when he left me all those years ago, but he wouldn't. I had hit rock bottom then. I had even taken an overdose in my desperation. It took me two long years to get over the break-up with Dane and, when I was through it all, I swore that I would never again let any man make me feel like that.

I was desperately sad and bitterly hurt that Pete had left me, but I was a mother with three young children. I had to be strong for them. I hadn't wanted my marriage to end but it had. Now I had to deal with it. But I thought I knew Pete. Whatever else was going on between us, I knew him to be a good and kind man, and trusted that he would never let any harm come to me, or anything bad be said about me, because I was the mother of his children.

CHAPTER FOURTEEN

IT'S OVER

As soon as Pete left me, I knew I had to get away. The press were bound to kick off big time and I wasn't up to dealing with them on top of the pain I was going through. The rest of the day passed in a blur of phone calls to my friends and family as I broke the news to them. But concerned as everyone was for me, I don't think anyone was that surprised. They had seen how much Pete and I had been arguing and how vicious those rows had become over the past months. I think many of them might have been secretly relieved that I was finally out of a marriage that had been causing me so much heartbreak.

I phoned the person who sorts out my travel arrangements for me and asked him to book me into the Maldives resort, to leave as soon as possible. I know this may seem like an ironic choice, given that it was where I went on my honeymoon, but it was the only place I could think of where I wouldn't be under siege from the media. Then I called one of my close friends and asked her if she would come away with me, as I really needed to be with someone right now. I had one more phone call to make and that was to my manager Claire Powell. Although I had given her formal notice she was still supposed to represent me until 23 June.

I think she was expecting a call from me as she'd had already had Pete on the phone. I told her Pete wanted a divorce, and that I wanted her to put out a statement to the press that he was divorcing me, saying that if she didn't put one out, I would. Claire sounded subdued. She said that she would do the statement later.

'I want it done now, Claire,' I insisted. Looking back, because Claire knew better than most people what Pete and I were like together, and because of what had happened in the past, maybe she wanted to delay putting it out in the hope that we might get back together. But I was adamant that I wanted it done immediately and I wanted people to know that Pete was the one who wanted to divorce me. Once she realised that I wasn't going to change my mind, she read out the statement that she thought should be put out: 'Peter Andre and Katie Price are separating after four and a half years of marriage. They have both requested the media respect their family's privacy at this difficult time.'

'Wait a minute!' I exclaimed. 'That sounds as if we

both decided on the split, but Pete is the one walking out on the marriage, not me. He's leaving me and that statement doesn't make clear how I feel about it.'

Claire assured me that it was better to make it sound as if the split was mutual; it was what all celebrity couples tended to do. I was in such an emotional state that I agreed. It was only as I was on my way to the airport that I changed my mind. But when I called her, it was too late. The statement had already gone out. I was really upset. The statement did not explain what had really happened nor how I felt about it. So I asked Diana, my book publicist, to put out another statement from me: 'Pete is the love of my life, and my life. We have children together and I am devastated and disappointed by his decision to separate and divorce me, as I married him for life. This is not what I want and the decision has been taken out of my hands. I will not comment further or do any interviews regarding the separation. But I will always love my Pete.' And it was true, I did still love him.

In hindsight, I wonder what would have happened if I hadn't pushed for that statement. I wonder if Pete would have punished me for a week or so by not speaking to me and letting me think our marriage was over. And then, once he had proved his point, would he have got back together with me, until the next time? It's impossible of course to know . . .

By the time I was at the airport the news had broken. As we waited in the VIP lounge to board our flight the story was on SKY news. Fortunately the sound was off as I didn't want Junior and Princess to hear anything. Princess was too young to understand but Junior perhaps wasn't. But I was stunned when I saw all these pictures of Pete crying and looking heartbroken. I thought, 'Hang on a minute! Why are they showing pictures of *him* looking so upset? He's the one who's dumped me! Why is there all this sympathy for him as the "broken man"? What about me, the "broken" woman he left? Why is there no sympathy for me?' Just because I wasn't going to allow myself to be seen crying in public – that's not what I do – it didn't mean I wasn't heartbroken.

I had already spoken to Pete and asked him if it was OK if I took the kids away with me, and he had given his permission. I would never take our children out of the country without his consent. I couldn't take Harvey as it was such short notice and there was no time to sort out his medication and make the appropriate arrangements with a nearby hospital, and nor could I take him out of school at such short notice.

I can barely remember the flight. I was still in a state of shock.

* * *

We were staying in the same villa where I had spent my honeymoon and the recent holiday with Pete, a time when Pete and I seemed to have everything before us and so much to look forward to. But all that seemed to belong to a different life now. I felt I was in the middle of a nightmare, especially when my friend and I looked on the internet the following day to see how the press were reporting the end of my marriage. I was completely stunned by the coverage. There were some reports that the break-up was a publicity stunt, which I thought was insane. What kind of people did the papers think we were? And there were plenty of other reports which portrayed me in a negative way. There seemed to be no sympathy for me at all. Instead it was Saint Pete and Sinner Jordan all the way. Yes, the press brought Jordan back pretty fast, as if she was always the bad girl waiting to come out of Katie Price.

The press were full of speculation about how another man had ended our marriage, and when they realised that Spencer was gay, their attention immediately turned to Andrew, as if he had something to do with the break-up. They even tracked him down to Spain where he and Polly were on holiday. They contacted Polly's friends on Facebook and tried to dig up dirt on the couple, but there was no dirt. There was no story. I spoke to Polly often during this time. I was so upset that the press had dragged them into it and ruined their holiday. They certainly didn't deserve that intrusion.

As I mentioned earlier, I had told Pete about the Maldives trip and couldn't believe it when I read that he was supposed to be devastated after arriving at the family house and discovering that I had taken our kids and he didn't know where we were! That was a complete and utter fabrication by the newspapers.

I still couldn't believe that my marriage was over and, what's more, the break-up triggered by a picture in the press. I felt that if Pete and I could only talk things through, maybe, just maybe, we might be able to salvage our marriage. For the sake of our children, I wasn't ready to give up on it. After all, this was the man I had thought I would be married to for ever. I'd believed he was the love of my life. We had been so close, closer than I had ever been to anyone before. Could it really be over between us?

So I phoned Pete and asked if he would fly out to the Maldives where we could be on our own, away from anyone else, away from management, away from the press, so that we could talk things through. But he refused. I knew then that our marriage was over. I knew, in my heart, that there was nothing I could say or do to change his mind and that I had better get used to being a single mother. There was no going back. I think I did my grieving for my marriage in the Maldives.

There was no way I was going to waste my breath begging him to change his mind. I knew from Pete's attitude and tone that we were finished. People will ask, 'How can you say this when you had so much together?' But I don't live my life thinking that if I had stayed with Pete then we would have even more money, maybe even our media empire. I could have stayed with him and we would have got more TV work, become a brand, but that would have been preserving our marriage for all the wrong reasons. You should be with someone because you love them and want to be with them, not because of what you can get out of the relationship.

Now I really was on my own, but I was determined to be strong. I would not let it break me. Nor would I let the press destroy me with their lies. The coverage of the split seemed to be getting even more intense and there were more stories that all seemed to heap the blame on me. Someone even came up with the Team Pete/Team Katie idea and various nobodies who thought they were somebodies were quoted as saying they were on Team Pete. And I thought, 'How pathetically sad is that? How can they not see that this isn't about taking sides, this isn't a game? This is about a family that has been broken up, and there are children involved.'

In spite of the emotional turmoil I was in, I knew I had done the right thing in coming away and I don't think I ever let on to the kids how upset I was. I saved that for when they were in bed and I could talk things through with my friend. During the day I played with the kids, went swimming with them, and sunbathed. I desperately missed Harvey and wished he could have been with us, but I knew he was being very well looked after by my mum and his nanny.

But unfortunately the press weren't going to leave me in peace to recover from the break-up. After a week they finally tracked us down. One day I was lying on the balcony. As I looked out to sea, I saw the very unwelcome sight of a couple of speedboats by the coral reef loaded with paps, all desperate to get shots of me. And then it got worse. Boats would come right up to my waterside villa, circling round it like greedy sharks. The hotel had to keep patrolling with a speedboat to get rid of them. 'Well, fuck you lot,' I thought. 'I'm not going to give you that picture.' So from then on we took to having meals in our villa. No way was I going to be photographed when I was trying to cope with the end of my marriage, so that someone could make a fat wad of cash out of me. And then I thought, '*I'm* going to make some money out of them for a change.' So I had my friend take a picture of me and the kids and sold it to the *Sun* for fifty grand. It paid for the trip and some, and didn't harm the kids in any way. I am not a victim, I am a fighter. Although it seemed like the press were doing all they could to break me, I would not be broken.

I had been in such a mad panic packing for the Maldives that I had forgotten to pack my anti-depressants. I had been on them since I'd had Junior and suffered from post-natal depression. Although I was long over the depression, I had kept on taking the medication, gradually reducing the dose. You're supposed to come off the tablets under medical supervision as there can be side-effects, but I didn't suffer from any at all. In fact, even though I was being battered by the press, and coming to terms with the fact that my marriage was over and I was going to be a single parent, I felt OK.

And by the time I flew back from the Maldives on 23 May I knew something else. I was terribly sad for my children that Pete and I were separating but I was starting to feel relieved that my marriage was finally over. I hadn't wanted to admit it before because I still thought we could make a go of it, but it was now brutally clear that Pete didn't want that. And nor did I. I started to feel as if a huge weight had been lifted from me. I wouldn't have to pretend to be someone I wasn't any more. I wouldn't have to walk on eggshells constantly, terrified that another row would be triggered if I did or said the wrong thing. I could go out when I wanted, with whom I wanted. I could be myself.

But back in the UK it was really tough as I was pursued relentlessly by the paps, and battered every single day in the press. I tried not to read the lies, but sometimes I would and I can tell you it's soul-destroying reading about yourself being described as the one who was to blame for the marriage breaking up, when all you ever tried to do was to be a good wife.

And on top of this Pete wouldn't speak to me. Everything to do with our children had to go through solicitors. It was so frustrating, never mind expensive – why couldn't we just sit down in a room on our own and talk about what was best for the kids? That was all I wanted to do, nothing else. I had no wish to get back with him. But I felt as if Pete was surrounding himself with people who had turned him against me.

Not once as far as I was aware, when all these negative stories were being printed about me, did Pete ever stand up for me and say, 'Hang on. This is between me and

Kate, and I don't want a bad word said against the mother of my children. She's a good mum.' I would have respected him more if he had stood up for me, rather than be photographed looking heartbroken. He had plenty of opportunities to defend me as he was doing so many interviews. Later on, in September 2009, when he did an interview for *OK!* magazine, he had the perfect opportunity to defend me as the mother of his children. *OK!* said of me, 'She gets a lot of criticism for not showing emotion – do you think she does it as a way of protecting herself?' And this was his answer: 'I have no idea – I don't think anyone can really figure someone else out. I have no idea about what's true or not true, there are new things every week so I try not to get involved.'

'But you did know me, Pete,' I thought to myself sadly. 'There was a time when you knew me better than anyone else. You did know that I loved you and that I tried to be a good wife. And you've always known that the children come first with me.' But in the weeks that followed I think my love for him died.

It was so sad that all this press attention was being focussed on our break-up. Ours might have been a story that sold newspapers, but for us it meant the destruction of a family.

After all that I had been through in the months leading up to our break-up and in the weeks after it, I can't say that I missed Pete as he was then – I missed the old Pete I had known. But I was sad for what we had lost and I missed being in a relationship and the family life that went along with that. Family has always been the most important thing in my life. Never mind money, big houses and expensive cars, if you haven't got your family then it means nothing as far as I'm concerned. But I didn't want to be reminded of him and had all the pictures of Pete and me taken down. I think that was understandable under the circumstances. After all, who wants daily reminders of the man who walked out on them?

And once I was back home the reality of our split really hit me when I realised that I would no longer be able to have our children with me all the time. That they would be spending time away from me when Pete had them. The first time I was without Junior and Princess, I found it very hard being in the house. I missed them so badly it was like a physical ache. I kept going into their bedrooms at night and expecting to find them tucked up in bed. The house seemed horribly empty with just me and Harvey in it. Talking to Junior and Princess on the phone several times a day wasn't enough, especially as they're both still so little you can't really have a proper conversation with them. It's just about letting them know that I'm there and telling them that I love them. I wanted to have them with me. I wanted to cuddle them. I missed my babies so much. But we were all going to have to get used to life as it was now. And when the children were with Pete, I didn't want to stay in and be reminded of their absence – I wanted to be out and about.

I was fortunate to have great support from my family and close friends at this time – I don't know what I would have done without them. But they were all brilliant and I'm grateful to them for getting me through some really difficult times. There were some so-called friends I didn't hear from at all after Pete left me. It was almost as if they had read the stories in the press and decided that I was to blame for the break-up. And there were some other female friends who became Pete's friends and didn't see me any more after that. It was to get even worse later on in the year when one of my best friends turned against me and sold a story about me . . . but more of that later.

I had once been so close to Claire and Nicola. They knew everything about my life and I found it incredibly sad that we didn't remain friends after Pete left me. We had been so close that Nicola had even filmed Princess's birth (for us, not for the reality show). It was a big shock to lose not just my husband but also two close friends.

But then other people came back into my life – one of them my ex-boyfriend Dane Bowers. He Facebooked me just after the news of Pete leaving me came out, asking me if I was OK, and we exchanged a few messages. Although my break-up with Dane had been bitter at the time, it was years ago and I didn't have any bad feelings towards him. To be honest, while I was getting such a battering in the press it was good to hear from people who seemed to care about me and knew that the stories were rubbish. Dane came over to the house for a party.

There were no feelings between us any more other than those of friendship. And back then, especially during those emotionally testing weeks after my marriage ended, I needed my friends more than ever.

CHAPTER FIFTEEN

I WILL SURVIVE

It had long been one of my ambitions to have my own production company. Now that I had left CAN Associates, I was free to do that. Just after I'd returned from the Maldives I'd asked Diana to get in contact with Zai Bennett, ITV's Director of Digital Channels and Acquisitions, and tell him that I wanted to film my own series. Apparently he was surprised to hear it. There had been so many negative stories about me in the press that he thought some of them might be true and that I might actually have lost the plot! But when he met me and saw how down-to-earth and normal I am, he realised what rubbish the stories were. I told him that I wanted to move on with my life; wanted to get on with filming my own series right away. And by 'right away' I really did mean in the next couple of weeks – starting with the children's birthday parties followed by my trip to Ibiza. I think he was pretty taken aback by how soon I wanted to start, but he was more than happy to sign me up.

I formed my own production company with Mark Wagman, a former ITV executive, calling it Pricey Media, and immediately began filming for *What Katie Did Next*. I wanted my new series to show the real me, and how I was living my life after my marriage had ended. I wanted to reveal my fun side and to prove that the press stories were complete bollocks – I was just a woman trying to get on with her life after a marriage break-up, not some bitch slapper from hell! While I wanted to have more control about how I was filmed, I was going to leave the editing to the director. I just wanted the show to be honest. I didn't want to be edited in a way which always made me look good; people could see both good and bad and judge for themselves.

I'd had such a miserable experience filming the final series of our reality show, *Katie and Peter: Stateside*. I found it especially painful watching the programmes when they went out after he and I had split up. And I think it made depressing viewing for everyone else, watching a dying relationship and all those bitter, nasty rows. But there was no point in brooding about it, however much it upset me.

*   *   *

Setting up new work projects definitely helped keep me

sane during the weeks and months that followed the break-up, along with the support of my friends and family and my own determination that I would not fall apart, or sit in my room stuffing my face with biscuits and crying as one celeb mag would have had you believe. I did go and see the therapist I had contacted when I was suffering from post-natal depression, just to make sure that I was staying calm and clear-headed. After we had talked, she told me it was clear that I had accepted that my marriage had ended. Now it was time to focus on a fresh start, a new chapter in my life – both in my private life and work-wise. I felt fired up with adrenaline as I contemplated my new role as a single mother – nervous, a little bit scared, but also excited about the many possibilities.

At the end of May I took part in the London Clothes Show at Olympia where I modelled my equestrian range and appeared on the catwalk. I needed the confidence boost the event gave me. As much as I was determined to get on with my life, my self-esteem was at rock bottom – as any woman's would be if her husband had just left her.

It was the first time I had ever appeared in a catwalk show with fashion models. The press picked up on the fact that I'd lost weight since I'd split up from Pete. I hadn't, in fact, it was just that I know how to breathe in to make myself seem thinner – a trick learned through years of glamour modelling.

When I first came on-stage I was dressed in a white

bikini and surrounded by other bikini-clad fashion models who were all younger than me. I'm not being bitchy when I say that they were so skinny, they looked like coat hangers. I really didn't think it was an attractive look. But they did know how to work the catwalk. As I was so much shorter than the other models, I had extra-high heels on and extra-big hair. I like to think I brought a touch of glamour to the show, even though I was a little stump compared to the other models!

Later I came on in glittery hotpants, over-the-knee pink boots and a blonde Afro wig – you know me, I always like to stand out! Probably the best part was when I got to model the clothes from my KP Equestrian range. It felt like a real endorsement of the company that I had been asked to model here. We'd been up and running less than a year and here I was on-stage in front of an audience of thousands, alongside well-established designers. For my press call I posed before a striking sand sculpture of a horse and a woman who was supposed to be me, in the hot-pink shorts and pink t-shirt from my range, along with a pair of black wellies with the pink KP logo. 'Please don't let me fall on the sculpture!' I thought as I posed away. And all the while the press were firing questions about Pete at me as I posed because this was my first public appearance since the split. But I said nothing. I still thought silence was the best policy.

The show at Olympia lasted for a couple of days and during that time I got to know some of the other models, including a stunning male model called Anthony Lowther. He'd caught Gary's eye first, I'm sure Phil won't mind me saying, as he rehearsed on-stage. Gary whispered in my ear, 'Have a look at him, he's gorgeous!'

I had to agree! Anthony, or Ant as I came to call him, had the kind of looks I love: dark hair, blue eyes, and perfect features. He appeared with me on-stage together with several other male models and I couldn't believe how tall he was, how manly, gorgeous and trendy. I've never been surrounded by so many male models before and, girls, let me tell you, it is quite a feeling!

I have to admit that I fancied Anthony – I mean, what woman wouldn't? He had everything going for him looks-wise plus he was a really nice guy and interesting to talk to. He was a total professional throughout the show and didn't flirt with me at all, even though secretly I wished he had. As I've already mentioned, my self-esteem was at rock bottom and it would have been good to know that men still found me attractive.

After one of the shows a group of us, including Gary, Phil, Anthony and another male model called Jo, went to the Boyzone concert at Wembley. It's very sad remembering this because that was the last time I saw the lovely Stephen Gately. He was a close friend of Gary and Phil's and I had met him several times over the years. The news of his tragic death later that year was a huge shock. It just shows that life is precious and that you have to make the most of every moment.

The gig was brilliant and afterwards a group of us went to the Red Lion pub in Highgate and then on to a gay club. I was just having fun with my friends. Ant was the first guy who'd caught my eye since Pete left me and I did enjoy being with him, but nothing ever happened between us apart from a couple of kisses. But right from the start the press were on our case, and after that night out there were stories saying that I had a new man.

'I just don't think I can handle the press attention,' Anthony later admitted to me. He's not someone who is interested in fame at all. I could understand where he was coming from: the press attention was still ferocious. The paps were camped outside my house all the time. Wherever I went I was photographed. And I still hadn't given any interviews, yet every day there seemed to be stories about Pete and me in the press. It seemed to me that while I was being slated, Pete was getting the best press he had ever had in his life. He was being portrayed by the press as the heartbroken victim and the perfect dad.

He was often photographed when he was out with the children during this time, so to some people it might have looked as if Pete was with the children more than I was. That wasn't the case at all. I always did my best to avoid being photographed with the children. The press were making up such shit about me, I would think, 'How dare you think that you can go ahead and take pictures of me and my kids and play me off against Pete, in some kind of sick competition about who is the better parent?' I know that I'm a good mum.

I felt as though the press needed someone to blame for the marriage breaking up and they had decided to blame me. I was seen as the bad guy and yet I was the one who had been dumped. One of my friends pointed out that it seems the press always blame the woman for a marriage breaking up, whatever happens. Maybe it's because the newspapers are mainly run by men? All I knew was that it felt deeply unfair.

And little did I know that the press stories about me were about to get a whole lot worse when I flew out to Ibiza in June for a holiday with a group of my closest friends. The trip had been planned before I had even split up from Pete. I had talked to my friends about how much I wanted to go on holiday to the island. I had even invited Pete to come along too but his reply was that it depended what else he was up to in the summer. He didn't sound at all bothered. Our relationship had become so stale by then. 'See what I mean?' I'd later commented to my friends. 'He's just got no enthusiasm for doing anything with me at all.'

I ended up booking the trip after he left me. Pete was going to have the kids in Cyprus and, as I knew they would all be well looked after by their dad, I felt I could relax and enjoy myself with my friends. And why would I want to stay at home on my own when I didn't have my children, knowing that I would still be slated in the press?

I flew to the island on easyJet with a group of my closest friends, including Gary and Phil, Julie, Melodie, Neil, Derek, and the photographer Andy Neil, as I was going to shoot my calendar on the island. They were all moaning about having to go on the no-frills airline but I was just thrilled to be going away! We had a really early flight, and while they drank champagne I stuck to mineral water.

It was also exciting jetting off to Ibiza because for the first time in years I wasn't with any managers who would be worried that I would say or do the wrong thing. I was thinking about having a PR company represent me but hadn't yet signed a contract. Nor did I take any security, though I was quickly to regret that when I discovered the press were on to me, from the moment I landed and throughout my entire stay.

The press made out my trip to Ibiza was a wild, out-of-control time where I behaved like a slapper and stayed up partying and drinking for twelve hours at a time, emerging from night clubs at 10 o'clock in the morning. Ibiza is renowned for people clubbing all day and all night, off their nuts on drugs, but I'm not into drugs at all. None of my friends are. By the time it got to around 2.30 in the morning, we were too knackered to stay any longer and had to go back to the hotel, so no way was I still clubbing at 10 in the morning – I was tucked up in bed alongside my friend Julie, with Melodie in the other bed. People said I was having a Jordan moment when in fact I was having a Mrs Andre split moment. I was just trying to deal with the situation I found myself in by having fun with my friends.

I was photographed in night clubs as I danced, and the press made out that I was off-my-face drunk when I'd just had a few drinks and was dancing no differently from anyone else. I did nothing to be ashamed of in Ibiza.

The picture the press painted couldn't have been more wrong. Honestly, it was just a week of fun with my friends, where we chilled out in the hotel, went for dinner, and went clubbing probably three times in total. Although I was still reeling from the break-up with Pete, this trip ended up being one of the best holidays of my life; I've never laughed so much as I did that week. I had spent so long being unhappy in my marriage that I think I needed the release, needed to let my hair down.

But the paps were everywhere and I couldn't do anything without them pursuing me and photographing me. I couldn't even relax by the pool in our hotel as they would be there – which is why we all ended up spending so much time in our hotel rooms. When I went down to reception there would be journalists in the lobby; reporters were staying on the same floor as me; I had cameras trained on my balcony, watching my every move. In fact, my friend Julie got whacked in the face by a pap's camera as he was so desperate to get a shot of me. We hired a speedboat one day as I was also shooting my calendar while I was out there and hoped that way we would escape the press for at least a couple of hours. But even then the paps got into other boats and pursued us. We did manage to shake them off one afternoon when we went on a gay beach, but it wasn't a real escape as there were so many other people on the beach trying to take pictures of me.

All I wanted to do was relax with my friends but my holiday was being portrayed as something seedy. I still couldn't believe the stories the press were coming out with. I was completely shocked. The stories were ridiculous! One caption in particular stunned me: 'Out of control Katie Price threatens to cut woman's face during Ibiza alcohol binge'. A journalist was claiming that I had threatened to cut her face because I thought she worked for a magazine in which Pete has a column. She had claimed that I had confronted her with a 'manic look' in my eyes and said: 'I'm gonna cut your f****** face. I swear to God, I'll f****** cut you.' Part of me wanted to laugh because it was so unbelievable. The other half was devastated. How dare they?

It was also claimed in news stories that I had been abusive towards my fans, but that was nonsense as well. I love my fans and would never abuse them or take them for granted. I know that they're the ones who've supported me and helped me get where I am now. When I went out clubbing I would get a really positive response from them. The press reported that I got booed when I went to a particular club, but as was revealed on my reality show in fact it was completely the opposite. Girls came up to me and said, 'We love you, Katie! We buy your perfume!'

But back home in the UK people believed the stories were true. I had my family and friends on the phone to me asking me what the hell was going on, but they quickly realised after talking to me that the stories were all made up. Meanwhile my reputation and my career were being damaged because of a pack of lies.

It seemed to me that because I had decided not to talk to the press, they were making up stories to fill the gap, stories I felt powerless to do anything about. I felt that there was no one to fight my corner, to put my side of the story to the press, to crush their lies. I realised that I did need some kind of management behind me. I felt completely victimised by the press, battered and under siege.

I just couldn't believe the amount of coverage I was getting, all these column inches over a few nights out. I mean, weren't there more important things going on in the world than Katie Price hitting a particular club in San Antonio? Also I was in Ibiza, party capital of the Med – what did people think I was going to do? Sit in my room, drinking tea and eating scones, watching *Minder*?

All the time my harmless nights out with my friends were being compared to Pete's behaviour. 'Wild Jordan parties until 10 a.m. while distressed Peter Andre takes care of the kids,' read one headline, as if as a mother I didn't have the right to have a good time. And it was a lie, as I've already said, I never stayed up all night clubbing. I remember seeing a picture of Pete crying and that did upset me because I could see how unhappy he was and didn't want him to suffer. I felt so torn, feeling upset for him on the one hand and then thinking, 'How can he be crying when he's the one who dumped me? He's the one who made that choice. He didn't have to put himself in this situation.' And if he thought he had made the wrong decision, he only had to ring me and say, 'D'you know what, Kate, I can't handle this. I can't handle not being with you. Can we meet to talk it through?' But I think because the press got involved in writing such lies so early on, Pete obviously came to believe them and it must then have got difficult for him to make contact with me. And l lost trust in him because of what I had been reading about him, and because of how he had been to me when I was in the Maldives and asked him to fly over. Looking back, I do believe that if the press hadn't got involved, and set us against each other, that Pete and I would have been able to talk.

And no doubt because he had seen the made-up stories in the press about my trip to Ibiza, when I called him in Cyprus to speak to the kids, he hurled abuse at me, telling me that I was a disgrace, a slag and a whore. In the press he was quoted as saying that I was a 'wild animal', that he 'didn't recognise me' as his wife. Other remarks he was supposed to have made included: 'What's this going to be like for the kids when they read how their mum behaves?' And, 'It was Katie who I fell in love with and married. But it looks like she just wanted to be her old self, Jordan. I can't believe what I'm seeing.' I was no different then from how I had always been; I was just on holiday with my friends, trying to cope with my marriage ending. And it was Pete's turn to have the kids, after I'd taken them to the Maldives, so why couldn't he have said that I was entitled to have a holiday?

I tried not to let it get to me but inside I felt so hurt by Pete's comments about me and by the way I was being portrayed as a bad mother. Pete had left me – he had walked out on our marriage. When were people going to take that on board? It was such a tough time.

There were other press stories that something was going on between me and Anthony Lowther who was out there running one of the club nights, but Ant was a friend, nothing more. I'd met up with him and his friends when I was out there and we'd gone out in a group a couple of times. I still fancied him but nothing happened between us. One of Ant's club nights was fancy dress and I went as a saucy Xena: Warrior Princess in gold hotpants, but as Ant was always surrounded by gorgeous fit girls in skimpy outfits, I think he would have noticed me more had I worn a gorilla costume!

He had been wary about press attention before he saw me in Ibiza, but out there it was even more intense and manic and I think it really scared Ant. He also happened to be very good friends with one of my exes, Matt Peacock, which made it even more unlikely that anything was going to happen. When I saw Matt things were fine between us, even though he had sold a nasty kiss and tell on me after we split. We're never going to be best friends, that's for sure, but we can at least be polite. For a fleeting moment I did look at him and think, 'You're quite fit actually!' But then I thought, 'Kate, reality check. He's already sold a story on you.' I wouldn't trust him again with a bargepole.

Ant was also concerned that I was on the rebound from my marriage, even though I said I wasn't, and he himself was getting over a bad break-up. So we remained just good friends. We text each other regularly, and Alex has met him and likes him. Ant has often been offered huge sums of money by the press to do stories on me, but he's loyal and he wouldn't – anyway, as I've already said, there is nothing to say!

* * *

One day on a trip to the old town I decided to drop into a tattoo parlour to see what I could do about the tattoo of Pete's name across my wrist – it was just above the crown I'd had done with red love hearts, above Princess's name. I don't think it could have been removed then and there but I decided to play a little game with the paps – their constant pursuit of me was driving me mad, so I came out with a bandage round my wrist to give them something to speculate on. Sure enough, the next day the papers reported that I'd had my tattoo altered and Pete's name inked out. At this rate

I was surprised they didn't report what I ate for breakfast! Two hunky male dancers actually . . . ha-ha, just kidding! (Better tell the editor to cut that out or the press will be saying that I had a threesome in Ibiza.)

Anyway the next day I went back to the tattoo parlour. I wanted to get the name blacked out, but the tattoo artist didn't think that was such a good idea. 'What about putting a cross through his name instead?' he suggested. I was still shocked after the break-up and about the way I felt Pete had turned on me; how he wasn't defending me when all these terrible things were being written about me. I didn't feel protected by him, I felt confused and vulnerable, and it made me hate him. I didn't want his name on me any more. Our marriage was over. And because I knew he was following my time in Ibiza in the press, I knew that he would read that I'd had his name removed. It would be my message to him, a way of saying, 'Yes, it really is over, Pete. I don't even want your name on me any more.'

'Are you sure about this?' Julie asked, worried that I was rushing into something. I think all my friends were concerned about me. They were surprised because I was so calm. Maybe they were still expecting me to break down; that this was only the calm before the storm. But I felt I had to be strong, and show that I was strong all the time, because I was so afraid that if anyone thought I was unstable, I might lose the kids. Although months later the press did manage to push me close to the edge . . .

'I'm sure,' I replied. The cross seemed like a good compromise. Pete was now my ex, but as he was the father of my children he would still have to be in my life. He'd had my name tattooed on his wedding ring finger – a permanent reminder of the marriage he'd walked out on. I wondered what he would do if he ever got married again. I mean, what new wife wants the old wife's name tattooed on her husband's finger? Maybe he would have it lasered off before then . . . I thought I probably would have more tattoos, but I will never again have a man's name. I never like to do the same thing twice and I felt I had already been there and done that, having Pete's name tattooed on me.

* * *

I wasn't just in Ibiza for a holiday, I was also shooting my calendar and this time I was going to do it in a beach location. The clothes I wore for this shoot were probably more expensive and classy than ones I've used before in other calendar shoots as they were my own. I wanted the calendar to reflect the newly single me – sexy, classy, strong and independent. I shot quite a bit of it on the famous Sa Trinxa beach and attracted quite a crowd as I posed by the sea. I know it stressed out my photographer Andy and the rest of my group, who were concerned about security, but I wasn't worried. The crowds were friendly. I didn't feel self-conscious at all while I posed in my bikini. When I'm in work mode, I go into my zone and totally focus on posing for the camera. I can shut out everything else around me. We also whizzed round in a speedboat, trying to find a spot away from the paps to shoot some of the other poses. I did one hanging from the mast and am rather proud of that one! The Pricey had still got it . . . None of this was a message to Pete to show him what he was missing: I genuinely had to shoot my calendar which I do every year and this was the perfect opportunity to do it.

Throughout the holiday I was being filmed for my reality series but that was a completely different experience from being filmed for the shows with Pete. I got on so much better with this crew, so it was so much more relaxed – even though in some ways it was harder work as I was now the main focus, whereas before I'd had Pete. And when all the bad press stories were coming out, I found some comfort in knowing that my reality show would reveal what had really happened.

In spite of the terrible press coverage and the negative impact it had on my career, to this day I have absolutely no regrets about going to Ibiza. I don't live my life according to what the newspapers say. They will write what they like anyway, twist anything for a good story. Even before I went to Ibiza I was getting bad press. But I should have booked a villa and not stayed at a hotel because I had absolutely no privacy there, nowhere to escape the press, and they wouldn't leave me alone.

But, looking back, Ibiza was the moment when the press about me was so bad that it really affected people's opinion of me. I feel they turned against me then and I certainly wish that hadn't happened. It was so unfair because the stories were all lies. I was being publicly judged when I hadn't done anything wrong. I had just gone on holiday with my friends. It felt as if, because I was a mother, I couldn't have any fun – and yet all my female friends who came away with me were mums too. There seemed to be a general feeling that I should have stayed at home and cried. If I wasn't seen looking heartbroken at every opportunity then that meant I had no feelings. Just because I chose to hide my heartbreak from the press, did that really make me a bad person?

So many people said to me back then, 'Why don't you sue the papers for all the untrue stories?' But back then I felt I couldn't take on the press. Lawyers cost a hell of a lot of money. I was a single mother and wanted to make money for my family, not spend it all on legal fees. I felt if I went down that path, I would have to challenge every single untrue story the press made up . . . and there are so many, every single day. I just hoped that the press would get tired of making up their lies about me eventually and change the record. I just wanted to get on with my life.

I told everyone that I was over Pete while inside I was still full of hurt at the way I felt Pete had treated me. It was as if he had become someone different, someone harder, someone who didn't defend and protect me as I had always believed he would. In a way this change I saw in him scared me as in five and a half years I had never before seen this side of him.

I think there were actually times when I hated him, which I know is a strong thing to say but I felt he had been very unfair to me. And there's a fine line between love and hate, isn't there? I still loved him because I don't believe you can switch off the love when you've spent so much time with someone and you've been through so much with them. When I thought of Pete I would still remember all the good times, but then I'd remember what had happened afterwards and I would hate him for what he had done. The love I'd felt for him once was overshadowed by my shock and hurt at him leaving me.

And, to me, Pete seemed to care a lot about his image, and his fame. What he didn't seem to understand was that one day his fame will end. Mine will as well. And are we still not going to be able to meet up and talk about the children? When Princess and Junior are teenagers, will Pete continue not to talk to me? He's going to have to one day. I was never just his girlfriend; I was his wife, and I am the mother of his children.

CHAPTER SIXTEEN

A FIGHTER FOR A FIGHTER

I still hadn't given an interview to the press about the marriage break-up but by July 2009 I felt as if I couldn't take any more of the bad coverage I was getting in the papers every single day. It seemed to me that the reporting of my Ibiza holiday had been the turning point. Now the press seemed to think that they could get away with printing whatever they wanted about me. I am tough and I was getting on with my life, but the negative publicity was taking its toll on me – I've got feelings like everyone else, however much the press tried to pretend otherwise. I hated knowing that people would read the stories about me and think that they were true when they were all made up. There were even stories that I had been texting and calling Pete, begging him to take me back – all totally untrue. If I had contact with him at all it was only to suggest that we meet up to discuss the children.

So when Piers Morgan approached me to be one of the guests on his chat show, I thought that this would be the perfect opportunity to tell my side of what had happened, without journalists putting their spin on it and twisting my words. I had no hidden agenda in doing the interview, no wish to slate Pete; I just wanted to tell my story. I was actually looking forward to the interview because as far as I was concerned I had nothing to hide or be ashamed of. My plan was to set the record straight once and for all. I had moved on with my life. I wanted to put my failed marriage behind me but it seemed that until I spoke about it in public, I wasn't going to be allowed to by the media.

I've been interviewed by Piers quite a few times over the years and I wasn't nervous this time, especially as I was being filmed at my house so there would be no live studio audience to cope with. I suppose I felt quite relaxed about it. But as soon as Piers began questioning me about my marriage I found the whole experience much more emotionally intense than I had anticipated. I think I had tried to block out the pain of the break-up. Talking about it was very upsetting. Then came the moment when Piers asked where I thought it all went wrong and I brought up our disastrous trip to LA. I suddenly found myself talking about my miscarriage, something which I hadn't spoken about since it had happened in April. 'I was pregnant in LA and the baby

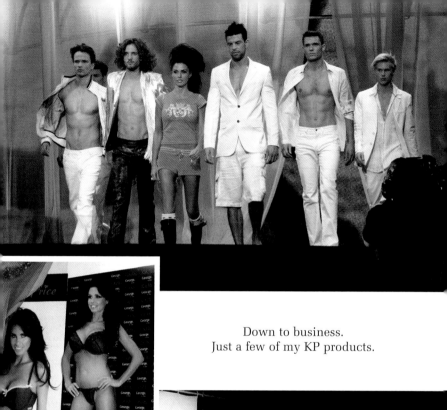

Down to business.
Just a few of my KP products.

Andrew giving me a lesson on my horse in Holland.

Happier memories with my horse, stateside.

Princess and Junior
on their horse, Harvey.

My beautiful children.

Just like her mum.

Harvey is such a happy
and loving child.

Harvey loves doing activities,
especially swimming.

Me, Andrew and Alex in Egypt.

Unwinding on holiday.

died,' I said. Feeling overwhelmed with emotion, I started crying. The interview had brought back so many unhappy and painful memories.

I wasn't trying to win sympathy from people, it wasn't an act. It was the first time I had cried since the break-up but it wasn't about Pete — it was about losing our baby. I knew that there had most likely been something wrong with the baby and that's why I'd had the miscarriage, but all the same it was deeply upsetting. I also thought about how very hard it had been that Pete had left me only three weeks later, while I was still coming to terms with the miscarriage, and how upsetting it had been reading all the vicious things the press had written about me as I was still recovering from the loss of my baby and from Pete walking out on me. I'd had miscarriages before, but then I'd had a husband to support me. This time my husband had left me, within weeks, and I had faced a battering from the press alone.

I think Piers was shocked to see me in tears. Even my brother said it was the first time he had seen me cry since the break-up. But maybe I needed to. Afterwards, on my own reality show, *What Katie Did Next*, Piers said that it was one of the most dramatic interviews he had ever done and that he was stunned by my revelation about the recent miscarriage.

When he asked me if there was room for a new man in my life, I told him that if I had my way, once the divorce was over, I would be remarried by next summer; that I wanted more babies and loved family life. In the end, of course, I beat my own prediction and got married the following January!

He also asked, 'If you could speak to Pete, what would you say?' And I replied that I wished we could talk for the sake of the kids, that I wanted us to be mature about our break-up and that I would always think of him as a brilliant dad. But when Piers asked if there was any chance of us getting back together, I didn't hesitate. 'Never. I've moved on. One day he'll know what a genuine girl he lost.'

*　*　*

I don't have any regrets about doing that interview. I think I was right to do it, and afterwards I was hopeful that people would finally see my point of view and understand how I felt. Now I had said everything I wanted to say, I'd got it out of my system and could draw a line beneath the past. I didn't want to talk about my failed marriage any more. I had moved on with my life. I gave the fee I was paid for the interview to the Vision Charity.

There were stories in the press saying that Pete was devastated that I had talked about losing the baby; that we had agreed we would keep it private. He was interviewed on *This Morning* saying he'd never wanted details of our loss made public. But I can't remember ever agreeing to such a thing and I thought, it's not a competition to see who has suffered the most . . . Also, in 2006 when I'd suffered a previous miscarriage, we had been filmed for our reality show at the moment when I found out the baby had died, because we had thought it was only going to be a straightforward scan. So why was this miscarriage different from the one I had suffered then?

Later, it was reported in the press that Pete had said he didn't want to see me because the situation between us was so complicated. What was complicated about it? He had left me, and we were getting divorced like so many other couples do. I just thought, 'Why can't he be an adult and talk to me?' There was also a story which said he was afraid of the lies I would come out with after any such meeting. When I read the story I thought, 'For fuck's sake, don't you know me better than that?' I was with Pete for nearly six years – he knows me and I thought I knew him. Of course, that story might not have been true, but the fact was he *was* refusing to see me and I felt this made the whole break-up even harder. It wouldn't have mattered so much if we didn't have kids, but we did. It was just so sad that things had come to this. I suppose I hoped that soon he would want to be amicable. But even by November 2009 he still didn't want to meet up with me, and in an interview with *OK!* where he was asked why, he said, 'If I sat down in a room and spoke to her, it would be in the papers the next day. Believe me.' I found that very sad.

* * *

Fortunately I had my work to keep me grounded and

was as busy as I had ever been, with *Sapphire*, my fourth novel, coming out in August, with my KP Equestrian range, and with filming my own TV series. I was also getting back into training again as I was determined to become fit and toned. I went to a gym specialising in kick boxing and mixed martial arts and had my own personal trainer there, Sol Gilbert, who I'd known for years. I really enjoyed the training, which was like a hard-core boot camp with punishing sets of sit-ups, boxing, running and skipping. The gym was not glamorous by any stretch of the imagination, forget about Jacuzzis and spa treatments, but on the plus side it was definitely having an impact on my abs.

During one session I was chatting to Sol about our mutual friend Michelle Heaton's forthcoming birthday party, which was going to be a big bash in London. I was looking forward to going out. Michelle had been a really good friend to me and given me a lot of support. I wanted to celebrate her birthday with her in style. That was definitely one of the advantages to splitting up with Pete: I had no one on my case now, telling me that I shouldn't go out, that I shouldn't have a drink. Instead I was free to do what I wanted. I caught sight of two lads working out in another part of the gym. 'They look cute!' I commented. Then I added impulsively, 'If they're single, why don't you invite them along to Michelle's party?' I just wanted a bit of fun and flirtation in my life. That's all, in case you're wondering!

* * *

A few days later I flew to LA. I had been invited to audition for the part of the nanny in the film *Sex and the City 2*. I've never had any ambitions to be an actress but as I was invited to audition, I thought, 'Why not? I'll try anything once.' The actual audition was going to be held in London, but the casting director wanted me to have a session with an acting coach in LA, to go through the script together. I can't say I enjoyed the experience, I found it very embarrassing, and it confirmed what I already knew: that acting really wasn't for me. I also used the opportunity of being in LA to get my hair extensions done. Yes, it is extravagant, I know, but the beauty salon at the Beverly Wilshire is the best place I've found and I wouldn't trust anywhere else to do them. And as I have to look good for my work, as far as I'm concerned it's money well spent.

Gary came out with me and we had such a fun time together. It was a very different experience from my nightmare stay there earlier in the year when my marriage had broken down and I had felt so sad and depressed. This time I was in the heart of Beverly Hills and I was reminded of all the reasons why I love LA: the sunshine, the shops, the laid-back vibe . . . the shops! I also found time to get my Botox topped up and teased Gary because he spent so long agonising about whether to have any himself then chickened out at the last minute. To me Botox is no big deal at all, it's just part of my beauty regime now and I love the results.

I was also loving my single life, and knowing that I

could do whatever I wanted. I realised that I hadn't been single since the age of fifteen! And in spite of the pain of the break-up, since I had split up with Pete, I felt as if a door had opened in my life and there were so many new and exciting possibilities ahead of me. Gary commented that I was the happiest he had ever seen me – but I was about to get a whole lot happier! Not that I knew it then . . .

Michelle's party was at the end of the week and I was keen to know if Sol had invited those cute guys from the gym. 'Change of plan,' he told me on Facebook. 'I'm asking my friend Alex Reid. Trust me, Kate, I think you'll like him. He's a cage fighter.' That instantly got my attention. I've always been interested in cage fighting. In fact, when we were together, Pete and I would regularly watch fights on TV and really get into the action. For those of you who aren't in the know, cage fighting is a full-contact combat sport where men fight using mixed martial arts. Believe when I say it is full on, raw and brutal. You can almost smell the testosterone in the air when the two fighters are attacking each other with such force and skill.

Looking back, I have to smile. I wonder if Sol ever imagined in his wildest dreams that he was setting me up on a date with the man who would turn out to be my future husband!

He also sent me the link to Alex's Facebook page when I asked what Alex looked like. But I couldn't really tell from his profile picture so I requested him as a friend. I think I sent my message on a Wednesday and only heard back from him on Friday. Two whole days later! 'That's a bit cheeky,' I thought. Was he playing games with me? But Sol assured me that Alex was definitely coming to the party. In the meantime Gary and I had checked out Alex's showreel on YouTube and were both seriously impressed. His fighting nickname was The Reidernator and I thought he looked like an incredible fighter, with the body to match. He looked so strong, macho and muscular, and he had a really hand-some face. He was gorgeous! Every girl likes to be protected and when I watched Alex fight, I thought, 'I could go out with a man like that.' He would definitely be able to protect me because he didn't just have show muscles, they were the real deal! And I thought if he couldn't protect me, then no man ever could.

Gary and I also watched a clip of Alex being inter-viewed about being a cage fighter and were impressed at how well he came across. He was well-spoken and sounded like a really genuine guy. I liked the fact that he was so dedicated to being a good fighter, and so passionate about his sport. When he was asked how he would like to be remembered as a fighter, he replied, 'Someone with heart, determination, and who was kind.' I was liking what I saw very much. Now I just needed to talk to the guy!

Finally Alex did get in touch with me and we exchanged a series of messages. He told me he was looking forward to seeing me at the party, and I replied that I was looking forward to seeing him as well. Ever the straight talker, I asked him what kinds of things he liked in a girl but his replies were frustratingly unflirtatious and nor did he text me that much. 'Maybe he's just not interested,' I thought, feeling disappointed. If he was, he would be on my case more. Being left by someone doesn't exactly do wonders for your confidence. I so wanted Alex to like me and find me attractive. And, yes, fancy me, because I admit that even from the brief contact we'd had, I fancied him.

On Saturday, 18 July 2009, the day of Michelle's party, I flew back from LA. I had texted Alex on the way to the airport, telling him that I couldn't wait to meet him, and he had replied that he was definitely going to be at the party. I felt nervous and excited at the prospect of meeting him. It was a bit like going on a blind date, I suppose, and I had never been on one before. Gary and I chatted about him on the flight home, wondering what he would be like, until we both realised that we would have to shut up and get some sleep or we'd be too knackered to go to the party. As soon as we landed, in the early evening, I had to dash off to appear on Fearne Cotton's TV show. To be honest, I was more concerned about getting ready for my date with Alex than talking on TV! After the show we didn't hang about but raced to the hotel. I got dressed up to impress in a revealing black basque and a little black tutu skirt I had bought from Trashy Lingerie in LA, which was very me, and Gary worked his make-up magic to give me the sultry look that I love. I hoped it was an outfit that would have Alex noticing me for all the right reasons.

My feeling of anticipation increased as I met up with my friends for cocktails in the bar of the St Martins Lane Hotel. There was Sol, his girlfriend, and the usual entourage of what I call my gay mafia, with Gary, Phil, and the top hairdressing duo Nick Malenko and Royston Blythe.

'He's not here yet,' Sol told me, seeing me scan the bar for Alex. That didn't sound like a good omen – maybe he really wasn't interested. Half an hour later, when I was beginning to give up on him, Sol whispered, 'Alex has arrived.' Instantly my heart started racing and I felt full of nerves, like some shy teenager, as if I couldn't look him in the face. But when I turned round and saw him I thought, 'Wow, he really is gorgeous!' I was immediately struck by how handsome he was, with lovely blue eyes and dark brown hair, and by the sheer size of him – at six foot two he towered over me. And while I could see that his nose had been broken and his ears had taken a battering from his cage fighting, I thought that just made him seem more sexy and manly.

Alex sat next to me after Sol had introduced us and right from the start there was a really strong attraction between us. You can always tell, can't you? You get that butterflies-in-your-stomach feeling, where you want to give them all your attention and to know that they're giving you all theirs. Whenever he was talking to someone else, I'd quickly whisper to Gary to ask if he thought Alex liked me. And then I put in some of my cheeky, flirty moves where I pretended to get something out of my bag. As I bent down, I'd be showing off my bum in my little tutu and I'd say to Gary, 'Is he looking at me? Is he interested?' I think it was pretty obvious that we both found each other very attractive. Not only was I impressed by his good looks, but he was such a lovely guy too. And by the time we left the bar and headed to the Mayfair Hotel for birthday drinks with Michelle, we were openly flirting with each other and I had taken pictures of the two of us together on my phone.

I didn't leave his side from then on and our flirtation continued as we all travelled by car from the Mayfair to Michelle's party, with me sitting on Alex's lap. By the time we reached the party we only had eyes for each other. Afterwards we hit several clubs, ending up at the Shadow Lounge, a gay club, with Gary and Phil. And there we had our first kiss. And . . . wow! Alex was such a good kisser. It was a kiss that felt full of promise. 'I really like him!' I thought. It was such an exciting, delicious feeling. Being with him made me feel so alive and special. I didn't want Alex to go, so when we left the club we went to Balans, on Old Compton Street, my usual haunt at the end of a night clubbing, for Thai green curry. Finally we all went back to Gary and Phil's house.

Those of you who've read my other books know that I've never been into one-night stands. I've always had relationships, and I've always made the guy wait a month before I sleep with him, wanting to know that he respects me and it isn't just about having sex with Katie Price or Jordan. But I didn't feel that I needed to be like that with Alex. Even though I had only just met him, something told me that things were going to be serious between us. And so, just hours after meeting for the first time, we spent the night together. Without going into detail, I can tell you that the sex was good, *really* good. I did have a moment's panic when I thought, 'Oh, no! I've blown it. He won't want to see me again because I've slept with him on the first date. He'll think that I'm a dirtbag.' But that concern quickly faded because being with Alex felt so right that it didn't matter we'd only just met. And, after all, was there anything to be ashamed of? I was thirty-one years old, my husband had walked out on me, my marriage had ended. I was newly single and free to do whatever I liked, with whomever I liked. The first time in my entire life that I slept with a man on a first date, I ended up marrying him! And I knew exactly what I was doing and what I wanted. I was definitely not on the rebound from Pete.

In the morning when I woke up I had no regrets, especially when I looked at Alex as he lay next to me. He was so big and muscular, such a strong and powerful man. I absolutely loved the way he looked and loved being with him. 'Fucking hell,' I thought, hardly believing my luck. 'He's got such a fit body! And he's gorgeous!' But it was way more than physical attraction.

Even then I felt really close to him emotionally. I felt I could be myself with him.

'I can't believe I just spent the night with you!' Alex told me as we cuddled each other. There was no awkwardness between us, though. Being together just felt right.

'I can't either,' I replied. I know people will be surprised and maybe even shocked that I felt like this after just one night, but I'm old enough to know how I feel about someone.

There was a knock at the door and Gary came in holding cups of tea for us. I'm so open with my close friends that I didn't feel any embarrassment at being seen in bed with Alex. In fact, I couldn't resist showing off how sexy he was. I cheekily lifted up the duvet and exclaimed, 'Gary, you have to see Alex's legs. Aren't they fit!' Some men might have felt embarrassed being talked about like this, but Alex took it all in his stride. He was so calm and chilled, I liked his style. Meanwhile Gary was saying, 'Phwoar! Love the legs, show us some more!'

But I kept the rest of Alex under wraps. Gary is a very good friend, but I'm not going to share everything with him!

'What are you doing today?' I asked Alex, immediately wanting to spend more time with him. I knew this wasn't just a one-night stand.

'I haven't really got any plans,' he replied.

'Right then,' I answered, 'you're coming back to mine.

I've got loads of friends coming over and I'm cooking a roast dinner.' Alex had to borrow some tracksuit bottoms and flip-flops from Gary as he only had his smart suit with him. And before we went back to my house, we had to call in at Sainsbury's to buy the food. Who says I don't know how to show a man a good time? And every so often, as I was pushing the trolley and he wasn't looking, I would be checking him out and thinking, 'Yes . . . you really are gorgeous!'

CHAPTER SEVENTEEN

FALLING IN LOVE AGAIN

Alex was a revelation to me that afternoon. He was such easy company; he got along with all my friends, fitted in with everybody. He was kind, he was generous, and a real gentleman. He was a man who had plenty to say for himself, which I liked, yet he was really good-natured about all my friends interrogating him. They do that with a new man as they are protective of me. My children were with their dad that weekend, but my friends had theirs with them as this was a family lunch. Straight away Alex was the one who got in the pool and played with the kids. He was brilliant with them and I liked him all the more for it.

'You're the manny!' I teased him over lunch. 'You're so good with kids.' He just laughed. He seemed so secure, so strong in himself. And I knew something else by the end of that sunny Sunday afternoon in July – I didn't want him to leave. I think Alex was quite taken aback that I wanted him to stay within forty-eight hours of our getting to know each other. But I'm very persuasive! I got my wish.

He pretty much moved in with me after that. For the first couple of nights, I always had friends round as well. I'm a bit of a contradiction, being forward at times and yet shy at others. So while I wanted Alex to stay, I felt I needed other people around us too. But it wasn't long before I felt completely happy to be left alone with him. I wanted us to be together, I'd completely fallen for him. It was a totally whirlwind, full-on romance. I'm an all or nothing girl when it comes to relationships; I always have been. I know when something feels right, and this felt so right. It might have seemed too fast to some people, but it was no different from how I was when I first met Pete. As soon as we were both back in the UK after appearing on *I'm a Celebrity*, Pete moved in with me and Harvey.

The better I got to know Alex, the more I fell for him and I came to see how well suited to each other we were. And, most importantly of all, when he met my children he was brilliant with them, so patient, so kind, so up for playing with them and reading to them. My friends commented that I certainly had the knack of picking guys who were good with kids! But my kids are the most important people in my life. I would do anything for them. They are so precious to me, no man comes near that and no man ever will. If a guy wasn't good with them, it wouldn't matter how much I liked him, the relationship would have to end; in fact, it wouldn't even start. Fortunately, when I met Alex's family, I got on well with them and they loved the kids too. Everything seemed to fall into place with Alex.

He is so in tune with other people and interested in many different things – from Greek mythology, to self-healing, to the pyramids. When I met him he was thirty-four. He was born in Aldershot and is from an army family. His dad was a paratrooper. Alex is the youngest child of six, three boys and three girls. He got into martial arts when he was fifteen. When he left school he joined the Territorial Army and also did some modelling. But he didn't really enjoy it, and so he started working as an extra in films. He was Tom Hanks' body double in *Saving Private Ryan*. After that he was keen to get into acting proper and so he went to drama school for a year and then landed a part in the Channel Four soap *Hollyoaks*. Throughout this time he was fighting too. When it became clear that he was going to earn more as a fighter than as an actor, he put his acting ambitions on hold. But, as he told me, fighting is a bit like acting anyway. It's a performance; it's a little bit like appearing in a show and going on-stage. It's just painful if it goes wrong! I wasn't looking forward to seeing Alex in pain, but I had to accept that he was a fighter because that was what he loved doing most.

* * *

I felt that Alex was my perfect match. After the split with Pete I had begun to feel that no man would ever want me again after they had read all the lies about me in the press, so it felt like a huge deal that Alex wanted to be with me and didn't take any notice of what had been written. He saw very quickly what I'm really like. I can be a bitch when it comes to my work and business, but in my personal life I'm completely different. Alex instinctively understood how insecure I am, how I need to be cuddled, how I need so much reassurance and love. We both knew very early on that we had fallen in love with each other. Within a matter of weeks we were talking about getting married and having children.

I'm the kind of person who thinks you only live once and that you should live your life the way you want to live it. It doesn't matter what anyone else thinks, it's about being true to yourself. I've also always had this feeling that I might die young – a feeling that has grown stronger thanks to the way the paps relentlessly pursue me whenever I drive anywhere – so I want to make the most of every minute, and know that I have lived my life to the full. And besides, there are no rules that say you have to wait a certain amount of time before you can fall in love with someone else after a marriage ends. There were some people who thought I had moved on too quickly after my break-up with Pete. But he had made it very clear that our marriage was over and we would never get back together, so what else was I supposed to do? Sit around and wait for him to give his permission and tell me, 'You can have a boyfriend now'? I don't think so! Anyway Pete no longer featured in my life except as the father of my children. I didn't feel the way I once had about him any more. All I knew was that I had fallen in love with Alex and it was a wonderful, exciting, liberating love.

There are so many things I love about Alex. I love the fact that he is so opinionated and his own person, with such a strong character. He also doesn't put up with any shit from me. For instance, early on when we went out together and I did my thing of having a few drinks and then going off and chatting to other people – and, yes I admit it, maybe flirting a little bit with the guys – Alex wouldn't stand for it. There was no big scene. He simply said very calmly, in a way which told me he absolutely meant it, 'Don't treat me like that. I'll only tell you once and then, it doesn't matter how much I like you, I will walk away. Of course I don't mind you talking to other people . . . I'm just like you, I'm interested in talking to other people too . . . but if I come up to you, I don't expect you to blank me.' That told me! And do you know what? I loved the fact that he'd got the measure of my character. It did make me wonder if I'd ended up losing respect for Pete in our marriage when I stopped listening to him. I respect Alex, and because of that I listen to everything he says.

It's true to say that I wish in many ways that I had met him six years ago. Not just because then I would have been spared the heartbreak of a bitter divorce, but because, just as I accept him completely for who he is, he accepts me for who I am. If I want to go out with my friends or go riding, he has no problem with that at all.

And right from the start of our relationship, I've had such fun with him – something that was sadly lacking in my marriage to Pete, especially towards the end. Alex and I go out together and socialise with friends at restaurants or clubs, or have people round for dinner, and play board games, and have a drink. I come from a sociable family where my mum and dad are always having drinks or dinner parties with friends, and finally I can do the same with Alex. I could never socialise like this with Pete because he had such a problem with me having a drink. I'm not saying I want to get off-my-nut drunk, I just want to be sociable like everyone else! Pete would always say that I acted like a twat when I'd had a drink. I'm exactly the same when I have a drink with Alex. The difference is, he can handle it.

Alex can't offer me anything in the way of money or material possessions, but I don't care about any of that. I can take care of myself. But he's got such a great personality, and so much love to give me, that he makes me feel secure and protected. Nor is he in the least bit bothered about fame. I never for a second got the feeling that he was with me just because of who I am. But here's a funny coincidence: Alex was lined up to appear on the 2004 *I'm a Celebrity . . . Get Me Out of Here!*, the same series I was first on, then the producers chose Pete instead! And now here I am with Alex after splitting up with Pete . . . It's strange how things turn out, isn't it? And wonderful, of course.

As well as our emotional connection being so strong, sexually we are a perfect match, the best I've ever experienced. I know you're probably waiting for me to go into all the juicy details of our sex life but I'm not going to do that because it's not fair on Alex and because I now realise that giving away too much about your private life isn't good for any relationship. Far too much of my marriage with Pete wasn't kept private – and look what happened to us! I'm not making that mistake with Alex. He has also agreed not to go into detail if he's ever interviewed. So all I will say is that there is a very strong physical attraction between us and our sex life is *amazing*. Let's just say that he's very different from any other man I've ever been with, in a very good way. And now that I am finally off my anti-depressants, which really suppress your sex drive, I'm as up for it as he is.

Alex was also honest with me right from the start about his previous sexual experiences. Sexually it seems he's been pretty adventurous in the past. I have certainly met more than my match there! He describes himself as having been try-sexual – as in, he's tried everything. I'm very open-minded and can honestly say that I wasn't shocked to hear this. Instead I admired his honesty. And that's not all. On the first day we spent together, he told me that he was a cross-dresser. It's not a huge part of his life and I know he plays it down, but the bottom line is that he has an alter ego called

Roxanne and he dresses as her in private for a sexual thrill. He doesn't go out anywhere dressed as a woman or have any desire to do so. He doesn't want to *be* a woman, and he doesn't want to have sex with men.

Was I shocked by his revelation? I can hand on heart say, no, I wasn't, and it didn't for a second put me off him. As long as it is something which is kept well away from the kids and stays private, I can accept it, because it's part of who he is. I think he can get away with cross-dressing because he is so manly and macho and because he is honest about it and is not ashamed. He didn't have to tell me, but he did and I respected him for that. So I knew what I was taking on from the word go with Alex, and if I hadn't liked it I'd have got out then. But if anything his confession made him even more intriguing. I like this side of him because it is extreme – and I've always seen myself as an extremist too.

As soon as we were on our own together I wanted to see what he looked like as Roxanne. 'Please let me dress you up and put make-up on you!' I said, already planning what clothes, wigs and make-up I could use on him.

'No, Kate,' he replied. 'I don't want you to.' His previous girlfriends had always had a problem with his cross-dressing, so no wonder he was surprised by my attitude.

'I can't get my head round the fact that you don't mind,' Alex told me. 'All my other girlfriends have absolutely hated it.' And there I was, asking if I could put make-up on him and dress him up!

'Most of the time I don't even think about it,' he told me. 'It's you who's making a big deal of it.' But I got my way, and I got to see Roxanne. What happened next is between me, Alex . . . and Roxanne.

My final word on the subject is that now I'm so used to that side of our relationship that if it wasn't there, I would really miss it. He has opened a door on a whole new experience for me and I love it!

* * *

Right from the start with Alex I felt that we had a very equal relationship. There weren't the competing egos that I think there had been in my marriage to Pete because we spent so much time working together, recording our TV show and doing shoots and interviews for magazines. Alex is a professional fighter and is very good at what he does. I have my work, and the two worlds are kept separate. Yes, Alex appears in my reality show, *What Katie Did Next,* but not all the time, and I have appeared in his series on fighting. But I don't want us to be filmed together all the time; it isn't healthy for any relationship. I've learned a lesson from my first marriage and it's that I can't be with someone all the time, like I was with Pete – in the end it does get too much.

Pete and I were both always so jealous of each other's exes, I lost count of the number of rows we had about them. But Alex and I are not jealous of each other's past at all. He accepts mine, I accept his. Because we met at a party, right from the start he saw me in social situations, out with my friends and entertaining at home. It wasn't like that with Pete at all. We met on a reality show and worked on a reality show. We ended up spending so much of our time together that I think we were fated to become more and more jealous and possessive of each other because it was only ever just us two.

One of the many things I really love about Alex is that he is completely his own man; he doesn't drop everything for me. He's been a professional fighter for the last thirteen years and is incredibly committed to the life. If I ever say, 'Don't bother training today, let's do something together,' he'll often say, 'No, I have to train, it's my job.' And he trains intensively three times a day – Jujitsu in the morning, boxing in the afternoon and weights in the evening. In the early days of our relationship he told me, 'It would be so easy to be sucked into your world and be with you all the time, but I want our relationship to work and last longer than five or six years. I want it to be for ever, so I need to be able to do my own thing. I need my own life. '

I really admire his drive, dedication and passion for fighting. And so when we meet up in the evening after we've both been working we have plenty to talk about – we're definitely not in each other's pocket. But right from the beginning Alex was really supportive of my work and came with me on some of my book tour at the end of July 2009 to promote my novel *Sapphire*. I really appreciated him coming – not only did I want to be with him because we were at a stage in our relationship when we wanted to be with each other as much as we could, but I felt really nervous about the response I would get from the public on my next tour. The recent press about me had been so relentlessly negative that I was worried it would have turned people against me and they wouldn't come to my signings.

However, I was determined to put on a brave face and had planned a spectacular press launch at which I was wearing a gorgeous glittery blue swimsuit, which I think had some 4,000 crystals sewn on to it – you know how I love my bling! And I was accompanied by a posse of hunky guys, including my friend Anthony Lowther, all stripped to the waist and showing off their six-packs – with the word 'Sapphire' inked on to their chests. I love my work!

The press launch went well and then came the book tour. It was so brilliant to have Alex with me on that. To throw the press off the scent he pretended to be my security guard, but I knew it wouldn't be long before they found out we were an item. I was trying to play down how deeply I had fallen in love with him in front of my friends and family, but I think everyone could see our feelings for each other.

Luckily my fears that people would have turned against me proved to be unfounded as huge crowds of fans queued to have their copy of *Sapphire* signed by me. It meant so much to me that they hadn't believed all the lies and I really do appreciate their continued support. I was absolutely thrilled when the book went to number one in the bestsellers list.

But it didn't take long for the press to get on our case. I did warn Alex what the attention could be like but I don't think he could ever have imagined just how intense it would become, and how the tabloids would try and rake up anything they could on him. Once they found out about our relationship it wasn't long before ex-girlfriends of Alex sold their stories, saying that he was vain and obsessed with his looks and being famous, and that he was obsessed with sex. There were even stories saying that I wanted him to have surgery on his nose and ears because I thought he could look better. Crap! I love Alex's looks. I would never want him to have surgery. I think he's really handsome just the way he is. His broken nose and battered ears are his 'badges' from fighting, as he calls them, and to me they add character to his looks, show that he's a man who's experienced life to the full.

There were also so many stories saying that I wasn't over Pete yet, that I was begging him to take me back – all lies. One particularly ridiculous article said that I had a shrine to him in my house! That was insane – I had taken every single picture of him down. Another said that I had been singing 'I Will Always Love You' down the phone to him. I couldn't even sing that Whitney Houston number if I tried! It wasn't even 'our' song, so why would I sing that to him? I was so sick of it. I had moved on, why wouldn't the press accept that? And I'm sure that the public were getting tired of reading it too.

Whenever the press turned their attention on my relationship with Alex and what we did as a couple, they managed to put a negative spin on it. If Alex wasn't with me when I went out there would be stories that we'd split up. I thought, 'Why can't they just let us be?' We weren't selling our stories to the press, we were just getting on with our lives, we weren't asking for this attention, we didn't want to be in the papers every day. But the stories would only get worse as our relationship progressed, and the lies more and more extreme. I felt extremely protective of Alex. I was used to being slated in the press, but he wasn't. He didn't deserve to be attacked in this way.

At the beginning of August 2009 Pete had the children and I flew out to Malaga with Alex and a group of my friends to stay at another friend's villa. We sunbathed, swam in the pool and generally lounged around chatting, behaving no differently from anyone else on a mini-break. But the press made it out to be sleazy and something it wasn't, calling it our 'X-rated' holiday. The only person being sleazy was the one who took pictures of me as I sunbathed topless by a private pool and then sold them to the press! Pete was quoted in *New* magazine as saying no way would he take me back now. As if there'd been any chance that I'd want to go back to him! I knew I never, ever wanted to go back to him.

By now the only reason I was sad about our marriage ending was because of the children and the breaking up of our family.

A couple of weeks later I was preparing to walk up the aisle in a stunning white wedding dress. No, not for my own wedding! Even I'm not such a quick worker, and anyway my divorce was yet to come through. This time I was Maid of Honour for my best friends Gary and Phil who were renewing their wedding vows. Alex and the children came with me to the *Midsummer Night's Dream*-inspired day – I love how my friends put on a show! There were cute white ponies with unicorn horns, women dressed as fairies, hunky men as fauns, and other people dressed as swans and peacocks on stilts. (Not sure where they feature in the Shakespeare play, but they looked amazing!) It really was a fairy-tale day. Though I joked that they should have called it *Two Gay Men and a Lady* because Gary, Phil and I are joined at the hip! They have been friends of mine since I was seventeen, and have stuck by me through everything. They've always been so loyal and have never sold any story about me. I trust them completely. They vet any guy I've ever been with, and if they approve it makes a big difference. I can be myself with them. They're my gay husbands really.

Even though I was so happy with Alex, I couldn't help thinking of my first wedding, and it did feel strange to be wearing a white dress again. I felt moved as my friends renewed their vows; it brought back so many memories of the vows I had once made. As the day went on I felt more and more emotional. By the time we'd had dinner and, yes, a few drinks and I was preparing to sing for Gary and Phil, I was in tears.

I was supposed to be singing DJ Sammy's 'Heaven', which I had been rehearsing and had recorded. Instead I impulsively took the microphone and started singing Whitney Houston's 'I Have Nothing', which was the song the choir sang at my first wedding as I walked up the aisle. I don't know why I chose to sing that number; maybe I needed to lay the past to rest. And, on top of that, it's a really tough song to sing! I just hoped that Gary and Phil would have more luck with the song than I did . . . Still, as they've been together over twenty years, I don't think there are any worries on that score! Fortunately one of the professional singers joined me as I sang with tears streaming down my face.

I couldn't help feeling a failure because when you marry someone, you expect to marry them for life and my first marriage hadn't lasted. But even as I cried, I knew that I would get married again. And then Alex was there at my side, taking me in his arms, and I thought, 'The past is the past; I've got so much to be happy about and to look forward to.'

But my new relationship was lived under the full glare of the media spotlight. I knew it wouldn't be long before the press found out about Alex being a cross-dresser. I felt very protective of him which was why I wanted to get there first, hinting that I already knew about it and it didn't matter to me. So when I bought my next horse, I called him Jordan's Cross Dresser. But I was still anxious for Alex, as I knew only too well how vicious and twisted some of the tabloids can be. And, sure enough, it wasn't long before he discovered that for himself.

It was the end of August when we came down to breakfast one morning and looked at the Sunday papers. 'Oh my God,' he said, as he picked up the *News of the World*. The headline proclaimed 'Secret Porn Shame of Jordan's New Lover', and there was a picture of Alex from a film he was in the middle of making. Before he became a professional cage fighter he'd been an actor, and I knew that he still had acting ambitions and was appearing in a film. The article went on to say that Alex was in a violent hard-core porn film with scenes that glamourised rape. For a few minutes I was completely shocked and then reason kicked in. I believed him when he told me that, while the film was violent, in no way did it glamourise rape, and that it wasn't porn but a gangster film. I trusted him. I knew that he would never sign up to a film that glamourised rape as someone very close to him had been raped and it had deeply shocked him. Part of the reason he became a martial arts artist and a professional fighter is because it is a nasty world and he wants to be able to protect the people he loves. He's also taught kids self-defence, but it's not just about how to fight – it's also about being better people and showing each other respect.

Both Alex and I believe that rape and sexual assault are serious things and we would never dismiss them. I would certainly never go out with someone who glamourised rape. When I was six, two of my friends and I were sexually assaulted. My mum was sitting close by while we were playing hide-and-seek in the bushes. Suddenly a man appeared and promised to buy us ice creams if we let him touch us. We were so young that we went along with what he said. He lined us all up, exposed himself, and then bizarrely began his assault by licking each of us. Then I think he touched us – I can't really remember, I must have blocked it out. I think we all knew that what he was doing was wrong but we were paralysed with fear. Thank God some older children saw what he was doing and he ran off. I rushed off to tell my mum what had happened but by then he had disappeared. She called the police, but I don't think they ever caught him. When I was interviewed by Piers Morgan in July 2009 I found myself getting emotional when I talked about the incident. I thought I had buried it, but it still had the power to disturb me, even years later. As a mother myself now, I appreciate how vulnerable any child is.

That wasn't the only time in my life that I came into contact with a paedophile. When I was thirteen I agreed to do some modelling for a photographer who said that he could get me jobs as a catalogue model. First of all he took pictures of me posing in my school uniform, being cheeky, sticking my tongue out or sucking a lollipop. I thought it was harmless, not realising his true intentions. From there he got me to pose in lacy underwear with stockings, suspenders and high heels. I just had to stand there with my hand on my hip, he didn't ask me to get into any explicit poses, and so I still thought it was harmless. The turning point came when I went round to his house for a shoot and he introduced me to a woman. Like him, she seemed perfectly ordinary, nice even. He said that she was his stylist and they were going to try out a new look with me. This time he wanted me to pose wearing a wet shirt with nothing on underneath. Suddenly this didn't feel like a game any more. I didn't want to show off my body in front of these people. I felt really uncomfortable with the idea and for the first time I was frightened. I was alone with them. I told them I didn't want to.

It was horrible, both of them by now standing close to me, trying to persuade me to do something I really didn't want to do. And they were very persistent, joking at first and then getting cross. The woman was the most persuasive, saying it would make a really good picture and didn't I want to be a model? And how I owed the photographer this, as he had taken so many pictures of me. But even aged thirteen, I was strong-willed and didn't give in to their demands. I left the house, saying I was going outside to wait for my mum. That was the last time I saw the photographer, I never went back.

A couple of years later two female Child Protection officers came round to our house and told us that he was now in prison for a series of indecent assaults on young girls and for taking pornographic pictures of them after he'd drugged them. The officers told me that they wanted to see me to check I was OK because his prison cell was plastered with photographs of me. My mum and I were completely stunned by the revelation. The police officers told me that if he tried to contact me, I must call them straight away. I'd had a lucky escape as I had not touched the drugged milkshakes he always offered me. But it was really shocking, knowing how close I had come to a man like that. I could have been one of those girls he assaulted . . .

But, back in the present, I knew I wasn't going to let the muck-raking about Alex's film role drive us apart. Instead I was going to show the world and the press that I was standing by him one hundred per cent. I was due to fly to Malaga that day to launch my KP Equestrian range at a polo event there. 'I want you to come with me,' I told Alex, 'I want to prove to everyone that I am supporting you.' So far as I'm concerned everyone has a past. I hated the way the press were trying to destroy us by putting a negative slant on Alex.

From the moment we landed in Spain the press attention was absolutely manic. In the end I had to cut short the signing as I was surrounded by fans pushing forward and paps surrounding the place where I was sitting and it was pretty scary. But at least the signing was a success and our appearance together showed that I was sticking by my fighter.

Some of my friends were really concerned about me seeing Alex when this story came out. They were already a little wary because the split from Pete was so recent. They were worried that I wasn't thinking straight, even though they knew I hadn't broken down and was getting on with my life and seemed happy. 'Kate, what are you doing with him?' some of them said to me. 'He's lied to you about this film.'

But I stuck by Alex. He hadn't lied to me, and I believed him when he said it wasn't a porn film. He had been honest about everything else in his past and even revealed the most extreme thing about himself, that he liked dressing as a woman, so why would he lie about a film? And as my friends got to know Alex better, of course they warmed to him and grew to like him, which was no surprise to me as he is such a lovely, loveable guy.

CHAPTER EIGHTEEN

THE PROPOSAL AND ROXANNE IS OUTED

September was a month of firsts. It was the first time in my life that I received a decree nisi – the first step towards finalising my divorce from Pete. In six weeks' time the divorce would be final and our marriage would officially be at an end. But I didn't need a court to tell me that my marriage was over. It ended when Pete left me. The last few months had been such a roller-coaster for me, with the pain of the break-up and then falling in love with Alex so soon afterwards, that it was going to be a relief when I could finally say I was divorced.

But life goes on, doesn't it? Along with the divorce proceedings came Junior's first day at school. I couldn't believe that my little boy was old enough! But there he was, looking all grown-up in his school uniform. I was so proud of him. He is such a lovely little boy, loving and full of fun. Both he and Princess were so young at that time, that I hadn't sat down and told them that Pete and I had split up. I don't think they would have understood. Instead, I always told them that I loved them, and that Daddy loved them too. My greatest concern was always that all my children should feel loved, protected and safe. And yet it was sad that Junior didn't have both his parents to see him off on his first day at school. Sadly that didn't happen and Pete missed out on a real milestone in Junior's life, which I think was a shame. There are some moments you can't buy back and seeing our son go off to school for the first time was a once-in-a-lifetime moment for me. I took Junior and he had his own mini-entourage of my mum, Alex, Gary and Nick.

September was also the first time I got to watch Alex fight live. He had been training intensively before the fight, and that included a two-week sex ban which wasn't to my liking! However, he still satisfied me . . . just not himself to the full potential. And, as he pointed out, some fighters abstain for a month, so I guess I was lucky. Anyway, so long as I still got all my cuddles with extras I wasn't complaining. I knew how important this fight was for him. I went shopping for some lingerie to show off to Alex as a reward after the fight, and also had a little black dress made by my friend Lamis Khamis with silver and gold sequins spelling out 'The Champ' across the front as I was sure that Alex would win. I intended to surprise him by putting it on when his victory was announced. But by the day of the fight – Saturday, 19 September – I was very nervous for him. The thought of him getting hurt was horrible! And along with that it seemed that a lot of people wanted to see him lose as a way of getting back at me. But I wasn't going to let any of the negative comments get to me; I was going to stand by my man. I took an entire entourage of friends on a coach to support Alex during his fight at The Troxy in East London.

I felt sick with anxiety as we took our seats. But at the same time there is such a brilliant atmosphere at fights it is really exciting. Everyone there has got such attitude, and I like the edge of tension and competition between the different supporters. I reckon it would be the perfect night out for a group of girls as there are so many fit-looking men there. When Alex came into the ring there were boos as well as cheers, but I ignored the boos and smiled and cheered my man. But it was so hard watching that fight! I felt as if I could feel every punch that he was taking and at times couldn't watch and had to cover my eyes, especially when he received a blow to the face which left him badly cut above his eye. After three rounds, which probably didn't last that long but felt as if they did, the judges announced that Alex was the winner. I went wild, shouting out his name and cheering, and then quickly stripped off the dress I was wearing and slipped on the little black number. I didn't care that everyone could see me in my underwear, I just wanted to show that Alex was my champ. And the night was about to get a whole lot better. As we all travelled to Movida to celebrate his win he had something to say to me: 'Kate, will you marry me?'

There were no scattered rose petals, no bottles of champagne and Alex didn't get down on one knee. Nor did he give me a ring. But I didn't need any of those things, I didn't need to be showered with expensive gifts, all that mattered was that I knew deep in my heart that I loved Alex and wanted to marry him.

'Yes!' I exclaimed, and threw my arms around him. A few of my friends heard the proposal but they all promised to keep it under wraps. We had already talked about marriage, so it wasn't a complete surprise, but all the same it was wonderful that he had asked me. We didn't want the press to know as this was just between Alex and me, there were going to be no big magazine deals. We talked then about how we would ideally like to get married before Christmas. I fancied a Caribbean wedding, but later we found out that if we wanted to get married so soon after my divorce came through in six weeks' time then it would have to be in Las Vegas. Everywhere else makes you wait a certain number of months after a divorce before you can marry again – and we knew we didn't want to wait any longer than we had to. In the meantime, we both had so much on. I had the launch of my style book, Alex had his TV series on fighting, and there was also the small matter of my returning to the jungle . . . but more of that later. And then the press found out about Alex being a cross-dresser.

I knew they would have a field day with the story and make it out to be something seedy and tacky, which it isn't at all. Sure enough, by the beginning of October the press were running stories on Alex. I know Alex is really secure in himself but it isn't easy having your name splashed over the papers in connection with something which is so incredibly personal and private. While lots of his friends knew about the cross-dressing, not all of them did. In some ways it must have been as difficult as coming out when you're gay, though at least his parents already knew and were absolutely fine about it.

'I suppose I'm going to have to get used to people shouting "tranny" and "cross-dresser" to me in the street,' Alex confided in me. I hated to think of him getting abuse for something which was nobody else's business and wasn't harming anyone. 'You should just smile and say, "Cheers, mate! Thanks for that!"' I advised him. 'Instead of letting it get to you. Otherwise those narrow-minded twats have won.'

But I know it hasn't been easy for him, knowing that something which is deeply private to him is now public knowledge. One of his friends was getting married and they sent him a text, taking the piss, asking him if he now wanted to come as a Roxanne the bridesmaid. I felt sorry for Alex and wanted him to put his point of view across so I arranged for him to do a shoot and interview with *OK!* Before he did it, I said, 'Don't joke about the cross-dressing because it is something private and unique to you, and if you joke about you'll just encourage other people to take the piss and you'll end up being hurt inside.' He took my advice and was completely open about what he did. 'So what? There are wars happening everywhere and people care about this, give me a break!' And he said that when he read those stories saying that he was a secret cross-dresser: 'It makes me laugh. There are no secrets, and there never have been between me and Katie. As far as the rest of the world is concerned? I've got nothing to hide and nothing to prove to anybody. I'm proud of who I am.' He also looked absolutely stunning in the shoot, dressed in a black suit and white shirt, especially when he lay back with the white shirt unbuttoned and showed off his gorgeous toned chest.

And I was so proud of him for standing up for himself. In this Alex is like me. Neither of us is going to live our life feeling worried about what other people think of us. His view is, 'I am, what I am, and if I don't fit into society, then bollocks! What does it mean to fit into society anyway?' Which is a view I share. When he comes across people who criticise him for cross-dressing and say that he is wrong to do it, he will immediately come back with, 'What's wrong with it? Why can't I cross-dress if I want?'

If they then reply that he's a man and therefore shouldn't dress as a woman, he'll say, 'Who says a man can't do it?' And he's so good at arguing his case that the people who object are often lost for words.

The only thing that does really get to him, and hurt him, is when the press knock his fighting. That is something he is totally committed to and passionate about, and he knows he is good at it.

I then had the idea of showing the world how much I truly didn't mind about Alex's cross-dressing at the launch of my style book, *Standing Out*. For once I could turn the press writing endless stories about Alex and me to my advantage and have some fun. I decided that I would dress the men closest to me in four of my most famous outfits. My brother would wear a pink tutu dress and tiara like I had for my wedding; Phil would wear a black and yellow jumpsuit like the one I had worn when I worked as a model for Formula One; Andrew would wear pink shorts and t-shirt from my KP Equestrian range; and Alex would wear a gold swimsuit like the one I had worn when I had dressed up as Xena: Warrior Princess in Ibiza. I myself was going to wear a blonde wig and scarlet dress, and vamp it up. It was our way of saying 'Up yours' to anyone who thought there was anything wrong with what Alex did. Plus it was an eye-catching way of getting publicity for my book.

The men were up for it and on 22 October Gary found himself very busy working his make-up magic on four hunky men, while Nick worked his hairdressing artistry on the wigs. I think some people were surprised that I was writing a style book as I've often been slated for what I wear but I've never set out to be a style icon. I've got my own unique style, and over the years I've been asked so many questions by fans about my style that I wanted to share the secrets of how I put my look together.

I thought the launch was a success; it was all tongue-in-cheek and a bit of fun. I felt I had made the point that I didn't mind about Alex's alter ego. But of course it wasn't going to end there and I found myself being asked about Roxanne during interviews about the book. Still, if that meant I could show that I was standing by Alex all the way, so be it. I wasn't going to go into detail, just make it clear that in no way was this a problem between us. I did have some cheeky banter with Graham Norton about it on his show, but that's what his show is like and Alex was fine about my comments.

By pure coincidence the launch took place on the day my divorce from Pete was finalised. It was such a relief! Finally Alex and I could start planning our wedding. Later, in the press, I saw pictures of Pete hugging Claire and his brother, supposedly after they had just received the news about the divorce. They all looked so happy, with big smiles on their faces, and I thought, if that photo is accurate as described, how can they celebrate such a sad experience? The divorce had damaged our family. All the fame, all the magazine deals, won't last for ever. They will fade away as new people come into the media and become popular. I felt that all the time Pete was getting such good publicity he seemed to believe it would last for ever, but it won't. The real test will be in years to come, when all the fame has gone and Pete's had time to think about what happened.

I was so happy with Alex and he definitely changed my outlook on life. Being with him was making me feel calmer and more chilled out. He's quite a spiritual person and into meditation and yoga. He introduced me to Bikram yoga – known as hot yoga for being done in a room heated to 105°F. I realised that I didn't want to hate anyone any more or be drawn into tit-for-tat slanging matches with other celebs. It doesn't get you anywhere, being bitter and twisted. Life is too short and I just want mine to be happy.

But it seemed that there were still many people who didn't want me to be happy, and in fact would go out of their way to make me unhappy. On Sunday, 25 October I couldn't believe my eyes when I saw the cover of the *News of the World* and saw that Michelle Clack, someone I had known for fifteen years and had counted as one of my best friends, and who had even been one of the bridesmaids at my wedding, had sold a story about me. She claimed that I was a 'monster', a 'selfish bitch', and a 'liar'. That I withheld sex from Pete and had been to blame for my marriage breaking up. She claimed that now I wanted to get back with Pete, and that I was unstable and needed psychological help. I was completely shocked that a friend could come out with such rubbish. When Pete had left me she and her husband continued to see him and I did find that difficult, especially as Pete was making the break-up even harder by not speaking to me. She would still come and see me, and when she'd just had her baby I went and saw her in hospital. But when I saw Michelle and her husband on Pete's reality show I did feel betrayed and I did say that she had to choose between being friends with him or me. But I think that's a normal reaction – my marriage had ended and I felt my ex-husband was being cruel to me.

I'd never in a million years imagined that Michelle would do this to me. I was bitterly hurt by her accusations and so upset. I'm not close to many people and had always counted her as one of my best friends. I'd trusted her and we'd been closely involved in each other's lives for years. We'd had our children around the same time, and practically every weekend she had come round to my house. In fact, I had only just lent her a crib that had been Princess's and various other baby things. In the past I had loaned her a horse – Jordan's Glamour Girl – and paid for its upkeep as she was also a keen rider. At one point her parents had even worked for Pete and me as our housekeepers.

I don't know what possible motive she could have had for doing such a story. All I can say is that I hope whatever it was she gained from betraying me, it was worth it. I vowed never to see her again. Our friendship was over. The press have written so many bullshit stories about me, but this one stunned and shocked everyone I was close to. They all knew Michelle and couldn't believe that someone close to me could behave like this. Wasn't it enough that my marriage had ended? Did I have to lose my friends as well as they turned against me? I also felt that Pete should really question some of the people he has around him and ask himself, if they would still be his friends if they didn't share the same management? I felt that Michelle could never have been a real friend of mine if she could sell a story like that which she knew would hurt me.

It was such a difficult time, having to deal with these endless setbacks. I felt as if I couldn't do anything right. I had been part of Asda's Tickled Pink campaign – for breast cancer awareness – and had posed for a series of lingerie shots to promote it. Money from my lingerie sales was also going to the charity. But I was dropped because people objected to comments about the scars from my breast surgery which I made on my reality show. I felt they had completely misunderstood these comments, which were entirely to do with me and how I felt about my own body and nothing to do with women who had breast cancer, who have always had my full support.

I had recently run a 10-kilometre race to raise money for a cancer charity because I know how devastating the disease can be. My mum's best friend Louise had battled breast cancer in the past and I saw how tough it was and the toll it had taken on her and her family, so I would never in a million years have wanted to say anything to offend women like her. Louise had been one of the women I had got to model my lingerie range a few years earlier, after she had cancer. She wanted to do a story in the papers about how supportive I had been to her during her illness. She managed to get a feature in one of the weekly magazines but none of the tabloids picked it up. No one wanted a good news story about Katie Price.

It felt as if people were queuing up to kick me, and whatever I said or did was blown up out of all proportion or twisted or was made up. At least on Twitter and my website I receive so many good messages of support from my fans. The haters who love to knock me can come out with their bitter and twisted comments, but I'm not listening to them.

Then in November things took a more sinister turn when I received a series of hateful letters threatening to torture and kill my horses, and heaping vile abuse on me – calling me a slag and a whore. I was stunned. I just couldn't believe that anyone would want to hurt an animal, but I know that there are some serious weirdos out there who have maimed and killed horses in the past. I took the threats seriously and called the police. Fortunately there are really good security measures at the stables where my horses are at livery, but even so it was horrible knowing that there was someone out there who wanted to kill an innocent animal. Later the police did catch the man concerned and he said he had sent the letters as a joke. Some sick joke that was.

I also read that a village in Kent were planning to burn

a giant effigy of me as part of their Bonfire Night celebrations. Apparently every year the village chooses a celebrity to put on the bonfire on 5 November – the year before it had been Russell Brand and Jonathan Ross. I'm sure it was only meant to be a bit of fun but I couldn't help wondering what exactly I had done to make people want to see that kind of spectacle. And as I was a mum of three young children, I really didn't think it was appropriate that they chose me. What if Junior had found out? He would have been really upset.

It wasn't just strangers who said hurtful things either. Pete's brother was filmed on Pete's TV reality show, saying that he was embarrassed to call me his sister-in-law. I found his comment so upsetting. He'd lived with Pete and me for a year, and I'd always made him feel welcome. Even when he was no longer living with us, we would often see him. How dare he disown me on national TV? He had a short memory, seeing as it was his brother who had finished with me.

It almost felt as if some people were trying to drive me to have a breakdown with their stories in the press. I did have some dark times when I feared that the stress I had gone through with my marriage break-up and then the endless battering from the press might cause the cancer I had previously suffered from to return. In 2002 I had gone to the doctor about a lump in my finger. Tests revealed that the lump was malignant, a rare form of cancer called Leiomyosarcoma or LMS. Fortunately for me it had been detected early on and the lump was removed. I am supposed to have regular MRI scans to check that it hasn't come back and up until now I've always been clear, but I know how bad stress can be for you. Fortunately I had Alex, my family and friends standing by me and helping me to stay strong through these tough times.

Still, it did get to the stage where I was looking forward to going back on *I'm a Celebrity . . . Get Me Out of Here!* just to get a break from all the shit the press were giving me. How ironic was that? In order to get a break from the paps, I was going to be filmed 24/7. I had agreed to go back on the ITV show, thinking it would be an incredible experience – especially as I knew what to expect after my first appearance in 2004. ITV had offered me brilliant money to take part and it seemed crazy to turn it down. I'm a single mum who works to support my family. To me this was just another job. Plus it seemed like a bit of an honour as I was the first person ever to return to the jungle. I knew I would really miss the kids but I couldn't take them over to Australia because it was important that Harvey and Junior did not take time out of school and I didn't think it would be fair just to go with Princess. I also thought it wouldn't be fair on Pete, though had we been able to talk amicably, I would have suggested that I did take the children over and then his parents, who live in Australia, would have had the chance to see them.

It was going to be strange, returning to the place where I had fallen in love with him nearly six years ago. I thought it would be a form of closure on my marriage, not that I needed it because as far as I was concerned it was over. But it would be like going full circle, right from the beginning of my fairy-tale love story with Pete to its end. I definitely didn't agree to go back so as to see if I was still in love with Pete, because I one hundred per cent knew that I wasn't. It wasn't a form of therapy, it wasn't facing my demons. I just wanted to go back so that I could feel like a stronger person, to prove to myself that I could deal with everything that had happened. And Alex, my family and friends supported my decision to go, though I knew they were all worried about me doing the trials and warned me I was bound to be voted in to do a lot of them.

ITV wanted to keep my appearance on the show a secret until I arrived in the jungle or at least until a few days before, but it was only fair that I should let Pete in on it. 'I want you to know that I'm not going to say anything bad about you. In fact, I don't want to say anything about you at all,' I told him on the phone.

His reply was that he would see.

'I swear on my life that I'm not going to slate you!' I exclaimed, frustrated by his attitude. 'If you read anything that says I have, it won't have come from me. It will be a lie.' He still didn't sound convinced but there was nothing more I could say to him.

Alex bonding with the kids.

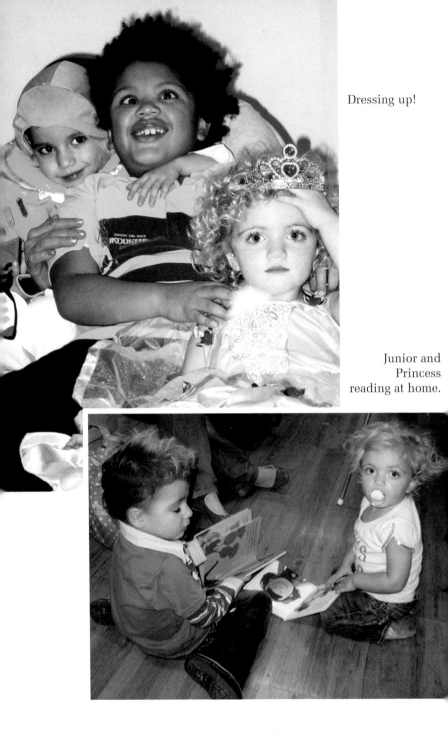

Dressing up!

Junior and
Princess
reading at home.

New Year's Eve 2009.
Party time!

Just before Alex went into the Big Brother house.

The happy couple.

What a fit body my hubby has.

Getting our marriage license in Las Vegas.

All glammed up.

Children's party at home.

Mr and Mrs Reid!

CHAPTER NINETEEN

RETURN TO THE JUNGLE

At the beginning of November poor Harvey ended up being rushed to hospital. He had 'flu-like symptoms: breathing difficulties, a very high temperature and sickness. Because of his medical condition he can't fight off infections in the way other children can; his medication levels need to be altered and we always take any illness of his very seriously indeed. He was suspected of having Swine Flu and taken to hospital as a precaution. Tests quickly established that he didn't have Swine Flu, but he still needed to be monitored. I was on a book tour, promoting *Standing Out*, when I got the call from my mum telling me how unwell he was. I quickly cancelled a signing and dashed to the hospital.

On the way I contacted Pete to let him know as I knew he would want to see Harvey. I made it clear that I didn't want anyone else in the room except him and me because of the risk of infection – nor did the doctors. I have to admit that it was strange seeing Pete again after so many months and everything that had happened with the divorce and all the lies that had been written about me since in the press.

When he first walked into the room, I thought, 'Bloody hell! He's tiny,' because he'd lost so much weight he didn't look like the Pete I knew or even act like him. It was as if I didn't know him at all, which was weird seeing as I had been with him for five and a half years. To me, he seemed to have lost his spark and was very gaunt in the face. When I had seen recent photographs of him I'd thought I could see sadness in his eyes, but this encounter was perfectly amicable. We didn't talk about our break-up, just gave Harvey lots of attention and swapped stories about the other children, the activities they did with Pete and what they did with me. And all the while Harvey was lying in bed, saying, 'It's Mummy and Daddy!' because of course he didn't understand that we weren't married any more.

Pete must have been able to see that I was still the same woman he had married. That I was genuine, vulnerable, concerned for my son . . . nothing like the monster the press had created.

Harvey was discharged from hospital the following day. With a bit of TLC and rest at home he was going to be absolutely fine. But, of course, me seeing Pete sparked the usual flurry of lies in the press. One story said that I hadn't told him about Harvey's illness and he'd had to find out from journalists; another that Alex had been in the hospital with me and Harvey, and that Pete had ordered him to leave – which was utter rubbish as Alex wasn't even there at the time. He had gone to see Harvey earlier in the day.

* * *

Two weeks later I was on a flight to LA, on the first leg of my journey to Australia. Harvey had made a full recovery by then. If he had still been ill there's no way I would have gone. I would have pulled out of the show.

When it was revealed that I was going back into the jungle there were some people who said that I was only doing it in order to win back the popularity that I worried I'd lost since the marriage break-up. I was asked in interviews if I was doing the show to get people to like me again, but that really wasn't the reason why I had signed up for it. However, I did want people to know that I was a completely different woman from the heartless bitch the press had portrayed me as over the past six months. When I went on the show for the first time in 2004 many people had the idea that I was just a Page Three bimbo, who spent all her time plastered in make-up and falling pissed out of night clubs, but they changed their view when they saw what I was like in the jungle. They saw that I was down-to-earth, ready to take on any of the challenges, and that I was a woman capable of falling deeply in love. I hoped people would see that I was still that woman. And maybe I did want Pete to watch the show and realise what a decent person I am, that I was still the girl he'd married. I hoped that if he did, he would stick up for me and help stop all the lies in the press. But I certainly wasn't looking for any more than that. There were stories that I would drop Alex in a heartbeat if I thought there was any chance of getting Pete back; how I would always love him. They couldn't have been further from the truth. I couldn't understand why the press kept going on about it when, as I've said before, Pete had made it crystal clear that he didn't want to be with me any longer.

The celeb mags even brought in behavioural experts to comment on my behaviour. They came out with a lot of crap about me being a 'desperate woman' who wanted to right a situation that had gone wrong, and said that I was 'desperate to win approval from Peter'. How I was only going back into the jungle to relive the past and be reminded of a time when I was happy. Even though I had said that I wanted closure, the opposite would happen – I would move backwards instead of forwards, a clear sign that I wasn't over the split . . . blah-blah-blah! Why wouldn't the press get off my back? My marriage was over. Pete was the father of my children and I would never want anyone to harm or hurt him, but all I wanted now was for us to be friends, for the kids' sake. But I admit that because I had been so battered by the press, and felt Pete had done nothing to protect me, that I did sometimes wish he'd find out what it felt like to be on the receiving end of so many lies, such criticism, such slating, every single day. He had walked out on me and received nothing but praise. Would he have been able to cope with the bad press I got?

Reporters had also asked if I was looking for romance, but no way was I! For a start I was deeply in love with Alex – not that the press knew that as we hadn't given any interviews about our feelings for each other. The producers of the show had told me that they had put a fit bloke into the camp, but I wasn't interested. I thought if I saw another couple fall in love that would be nice. I had been there, done that, bought the t-shirt and had the divorce. I could give them plenty of advice . . .

When we stopped off in LA for three days I took the opportunity to get my Botox done – I might be going to rough it in the jungle but I still wanted to look halfway decent. I had decided not to get my hair braided this time round. During my first jungle experience I'd had long blonde hair which I'd had braided, but I thought everyone would criticise me for trying to relive my last experience if I went for the braids again. So God knows what my hair extensions would look like by the end of my time in the jungle! I wanted to take Gary Cockerill as my luxury item, so that he could do my hair and make-up, but of course they wouldn't let me!

I also appeared on the *Chelsea Lately* show – I had been asked to go on it but you'd never believe that if you saw the interview. Chelsea Handler has a reputation for taking the piss out of her guests and she certainly did that with me – but not in a funny way. She was just vile and used me as the butt of her crap jokes. I felt like walking off. Looking back, I wish that I had but at the time I thought, 'Just tolerate it. It's only for a few minutes and will soon be over.' Then I was back on the plane and, after a stop-off in New Zealand, landed at Brisbane. I wasn't feeling particularly nervous then. As far as I was concerned, I wanted to go into the jungle and get on with it, but as I landed I still didn't know when I would reach the camp. The press made out that I was desperate not to go in straight away and had thrown some diva fit, which is bollocks. They were most likely pissed off with me because I wouldn't give them the shots that they wanted, nor would I talk to any reporters. Instead I kept my mouth shut, ignored them all and pretended to be permanently on my phone.

Things were great between me and Alex and we'd been in touch regularly since I left the UK. I was expecting him to fly out to Australia on 22 November with a group of people including my brother.

I was staying at the Palazzo Versace hotel, which was where I'd stayed first time round in the jungle. I'd also stayed there when I came out for a holiday later on with Pete and the children. As I travelled along the Gold Coast, memories of my marriage began flooding back as I thought about being in Australia with Pete. The hotel is really close to where his family live, though I hadn't seen or been in touch with them since the break-up. But

I didn't want to cry. It wasn't as if I wished things could be different, it was just an emotional experience thinking back over the past. I wondered if Pete's parents would watch the show. If they did, I hoped that they would also think, 'That's the Kate we know.'

As soon as I was checked into my room, the show's producers came to see me and told me that I would be going into the jungle the following day at 11 a.m. I was absolutely fine about that. I planned to fit in some last-minute beauty treatments so I had a sunbed, got my eyebrows tinted and had my nails done. Then I planned to have a long sleep so that I could be fully rested for whatever lay in store for me the following day.

Instead I woke up at 4 a.m. because I was still jetlagged. I called the kids. I had set up Skype on my computer and had asked Pete to do the same on his so that I could see the children before I went in. It would have meant a lot to me, but unfortunately Pete said he couldn't get it to work, which did upset me. All I had now were the photographs of them which were going to be my luxury item. Before I'd left the UK I'd had a set of string bracelets made, each with a different object on it that meant something special to one of the children – so Harvey had a train on his, Princess a dummy and Junior a car. The plan was that while I was away they would each wear their bracelet and I would wear three matching bracelets to remind me of them all.

I put on my kit, the khaki shirt with 'Katie' written across the back – last time it had said 'Jordan' – and the red trousers. And as I looked in the mirror, once again memories of Pete came rushing back and I felt sad about the way things had turned out for us. Was I doing the right thing going back into the jungle? For the other contestants it was just a game show, but it meant so much more to me. I was going back to the place where a fairy tale had begun for me. I had met my future husband there, I'd had two more beautiful children, and five and a half years on the fairy tale had ended and I was going back in.

Once I was wearing my kit and the producers had checked my bag to make sure I wasn't smuggling anything in – I managed to get some hairbands past them – I started to feel apprehensive about returning to the jungle. I had heard, whether it was actually me or not, that other contestants had been slagging me off and saying they didn't want me in there. I suddenly realised how horrible it would be if I turned up at the camp and they were all vile to me. In particular I'd heard, whether it was true or not, that the interior designer Justin Ryan didn't like me and had said that I wasn't welcome in camp. But I'd signed up for it, I'd better get on with it. Before I left the hotel I sprayed my entire kit and bag with Coco by Chanel, which as it turned out was a completely pointless thing to do as within a matter of hours I would be smelling rank!

When I arrived at the helipad to get the helicopter which would take me to the camp, I saw the same guys I'd met the first time round when I'd been with Pete. It felt strange not having him with me. I said goodbye to Diana, who had come out with me, and did get tearful then. It was from a mixture of nerves and feeling emotional because I knew I wasn't going to see the children for a while, and mixed in with that were all the memories of last time. Everything was swirling round in my head – thoughts of the children, of Alex, of Pete. On the flight to the camp I remember looking down at the land below and all the houses, wondering if I had flown over Pete's parents' house.

As soon as I landed, my jungle experience kicked off for real as none of the crew would talk to me and all their watches were covered up. I said goodbye to the woman who had flown with me, trying really hard not to cry. I hadn't expected to feel like this! I tried to pull myself together. I felt upset about missing the children, nervous about what to expect, worried what the public would think of me – not that I really cared what they thought, but I knew that from now on everything I did was going to be watched and judged.

I was told by the crew that we had to start walking, though they wouldn't tell me where we were going. It was boiling hot by then and it felt as if we walked for ages. And then we arrived at what was to be my first challenge. Looking back, I don't think I had mentally prepared myself for the trials. I'm afraid of anything involving water, heights or spiders, and I didn't want to do any of the gross eating challenges either. The first time I went into the jungle it was a brilliant show for me to do because it helped people to see the real me and I did want to do well and maybe even win. But this time round I was thinking, 'I'm not actually going on the show to win. I don't need to. I don't need the money, and if I don't want to do something in a trial then I won't!' Which probably wasn't the attitude that was going to get me through.

My heart sank when I saw that the challenge involved collecting a number of yellow balls that were submerged in a murky pool. I have a real fear of going underwater, as I said earlier, dating back to when I was a teenager and had a panic attack while swimming. I actually thought I was going to drown. The water in that pool looked deep and absolutely stank; I don't think I've ever smelled anything quite as foul! I think it had fish guts and other yucky things floating about in it. 'I don't want to get in that fucking water!' I thought. I was terrified because I didn't know how deep it was. And while I was working myself into a state of anxiety, the crew didn't say anything to me, just kept on filming. It was exactly what had happened the first time round, but it felt horrible, as if I was nothing to them and all they cared about was filming me. I do realise that it is a TV show but it felt as if there was no humanity in their approach to me.

I just couldn't bring myself to get in the water – I was petrified about how deep it was. The more I tried to psych myself up to get in it, the more fearful I became until I could feel myself going into a panic attack. My hands went into spasm, and one of the crew had to give me a paper bag to breathe into. They had to abandon their policy of not talking to me then as it was obvious that I was having a panic attack and that I wouldn't be able to get into the water unless they told me how deep it was. So finally someone told me that the water wasn't deep and I would be able to stand in it.

'You're lying!' I exclaimed, and they had reassure me again that the water really wasn't deep. 'What the hell have I got myself into?' I thought. 'Why did I ever agree to do the show!' But somehow I did pull myself together, telling myself, 'The game starts now. Just get into the water, get the balls and get it over and done with!'

As soon as I got into the water I wanted to retch because the smell was so vile, especially when I had to put my head underwater to reach the balls. It was also freezing cold and so murky I could hardly see what I was doing, but somehow I collected them and then had to decide whether I should let the other contestants keep their luxury item or whether I should choose some food items instead. I went for the food items and chose tea, coffee, biscuits, chocolate, sugar and milk. And as soon as I'd done, I thought, 'Oh, God, I hope I've done the right thing and they won't be cross with me.' Then I had to walk to camp, stinking and freezing cold, and the crew didn't even give me so much as a towel to wipe off the gunk!

It was getting dark when I got close to the camp. I

recognised the waterfall and could smell the campfire – no doubt the other contestants could smell me as I approached! And once again I experienced a rush of memories about how it had felt to be here with Pete. Then I thought of my kids, Mum and Alex, watching me on the show, and wondered whether I really could go through with it.

'Right, we're going to leave you here,' the crew told me. 'Just follow the path down and it will take you to the camp.' As I got closer I could hear laughter and felt apprehensive about the kind of welcome I would receive. But I need not have worried because as soon as I walked into camp, in my swimming costume and shorts that were caked with God knows what and with my hair matted with gunk, everyone stood up to greet me, smiling as they said hello. My fellow contestants were: Camilla Dallerup, George Hamilton, Gino D'Acampo, Jimmy White, Kim Woodburn, Lucy Benjamin, Sam Fox, Sabrina Washington, Stuart Manning, Colin McAllister and Justin Ryan. I waited for Justin to tell me that I wasn't wanted there, but he was smiling too. It was such a relief that everyone seemed to be so friendly.

And then all I wanted to do was to have a hot shower and get rid of the foul smell, but of course there was no shower – I had to make do with the cold water in the pond. But I simply could not get the smell out of my hair or out of my costume. My hair stank the entire time I was there – everyone commented on it! As soon as I got out of the jungle I had to take my extensions out because they had been ruined by whatever gunk had been put in the water. I'm not being a primadonna but those extensions had cost me six and a half grand so I was well pissed off. And I think whatever gunk they choose to put on the contestants, they should at least make sure you can wash it out!

I actually ended up with the same campbed I'd had last time as no one had wanted that position since smoke from the fire drifted that way. But it didn't bother me. In fact, having that bed made me feel more at ease because it was familiar. The first time I was in the jungle Pete's bed had been just above mine. Now, every time I looked over, I almost expected to see him lying there. In fact, everything to do with the camp . . . the smells, the sounds . . . triggered memories of him and of how we had fallen in love here. It really had been love at first sight and it was emotional for me, being back in the place where it had all started. They were all such happy memories. Then I'd think, 'But it's over.' The good memories had been overtaken by all the bad things that had happened since . It was so sad to think that we were barely talking any more. We had been so deeply in love from the moment we first met.

But while my head was jumbled with thoughts of the past and of Alex, I was, after all, there to take part in a TV show. When Ant and Dec appeared later to give the results of who the public had chosen to do the first bushtucker trial, I suppose it should have been no big surprise that they had voted for me. But I never guessed that I would be voted in every single day. And I hated the sound of the latest trial – The Deathly Burrows.

I think when I was in the jungle the first time, I was much better mentally prepared and up for doing whatever they threw at me. But now I was a mother of three, I was older, I'd just been through a divorce . . . I didn't have that same hunger to prove myself. I was also very successful in my work. Although the fee for appearing on the show was good, I didn't actually need it. And I really missed my children. Right from the start I had a voice in my head saying, 'If you don't want to be here, why not just go home?' But then I'd try and tell myself to play the game, be a team player.

And so the following morning found me walking over the bridge to meet Ant and Dec at the site of the trial. However, as they both explained what it involved in their typically cheeky way, I felt my resolve waver. I would have to bash my way through earth walls into a series of chambers to find the stars, which were surrounded by cockroaches, spiders, and God knows what else. Ugh! I didn't want touch any spiders! And if I had to scrabble about like that, what the hell would be the state of my nails? I'm so obsessive about having perfect nails that I wasn't even wearing insect repellent because someone had told me it stripped your varnish off, and I would rather get bitten than ruin my nails. I thought, 'Oh, no! I just don't know if I can do this,' which hadn't been my attitude last time. But then I thought of the kids, and about doing it for them and making them proud of me.

I took a deep breath and started. I bashed my way into the first chamber. It was pitch black and I couldn't see anything. Straight away I almost wimped out as loads of cockroaches fell on me. Before, when I did the bush-tucker trials, the adrenaline would always kick in straight away. This time it just didn't. I found it really tough to get into trial mode. But somehow I pressed on and got four stars.

Then it all went horribly wrong. I could feel a torrent of water swirling around me, and Ant and Dec told me I had to lie on my back. I was petrified. I couldn't see and was panicking that I wouldn't be able to get out of there and I would end up submerged underwater – my worst fear. There was no way I could carry on. I had to shout those infamous words 'I'm a celebrity . . . get me out of here!', and they had to bash open the tunnel and pull me out. I was shaking, hyperventilating and crying. I was gutted that I hadn't been able to collect more stars but I can't help how I am with water. I think Ant and Dec could see how upset I was because at one point Ant held my hand, and you know what those two are like. Usually they're giggling like schoolboys when the celebrities do the trials.

Back at the camp everyone was sympathetic even though I'd got so few stars, but then Ant and Dec came into camp and revealed that, surprise, surprise, I had been chosen to do the next trial too. I thought, 'Do people really want to see me suffer like this? Or is it just that they like watching me?' I felt bad for the other contestants who were all dying to do a trial. It really is incredibly boring being in camp if you don't do one – there's bugger all to do apart from cleaning up, washing and chatting. And so the following day I was off to what would be my second trial, excluding the one I had to do before I even arrived in camp. It was called Celebrity in a Bottle and, as the title suggests, I had to lie down in a giant bottle and answer a series of questions while some 60,000 cockroaches crawled all over me – when one would be bad enough! In those numbers it was a truly vile experience. However, I managed to get six stars, so I was quite proud of myself. Surely three trials would be enough?

Back at the camp, as we sat round the campfire talking, I asked if the others thought I was different from how the media portrayed me and Kim Woodburn had a bit of a pop at me, telling me that I was a publicity-seeker and that I shouldn't pretend to hate the attention when actually I love it.

'I used to love it,' I told her, but didn't take her comments seriously; she was entitled to her opinion. Before I had gone into the jungle I had decided that if anyone had a go I would simply agree with them. I wasn't going to start any arguments. I didn't need to. I don't try to be seen in any particular light. I am what I am. This is partly Alex's influence, I'm sure. He has definitely helped me be more chilled out. And I think all the contestants could see within a day or so that I'm actually a nice girl, with a warm heart, and a genuine persona – not this devil woman the press make me out to be.

But I wasn't feeling quite so chilled out when I discovered that I'd been voted to perform yet another trial, this time with a gruesome school theme. And just to make me feel under even more pressure, the other contestants had to come along and watch – though actually they did give me much-needed support. I was so nervous before the trial I could feel myself shaking. I remember saying, 'Kids, if you're watching, I love you!' I had done a shoot before I went into the jungle with the children and various spiders and snakes, and I knew how fascinated they were about what I was going to do and how excited they were about seeing me on the show.

And then it was time to get stuck into the different disgusting tasks, from putting my face into a tankful of slime and stinking mealworm larvae and collecting the star with my teeth, to swimming with baby crocodiles and then putting my hand into a globeful of writhing snakes. There was even a foul eating task called the Bush Tuck Shop where there was a choice of disgusting things to eat and drink. I thought the least repulsive thing would be the beetlejuice smoothie but after one tiny sip I retched and I had to pass. The finale involved me being dressed in a plastic jacket and boots, and having what seemed like thousands of cockroaches poured on to my head and into the jacket and boots. Ugh! But I did it, and succeeded in winning nine out of twelve stars for the camp. And my fellow contestants were all lovely to me, telling me how incredibly well I had done and how proud they all were of me.

But by now I was feeling that it was getting to be too much. I was really missing the kids and Alex. I've been away from the children before, but I've always been able to phone them or talk to them on Skype. Not being able to do that was very hard.

In fact, from the moment I woke up in the morning I wanted it to be dark again so I could go to sleep and be one day closer to getting out of there. It was nothing to do with the other contestants. I got on really well with all of them, especially Jimmy White. I'd say to him, 'Jimmy, breakfast is on, next it'll be lunch.' Of course, then I'd be sent off to do another terrifying trial and by the time I got back we'd hear the frog chorus and I'd say to him, 'The frogs are at it, it must be nearly dinner-time, then it'll be bed!'

It felt like my days consisted of staring into the campfire, thinking about Pete and the past, missing the kids, and then being traumatised by a new trial . . . and all the time wanting to get the fuck out of there! But I did have plenty of time to reflect on the past. Especially at night I would look into the fire and picture Pete sitting next to it, and they were such good memories. In fact, the whole place reminded me of him. From first thing in the morning till the moment I went to sleep, it was Pete,

Pete, Pete. But then I'd think, 'How fucking sad that it's all over and we're not even talking.' I talked to other people in the camp about him – recalling our whirlwind romance – how as soon as I saw him it was love at first sight, and how I kept expecting to see Pete in the camp. As I had told him on the phone before I went in, I had nothing bad to say about him, only good things.

I also had time to think back over the last six months since he'd left me. It had been a tough time for me but I realised that I might not have acted in the way people expected me to. I felt sorry if I had offended some people, but I couldn't regret what I'd done in the past because at the time it had felt right for me to behave like that. Perhaps I'd acted immaturely but I was so shocked and hurt when Pete walked out on me, and that's just the way I chose to handle it. I can't change how I am. I've always been outspoken and am probably my own worst enemy because I won't play games and pretend to be someone I'm not, just to please other people.

After three days of me being voted to do the trials, the crew who filmed me on my way to the next one would joke, 'Not you again!' And I would joke back, 'Yep! See you tomorrow.' But I swear, on my life, I did not want to be chosen to do them. Maybe there were some people who thought that I loved it and wanted to be on TV all the time, but I can one hundred per cent say I did not. I was scared of doing another trial. My clothes all stank as we'd only been given two pairs of trousers and shorts, and mine had been wrecked in the trials. It wasn't worth washing any of the kit as it took so long to dry, and I would be so cold I would have to put everything I had on and try and ignore the smell.

But I had always planned to stick it out; I certainly did not have a game plan to leave early. I'm usually such a trouper, but I was missing the kids so much and I don't think I was physically or emotionally prepared for doing so many trials. I started telling the other people in the camp that I wanted to go, that I just couldn't take any more. I think they all thought that I was saying it in a bid for attention, but I wasn't. I really meant it.

And then I got voted in to do the fourth trial – Hell Hole Challenge. My heart sank. I didn't think I had the stamina or the energy to go through with it. I felt drained, physically and emotionally. When I got to the trial I almost bottled it when I saw that it involved climbing a 60-foot wall. I'm petrified of heights and just climbing that would have been a challenge in itself, but then I had to stick my hand into a series of holes, when I couldn't see what was inside them and grab a star. But I did it. I put my hand into holes full of spiders, snakes, frogs and rats, winning nine stars. It felt as if the public *really* wanted to give me a bad time by voting for me. I tried not to take it personally even though it was hard not to. They'd seen me battered and terrified for the last four days. I thought it was time for someone else to have a go. Later, when I did get out, my mum told me how she and my brother Daniel had gone on ITV's *This Morning*, to talk about my jungle experience and say how painful they'd found it to watch me doing all the trials. To them it had felt as if I was being punished, and my mum had compared my treatment to that received by the gladiators in Ancient Rome where the crowds delighted in seeing them get hurt. Perhaps that comparison is a little extreme but as she's my mum I guess she felt protective of me. But it did feel to me that I was being punished. I knew when I went in that I would get voted into some trials, but I didn't think it would be so relentless.

Still the punishment didn't stop. I endured a further two trials – a disgusting eating task called Vile Vending where I drew the line at chewing on a kangeroo's testicle, and then the sixth task, Car-lamity, which actually wasn't too bad compared to all the other trials. I had to drive round a circuit, going through slime and spiders' webs, with the usual disgusting eating challenge thrown in too. I got eleven out of twelve stars. I don't think they'll be setting that trial again as I told Ant and Dec that I'd quite enjoyed it! But by then I felt as if I'd had enough. I wanted to go.

I told the others in camp that I was sorry but, physically and emotionally, I just couldn't do any more trials. I asked if they would support me and go the Bush Telegraph to tell the production team that I had done enough and shouldn't have to do any more. They all agreed to do it. I'm sure that, proud as they were that I had done so well for the camp, they must have been pretty pissed off as well that I was getting to do everything. And then I went to the Bush Telegraph myself and said, 'I'm telling you now . . . and I swear . . . that I am not doing any more trials.'

'OK,' the producer or whoever it was said – you don't get to see them, 'we've taken note of your views.' But I could tell that they didn't believe me. I returned to the camp, and not long after that Ant and Dec came bouncing in to reveal that I had been chosen for the seventh trial.

'I'm not doing it,' I told them. 'I'm ready to go.' Of course, they couldn't really say anything as we were live and time was running out. So as soon as they'd stopped filming I returned to the Bush Telegraph and said, 'Look, I'm serious about not doing the trial. I want to go home.' I didn't care about losing the money or not winning. All I wanted to do was go home and see my kids and Alex.

For two whole hours the producers tried to persuade me to stay. I even saw the psychologist and said, 'I'm not being funny, but you lot are making me feel that I'm in a nut house by trying to convince me to stay. I want to go! I've made my mind up and nothing is going to change it.'

So then the producer said, 'OK, we understand but please could you go to the trial with Joe Bugner [the other contestant who had been voted in for it], and then say, "I'm a celebrity . . . get me out of here!"' They told me that I didn't have to do the trial but, for filming purposes, it would be great if I could at least go along and deliver that line. I felt as if they hadn't listened to a word I'd been saying! 'I've just sworn that I won't do the trial! There is no way I'm even walking to the trial and wasting my breath, unless I've got my rucksack on my back and I can say that I'm leaving. In fact, no way am I even going to the trial because I know that I'm a trouper and I will end up wanting to help Joe. I've sworn I won't do it. Please, just let me go!'

But they didn't give up easily. Their next tactic was to line up my family and friends on the phone, no doubt to try and talk me out of my decision. 'Your mum's on the phone, will you talk to her?'

'No!' I told them. 'I'm thirty-one years old, I'm an adult. I've made my decision . . . I want to go home.' Then they got Diana on the phone and I wouldn't talk to her either; they got Mark Wagman, one of the directors of Pricey Media, and I wouldn't talk to him. They told me that Gary had arrived and said that he really thought I should stay, and did I want to talk to him?

'No! I don't want to talk to anyone, I just want to fucking go! You're making me feel mad by trying to talk me round!'

'But maybe you could win if you stay on,' one of the production team said.

'I don't care! I just want to go. Let someone else win. I'm really missing my kids. I can't bear not to be with them.' Surely I could not have been any clearer!

'OK,' they said. 'What can we do to keep you in here?'

'Nothing!' I exclaimed. 'I just don't want to be here

any more. It wouldn't matter if you offered me a million pounds!' By now I was face to face with the producer and he said, 'Could you just stay in for another twenty-four hours?'

'No, I'm going. Please don't make me go through the barriers on my own, because I will.'

So after those two hours I returned to camp and, thankfully, fifteen minutes later the producer told me that I could go within the hour. Thank Christ for that! I thought.

I said my goodbyes to the other contestants, and genuinely wished all of them well. As I left camp and walked across the bridge that would lead me to freedom I was so happy! I could go home and see the kids! I didn't for a second regret leaving though I felt I might have let my friends and family down, and I suspected that my mum would probably bollock me for not sticking it out. But I knew I was doing the right thing. I was missing the kids too much; I didn't need to prove anything more to anyone. Although the money would have been great, I didn't actually need it, nor did I need the fame. I'd gone in there and tried my best; I'd done my trials and proved I was a trouper.

But as I walked out it was a very different feeling from last time when I had been on such a high. Even though I was relieved to be going, I felt nervous and self-conscious, as if the crew were looking at me in a way which said, 'You're such a failure for walking.' I didn't feel any warmth from them and thought, 'Bloody hell, it's only a game!' Because I had chosen to come out of the jungle rather than being voted out, there was no one to meet me at the end of the wooden bridge, and no press call. The studio was deserted. I suppose they want to make it feel like you are a loser who doesn't deserve any attention.

Once I was out of the studio I had to get straight into a van which took me down to the catering tent. Thank God I wouldn't have to face another a trial! I was so looking forward to being reunited with Alex. I was sure he would be there because he was supposed to have flown over with my brother and Gary and Phil. However, when I walked into the tent he wasn't there. I felt really disappointed but was sure I would see him soon. At least there was a close friend to meet me – Michelle Heaton. But she didn't have good news for me. I was stunned when she told me that it looked as if Alex had been giving stories to the press while I was in the jungle. Apparently on Sunday there had been a front-page story in a tabloid that he was flying out to Australia to propose to me and had already picked out a pink diamond ring.

I felt sick to my stomach at the betrayal but couldn't let on how upset I was because ITV were still filming me. I just didn't believe that Alex could have done this to me. From the moment we got together, I'd told him that I didn't want another 'Katie and Peter' relationship where all our personal life was constantly splashed across the papers. Alex had talked about me to one paper early on, and even though he had said really lovely things, I'd told him I couldn't be with him if he talked to the press about me. That if it happened again then we would be over.

I was adamant about this. I didn't want to marry anyone who'd try and get famous by using my name or make money by selling stories about me. And he knew exactly how I felt. There had been several times over the past months when Alex had said that an interview in such and such a magazine had been lined up for him, and I would say, 'Excellent . . . if they want to do an interview about what you do, then you should do it. But don't get famous on the back of doing interviews about me. And if the magazine only wants to do the interview with you if you answer questions about me, then don't do it. It means they want to know about me, and this should be about you.'

Straight away I wanted to talk to Alex to find out what the hell was going on, but I didn't have my phone and I was being filmed as I was driven back to the hotel so I didn't want to say too much or show how shaken up I was by the news. I felt very confused and upset. I loved Alex so much; I wanted to marry him. Why had he done the one thing that he knew would end everything for us?

Back at the hotel I was no closer to finding out what had happened; all I knew was that Alex hadn't flown out with my brother as he was supposed to but was on his way to Australia separately. I was being filmed for my own TV reality show and made it clear that I wasn't going to talk about Alex on camera; I needed to find out for myself what was going on first.

Once the camera was off I phoned him. 'I can't believe you've done a story. It's over between us,' I told him straight out. But inside I was willing him to tell me it wasn't true and that he loved me, this was all a misunderstanding. But while Alex sounded really upset about me ending our relationship, his explanation of what had happened was very confusing. He didn't tell me why he hadn't flown out with my brother, for instance, or why he hadn't told anyone else what was going on. I wasn't getting clear answers to my questions and felt very confused by what he was telling me. It just didn't ring true. I am quick to react to things and tend to jump straight in, without taking my time, so I ended the call by telling him again that we were finished. I don't know quite how I found the strength, because I was devastated, but I did. Alex sounded very upset too and told me again that he hadn't done any story, but by then I didn't know if I could believe or trust him.

I was still reeling from what had happened when I had my interview with Ant and Dec. I told them that I had finished with Alex and wanted to be single again. Looking back, I realise I was too harsh, dumping him in such a public way, even though I had already told him on the telephone. I really regret humiliating him like that, but at the time I felt so hurt by what I thought he had done. I am trying not to be so impulsive in future.

The only good thing was that I was able to talk to the

kids. I couldn't wait to go home and see them but was going to have to stay for a few days more while my contract with ITV was sorted out. As I had walked from the show I lost a lot of the money, but really wasn't concerned about that.

I'd been so in love with Alex and we'd had such a good relationship that this problem had come like a bolt from the blue. We had never had rows before because we'd had nothing to argue about! In stark contrast to how I felt when Pete dumped me – when even in the middle of being so shocked and upset I still felt a sense of release – this time I was utterly heartbroken. I just wanted to curl up in bed and cry.

Two days later Alex arrived. He came straight up to the suite and as soon as I saw him I realised how much I still loved him. I thought he looked gorgeous and longed to cuddle him and for everything to be put right between us, but I was still so angry with him that I made myself be cold and a bitch and kept him at a distance. We went up on the terrace to talk while my friends waited below. They were pretty sceptical about me seeing Alex again, and had already said that I shouldn't – that he hadn't been there for me when I came out of the jungle, and how if he loved me he should have been on the plane straight away to come and see me. But I wanted to hear what Alex had to say. Deep down, I didn't want to let him go. If I made up with him, it would be my decision and nobody else's.

It was an intense and emotional meeting. We were

both hurting. Alex said, 'I can't believe you dumped me on national TV!'

And I said, 'Yes, I fucking did, Alex, because I thought you'd done that story on me! You didn't fly out when you were supposed to, and you didn't let my brother know where you were staying, so you have to admit that it looks like you might have been doing a story.'

He told me yet again that he hadn't sold the story, he hadn't bought me a ring, and he wasn't going to propose. We talked it through and by the end of it I just knew I wanted to be with him, that we would get over this. We spent the night together and made love, and being with him again felt so perfect. I felt complete now that he was with me.

We should have talked it over straight away and I shouldn't have been so quick to tell him it was finished, but he wasn't there and it was such a crazy time with me being told so many conflicting things. Now I look back and just think, 'Thank God we did sort it out.' I might have lost him otherwise and I can't imagine my life without Alex.

Over the past months I'd had many arguments with my friends and family who thought I shouldn't be with him because he was a cross-dresser. But I couldn't give a fuck what other people thought. I loved Alex, and I knew he loved me. I felt so right with him, felt protected by him, and more than that even the kids loved him to bits. I had found a man I could be my absolute self with. Only I could judge the strength of our relationship. I couldn't live my life according to how everyone else wanted me to. I wasn't going to be with a man just because other people thought he was right for me. I was old enough to know how I felt, to know what I wanted out of life and who I wanted to live it with.

I wanted to be with Alex.

CHAPTER TWENTY

GOODBYE 2009

Back home it was wonderful to be reunited with the children. I had missed them so much and never, ever wanted to be away from them so long again. And ever the straight talker, I told my family and friends that I loved Alex and didn't care what any of them thought, my relationship with him was right and I wanted to be with him. I felt very sure of this. But I also made the decision that I didn't want the press to know anything about us. Of course, the paps were bound to see him coming and going from the house as they were always parked outside, but I didn't want to give them any chance to photograph us together. And once again I told Alex that I didn't want him to do any interviews about me; that if he was interviewed then I wanted it to be about his fighting, not about me, and he agreed.

Meanwhile, just as I was reunited with Alex there were stories in the press that I had phoned Pete as soon as I'd come out of the jungle, begging him to take me back. They were complete lies. In fact, Pete had phoned me as I was travelling home, saying that he had posted a message on Twitter that we weren't getting back together as he was so sick of the rumours. I think a story had just come out saying that I wanted to get back with him – the same old, same old. I said, 'Pete, I don't even bother saying anything any more when the lies are printed. What's the point?' It was a perfectly friendly conversation. I had thought about him so much when I was in the jungle and now I had something to say to him. 'I'm really sorry if you think I was a bad wife to you, and I'm sorry for anything I've done since we split that might have upset you, but I'm still the same person you married.'

I felt I had to say these things. Maybe it was my way of finally closing the door on our past, and letting Pete know how I felt. 'I want you to know how sorry I am. I genuinely did love you and I'm sorry if I wasn't the wife you wanted me to be.' And I went on to say, 'You will see a different me from now on. I'm not going to mention you, and I'm going to cut down on doing interviews in magazines.'

I really hoped things could be amicable between us, though only time would tell. And I still felt, and think I always will, that if only Pete had stood up for me when we broke up and said, 'She's the mother of my children and I don't want a bad word said about her,' then I wouldn't have received the battering I did from the press. Writing this now, over a year on from our break-up, I can honestly say that I do forgive him, but I don't think I'll ever forget. I don't think I deserved to be treated like that by the press.

* * *

I'd had time to do a lot of thinking while I was in the jungle and had come to the decision that I was going to cut back on the interviews I did in future. I was sick of the gossipy slanging matches I had got involved with in the past. I didn't want to do any more trashy interviews slagging other people off. If I did interviews now I wanted them to be more grown-up, based around things that were actually worth talking about. I'd had such negative press, seen so many lies written about me, that now I'd had enough of it. It didn't seem to matter how many times I pointed out that something wasn't true, no one seemed to want to believe me. I felt that if people wanted to believe instead that the sun shone out of Pete's arse, then let them. I couldn't defend myself any more than I had. Every single day the tabloids wrote made-up stories about me, such lies I didn't even know how they could fool the public into buying the papers. But I didn't want to be part of that world any more. I wanted to be more mature, to concentrate on doing things with the kids, on my relationship with Alex, on my business interests and on my riding. I wanted to be happy!

I felt that some of the tabloids and celeb mags had treated me like shit. Why should I do an interview with them which they would end up twisting and turning into something horrible? I felt they didn't show any respect for my feelings, or even treat me like a human being at all. I was sick and tired of doing an interview about something good in my life one week, only for them to print something hurtful and untrue the following one. I wasn't going to be abused like that any more.

In future I would still do press calls and interviews when I had a new book, TV show or product to launch because I enjoy doing them, but I didn't want to continue in the same rut of giving the paps pictures which they could then write a pathetic story around. After returning from Oz I'd had a couple of nights out in London, including attending Piers Morgan's the Morgan Awards, and because I was still jetlagged and hadn't eaten much I did get a little drunk and I looked absolutely horrendous in the pictures. It was no big deal, but of course the press made it out to be worse than it was and I ended up on the cover of various celeb mags. I knew that I was an idiot when I had too much to drink and didn't like what I became then. It was silly to let myself do that. All I wanted to do was be a good mum, have a good relationship with Alex, and buckle down to my work and my riding. I felt as if I had turned over a new leaf.

I also decided to stop writing the column for *OK!* magazine where I talked about my week. It was supposed to be a fun column but, increasingly, I felt the magazine turned it into something bigger. They would put headlines about me on the cover and make it look as if I'd done a photoshoot for that particular column, and that just seemed to filter into the other tabloids and then everything would be blown up out of all proportion. Meanwhile one of the tabloids in the same group as *OK!* would write the most hurtful, hateful rubbish about me. I agonised over the decision, especially since I had done so many interviews and photoshoots with *OK!* over the years – including my first marriage and photoshoots with the children – and had allowed them special access to my life. I had trusted them. Also I'm a very loyal person. I knew Richard Desmond, the owner of the Express group which included *OK!* and had socialised with him and his wife many times over the years – in fact, he had come to my wedding to Peter, and I had been to his house for dinner and he had come to mine. So I wrote him a letter, setting out my reasons for deciding to leave my column in *OK!* and saying how hurt I had felt by some of the stories which had appeared in other publications in the Express group. At the end of the day it's not just about money for me, it's got to be about personal loyalty.

And I'd also decided while I was in the jungle that I didn't want to read the tabloids and celeb mags any more so I got my mum to cancel all my subscriptions, except to *Horse and Hound* – they don't make up stories about people! In the past I would come down to breakfast and there would be a whole pile of news-papers and mags on the kitchen table, and more often than not there would be a story about me in them – a made-up story – and I couldn't stand it any more. I asked all my friends and family not to text me about anything that they saw in the press. I didn't want to know. I didn't want to get wound up by a pack of lies. That was such a good decision! It meant I didn't start the day on a bad note, upset and pissed off because of what had been written about me. My head felt clearer because I wasn't getting up every morning and reading a load of shit about myself. Nor would I go online and look at stories there. Free at last! I felt strong about it back then, though in the New Year everything caught up with me again and I was at breaking point once more because of what the press put me through . . .

* * *

It was Christmas 2009 and I was gutted not to have all the children with me. It's such a special time for me and has always been about having a traditional family celebration, but this one ended up being my worst-ever Christmas. Yes, I had Harvey with me, of course, but he doesn't really understand Christmas and doesn't like opening presents because he's so sensitive to noise and hates the sound of paper ripping. I was with Alex and our relationship and the bond between us was getting stronger all the time, but I missed Junior and Princess so much. I just couldn't get excited about a Christmas spent without them. And much as I wanted things to be friendly between me and Pete, I did end up resenting him for having the children then.

I felt that I couldn't wait for 2009 to be over. It had been such a difficult year for me. I'd gone through a traumatic miscarriage, a bitter break-up and divorce, all under the full glare of the media spotlight. I decided to throw a fancy dress party on New Year's Eve – I wanted to end the year on a high. I had come to the conclusion that nine is not a lucky number for me: it was September, the ninth month of the year, when I got married; 2009 was when I got divorced; and I think Dwight Yorke sometimes played in a number 9 shirt . . . and what a disastrous relationship that was!

So New Year's Eve found my house transformed into a scene from Narnia, a sparkling enchanted winter wonderland with plenty of glitter and bling and with me dressed as a giant pumpkin! The theme of the fancy dress party was 'fairy tale' and I imagine people expected me to be wearing some big Disney princess number or else a cheeky little outfit flashing suspenders and loads of cleavage. But I thought the huge orange suit was hilarious, especially as I had to be pushed through the door since the costume was so bulky! Junior came as one of his favourite characters, Buzz Lightyear, and Princess was Belle. Alex had been debating whether to come as a Greek god while we were in the costume hire shop and I had to say, 'Not the Greeks! Please stay well away from the Greeks!' Not because I've got anything against Greek people, it was just that I'd had a gruelling year getting divorced from a guy who was Greek! And so Alex came dressed as Alexander the Great and showed off his gorgeous body. All my guests had made an effort and the party was full of Prince Charmings, Snow Queens, Tinkerbells, Wicked Witches and Captain Hooks. I loved it!

The fire alarm went off because of the smoke machine at the disco, but luckily one of my guests was Greg, the man who'd built the house, so he knew how to switch it off before the fire brigade turned up!

After an hour or so I was boiling in my pumpkin outfit and so got dressed up again as Cruella de Vil – all fake fur and a black-and-white wig. There was plenty of dancing and I had a good old go on the karoke machine – I'm always like a moth to the flame with those, especially when I've had a couple of drinks and any self-consciousness I have about launching into song goes out the window. Before the party I'd told my friends that I was going to be singing more ballads than they'd had hot dinners because I love them! Luckily they're used to me doing that by now.

The closer it got to midnight, the happier I was about saying goodbye to 2009 and hello to a new year which I knew had many brilliant things in store for Alex and me. Another quick costume change and this time I was a sexy Minnie Mouse and it was time for the countdown to midnight. I had the microphone. 'I hate 2009!' I shouted out. 'I hate it, I hate it, I hate it!'

And then the worst year of my life was officially over.

Now I had 2010 to look forward to, where one thing was for certain – I was going to marry Alex Reid! But first of all he had an appointment with Big Brother.

CHAPTER TWENTY-ONE

MY *CELEBRITY BIG BROTHER* HUSBAND!

I had known as far back as October that Alex had been asked to go on *Celebrity Big Brother*, and when we'd discussed whether or not he should go on it, I'd told him that it would be great for him to do it so people could see what he was really like. But I also warned him that the show could possibly be edited in a way which might show him in a bad light, especially as the press stories about him had already been so negative.

I did have some concerns for him. He is such a lovely, open and friendly guy, but he hasn't had much experience of dealing with the media and I worried that he might be stitched up. I know only too well how devious and manipulative the media can be. I also told him: 'If you do go on the show, try not to talk about me. Let people see what *you* are like. You don't just want to be known as being Katie Price's boyfriend.' Later some of the press would make out that I had been a total control freak about what Alex could or couldn't say about me on the show; how I had written out a list of commandments for him, telling him that he would be dumped if he said anything out of turn, which was complete rubbish. All I wanted was for him to be himself.

On Sunday, 3 January 2010 Alex went into the Big Brother house to a chorus of boos. I felt gutted for him when I heard the crowd's reaction. I knew they were booing him because they had believed all those negative press stories about both of us. But I also knew that Alex was strong and wouldn't let it get to him. Before he went in I told him, 'Whatever happens, I'll be here waiting for you. I love you.'

For the next four weeks I missed him so much! I was pining for him: missing talking to him, missing having cuddles, missing our banter, missing all his love. I drove everyone around me crazy by asking them all the time if they thought he still loved me, and were they sure he hadn't gone off me? Then I'd try and be rational and say to myself, 'Of course he hasn't gone off you! He wants to marry you, Kate!' I was also in a constant state of nervous tension because I so wanted him to do well. I was glued to the TV in the evenings and couldn't go to sleep until I knew he was tucked up in bed, which I could see for myself as there was a live feed through the night.

Once I saw that he wasn't immediately nominated for eviction by the public, I started to think that he was in with a very good chance of winning the show. He was coming across so well, showing all the qualities that I loved about him – how easy-going he is, how kind, what a gentleman, how up for every task, how he doesn't take himself too seriously and always tells it like it is. Basically what an all-round loveable guy he is. And very soon everyone else seemed to pick up on those qualities too and realise that you can't actually say a bad word about Alex. Which was ironic as practically from the moment we got together the press were trying to make out he was some cross-dressing pervert, and all along I stuck by him because I knew what a wonderful, decent guy he really was. I recorded a message for him, telling him how proud I was of him and how I hoped we could do the thing we didn't have time to do before he went in . . . which only he would understand, hopefully!

I spoke regularly to his mum about how he was getting on and posted my thoughts on Twitter about how well I thought Alex was doing and how very much I missed him. And then I thought, 'Why the hell did I tell him not to talk about me too much?' All I wanted was to hear him say that he loved me – Katie Price! Alex did talk about how in love he was, referring to me as 'the other half'. But he didn't use my name, and before long I was desperate to hear him say that he loved and missed me. It was torture!

Meanwhile in the outside world I was busy filming

my TV reality show and having meetings to set up my other work projects for the year. Since 2009 had been such a difficult time quite a few of my planned launches for new products didn't happen. But I was determined to make 2010 a more successful year than ever work-wise. I had plans for a new perfume, a make-up range, and a collection of baby clothes. I couldn't wait to get started. And I wanted to get back on track with my riding, hopefully so I could compete again.

A few days into the New Year I flew over to Holland with the film crew and Andrew and Diana to buy a new horse. By the time we flew back, the UK was in the grip of one of the heaviest snowfalls for decades. In fact, Andrew, Diana and the film crew got snowed in at my house for two days! The kids all had a great time, sledging and making snowmen in the back garden, but I had 'flu and could only lie on the sofa, sniffing and coughing. Meanwhile the press were busy twisting the facts so as to come out with the story that Andrew and I were snowed up on our own together in my house! It was so ridiculous I didn't let it get to me. It was just another made-up story in the whole long line of them, and once again I knew that people would see what had actually happened on my TV show. But I was concerned for my friends Andrew and Polly, who were innocently caught up in it all.

Other stories at the time included my appearance at my friend Danielle Lloyd's engagement party, where the press made out I was flirting with Olly Murs from *X*

Factor when I was just chatting to him and giving him some advice about management. Because I've been in the business so long, I know how the world works and always tell any young person I meet in the media that they need to be very careful because management will take a cut of everything they do when in fact they can actually set things up themselves and cut out the middle man. And I was supposedly flirting with some Spurs footballer I had never even heard of, never mind met. Oh, yes, and apparently I was also going to dump Alex and go off with Jermain Defoe. You couldn't make it up! Except they had. Never mind all the made-up stories about my reaction to seeing Alex in the Big Brother house – ranging from being angry that he had mentioned me and our relationship, when as I've already said I was desperate for him to tell the world that he loved me, to the fact that I was fiercely jealous of his friendship with fellow housemate Nicola T. I wasn't – not one little bit. After she was voted out of the house, she actually sent me a nice lot of goodies, including some tops with her logo on them.

By the time *CBB* was coming to end I was almost driven mad from missing Alex so much. I needed to see him so badly it hurt! I even lost a bit of weight through pining for him. But I was thrilled that he was doing so well. On the day of the final I was so nervous for him. I wanted him to win and was absolutely thrilled he had made it this far. I went to the *CBB* studio with his mum, his two sisters, his sister-in-law and his best friend, and we were all sitting in the green room watching the huge TV screen, willing Alex to be named as the winner. Vinnie Jones came third, leaving Alex, my fiancé and Dane Bowers, my ex. I thought, 'That must prove that I always go for genuine guys, seeing as the public like both of them!' I also saw Dane's dad, brother and sister there, and it was the first time I'd seen them since I'd split up from Dane all those years ago. I went over and said 'hi' and it was all perfectly friendly, but it was quite weird being in a room with Alex's family and my ex's.

Earlier I'd chatted to Davina and asked if she would pass on a message from me to Alex. 'Will you tell him that I love him and that I'm here for him?' I wanted him to know how I felt the moment he came out of the house. Later, Alex told me that as soon as he met up with Davina, she told him what I'd said and he was really relieved.

When she finally announced that Alex was indeed the winner, I was over the moon, jumping up from my seat and hugging his mum and sisters. Now I just had to see my man! As Alex came out of the house he was cheered by the crowd – such a difference from a month earlier! 'I'm a man in love!' he told the crowd. 'I love Katie Price!' My heart leaped, and everyone in the green room cheered. He got booed by the crowd, though, when he mentioned my name. 'Hang on! he exclaimed. 'Why are you booing her?' I think he went on to say something along the lines of how, four weeks earlier, they had booed him because they didn't know him when he went into the house. Now they were booing me, but that was because they didn't know me either.

But I didn't care about the crowd's reaction – to me it is like a panto. While it isn't very pleasant to hear yourself booed, I didn't let it get to me. All I wanted to do was see Alex. But one of the production team told me that I couldn't see him until the end of the night, after he had done his press call and after his de-briefing session with the psychiatrist. 'Bollocks to that!' I thought. 'I *am* going to see him. I'm his fiancée, they can't keep me away from him!' By now I was outside the studio and watching Alex on-stage with Davina. I had wanted to look good for him and was wearing a little black dress, sheer socks and heels, and was absolutely freezing! 'How do you think he will greet me?' I kept asking everyone around me. 'D'you think he will hug and kiss me or ignore me?' I felt like a groupie, waiting for him.

As I went to walk towards Alex, security tried to stop me. 'None of you lot can tell me what to do!' I declared, and carried on walking past them. I was a woman on a mission, and my mission was to be reunited with my man! I think they realised that it would be more trouble than it was worth to hold me back. I felt as if I was in a movie at that moment because as soon as our eyes met, Alex and I ran to each other and hugged and kissed – really it should have been in slow motion with romantic music playing in the background. We didn't care about anyone else; we were together and that was all that mattered.

From then on I didn't leave his side. I went and saw the psychiatrist with him, and did the press call with him. And as soon as we were on our own in his dressing room, we couldn't hold back any longer and we did have a cheeky quickie. We were both dying for each other! It was naughty, though, as the production team were all outside . . . We were so excited to see each other, we could hardly get all the words out that we wanted to say. Amongst many other things we both said that we couldn't wait to get married. There was nothing stopping us now – my divorce had come through, we had a small window in our work schedules. It was time to tie the knot – Vegas-style!

* * *

So on Monday, 1 February 2010, a few days after Alex had been crowned the winner of *Celebrity Big Brother*, we flew to Las Vegas. I did have my film crew with me but the plan was that they would only film some of the run-up to the wedding and our mini-honeymoon in Vegas. I did want them to film the ceremony, but that would be for Alex and me and our family and friends. It wasn't going to be shown on my ITV series. Gary and Diana came with us too. I couldn't take the children as they were with Pete, but Alex and I had already decided that we would have a blessing ceremony later in the year to which all our family and friends would be invited.

We kept our wedding plans a secret from our friends

and from the press, but we had told our families on the way to the airport and they were really happy for us. Though I think my mum already knew what I was up to as earlier in the week I had asked her if she knew where my decree nisi was, and I had asked one of her friends who had tied the knot in Vegas what it was like getting married there.

It had to be Vegas. As I've already explained, it's the only place you can get married so soon after a divorce, but it was also perfect for us as Alex knows Vegas really well. It's the centre of UFC (Ultimate Fighting Championship) and so he has lots of contacts there. And Vegas always seems like such a fun and happening city where anything is possible, which suited us as a couple very well. Vegas is certainly Wedding Central as apparently some 120,000 couples get hitched there annually. And so many stars have got married there – from Elvis Presley marrying Priscilla to Angelina Jolie and Billy Bob Thornton. Though let's hope that my marriage to Alex lasts longer than Angelina and Billy Bob's . . .

We touched down at 10 o'clock at night and had to dash to the special marriage bureau to pick up the licence which would allow us to get married at any chapel we chose in the city. Again I had the feeling that we were in a movie as there we were, two people who were so in love, trying to evade the paparazzi and prevent anyone finding out what we were up to. It was like *Mission: Impossible* meets a rom-com! We had already looked at a selection of chapels online back home. There are so many to choose from but if you don't want a traditional venue you can even get married on top of the 'Eiffel Tower', overlooking the Strip! But we were keeping things simple. We had chosen the wedding chapel called the Lilac Salon at the luxurious Wynn Hotel. When we stopped off at the hotel to check it out, after getting the marriage licence, we were really impressed by the venue – it was beautiful, and so romantic. I couldn't wait to walk up the aisle, which was lined with gorgeous bouquets of white flowers, and say, 'I do!' Now we just had to get the rings and our wedding outfits. We literally went into the first jeweller's shop that we came to on Sunset Strip and bought the rings in a matter of minutes.

The following day we had just five hours before the wedding ceremony at 4 o'clock in which to choose our outfits. In the first menswear shop we tried, Alex bought his outfit – white shirt, trousers and shoes. He looked so handsome. So then it was my turn, but when we went into a boutique I couldn't see anything I liked and the clock was counting down. I ended up popping into a sex shop as I thought they were bound to have a short white dress. 'It is Vegas after all,' I thought, 'anything goes.' I found a dress, and with it I bought a pair of diamanté high heels. We were on the way back to the hotel to get ready when I spotted a wedding dress store. 'Stop the car!' I called out. 'I want to see if there's anything for me in there.' While I didn't want a big white number, the little white dress I'd just bought didn't seem special enough.

We dashed into the store and I told the assistant that I had to get a dress, like now! So she quickly pulled out a few for me, but they were all full-on wedding dresses, which weren't what I wanted at all. Maybe it would have to be the short white number after all? But then Gary held up a dress and said, 'What about this one?' It was a similar style to dresses I've worn in the past and I instinctively knew it would suit me. It was a simple, long, fitted white dress with sequins. Yes, even though I wanted simple, I still wanted sparkle! 'Grab me a Small,' I told him. Then I saw a veil and asked the assistant to steam it for me to get rid of the creases. And that was it! I didn't even try the dress on! We were having such fun getting married this way. There was no agonising over expensive designer outfits, venues, guest lists, catering, cakes and all the other baggage that comes along with a big wedding. Because we were keeping it small we were free to think about what our wedding day was really about – just us expressing our love and commitment to each other.

Gary quickly did my hair and make-up, and ten minutes before we were due at the chapel I put on the dress. It fitted perfectly, as did Alex's outfit. He had already phoned up his friend John Hathaway, who was also a fighter and was out in Vegas, to ask if he would be best man. I think John was pretty surprised as he'd had no idea what we had been planning. Funnily enough, he was one of the guys I had spotted at the gym just before I met Alex, and had suggested that Sol ask along to Michelle Heaton's birthday. The fighting world is a small one apparently . . . At the hotel chapel there was another lovely surprise when I discovered Phil had flown over to be at the wedding.

And then it was time to tie the knot! Gary and Phil walked me up the aisle to meet Alex, accompanied by the song we had chosen, Whitney Houston's 'I Believe in You and Me'.

I was bubbling over with happiness and excitement as we exchanged our vows. I felt really emotional and knew that this was what I wanted more than anything. The fact that it was just Alex and me, a few of our friends and the minister made it even more special because we weren't having the wedding for anybody but us.

I couldn't stop smiling at Alex. I, Katie Price, most certainly did want to take Alex Aristides Reid as my husband! As he gently slid the ring on to my finger it was the culmination of all I had longed for these past months. I was Mrs Reid and we belonged together now – I was his and he was mine.

Arm in arm, we walked back down the aisle to the music of 'Ordinary People' by John Legend. The photographer had been taking pictures of us throughout the ceremony, and he continued to take photos as our friends congratulated us and Alex and I hugged and kissed. There was no glossy magazine deal, I hadn't wanted that. I wanted everything about this wedding to be as different as possible from my first marriage. So there was no endless posing for formal pictures. When I saw the photographs of our wedding the following day, I was struck by how incredibly happy and carefree I looked – just the way a bride is supposed to be. Alex, of course, looked very handsome. And the pictures were all so romantic, informal and natural.

I can't help feeling that my wedding to Pete had been more like a show. I was in love with him, and wanted to marry him, but we seemed to get overtaken by the big event that our wedding became. Whereas my marriage to Alex was far more intimate and laid-back; we went with the flow. It was just about us, no one else, and it was so romantic.

We issued a press statement saying that : 'We are very much in love and look forward to the future together. We can't wait to get back and celebrate our marriage with our friends and family who we know fully support our wishes.'

Our wedding day was perfect, completely stress-free and happy. After the ceremony we went out to celebrate with our friends. We had dinner and then hit the Vegas night life. One of Alex's friends owns the Sapphire Gentlemen's Club there, which is an upmarket lap-dancing place with VIP areas. It may sound tacky but it wasn't. Back home the press slated us for our choice but we didn't care. We were celebrating our wedding, stag and hen nights all in one go – and it was fantastic! And we were in Vegas, what else were we going to do?

Back at our five-star honeymoon suite at the Planet Hollywood, I can only say that things got even better when we spent our first night together as Mr and Mrs Reid. Put it this way, we definitely consummated our marriage in style!

We only had two more days together in Vegas, so it really was a mini-honeymoon. Alex was due to fly to India for a week to learn a new fighting technique for his show on Bravo; he would be back in the UK for ten days and then he would be off again to LA. So that made our time in Vegas even more special as we knew we would soon be spending some time apart.

Alex had to fit in some training at the gym but I didn't mind going along and watching him. The paps, of course, did track us down, even though we had done our best to dodge them. They really are like vultures and it was pretty hard to shake them off. But we did manage it a couple of times – including our trip to go dune buggy racing when Gary and Phil went in the limo and pretended to be Alex and me, fooling all the paps into following them. The photographers twigged pretty soon but couldn't exactly pursue us when we were racing across the desert. I loved buggy racing, of course, as I'm such a daredevil – and Alex loves that about me. Gary hated it. Said he thought it was like the worst fairground ride ever!

But all too soon we were on our way back to the UK. We had flown out as boyfriend and girlfriend and were flying back husband and wife. I felt as if we were starting a new life together.

I really do feel that Alex is the love of my life. I know people will be cynical and say, 'Oh, yeah, we've heard that one before.' And, yes, you have heard it before, because I was in love before! But who says you can't fall in love again?

I wanted to show that this relationship was different so I decided that I would change my name to Katie Reid – except for work, where I will always be Katie Price. But the name Katie Reid would be on my passport, driving licence and cheque book, and it would be how I wanted to be known outside of work. I had of course promised Pete that I would change my name when we were married, but somehow I never got round to it as we were always flying off somewhere and I needed my passport.

Everything is different with Alex. In every other relationship I've had, I would never buy a house with the man. I've always been fiercely independent and wanted to own the house myself. I suppose I worried about what would happen if we split up and I ended up losing my home. But when we got back from Vegas I said to Alex, 'Forget about my house, we should buy a house together.' Having a big house no longer seemed so important to me. I was thinking of downsizing and buying a house we could both afford. I wanted us to have a joint account and for whatever we both earned to go into that account. It would be used completely equally and there would be no egos about who earned the most. I've never done that with any other guy before Alex.

CHAPTER TWENTY-TWO

MR AND MRS REID

Back in the UK, our family and friends were thrilled for us. Everyone who mattered to me could tell what a wonderful relationship I had with Alex and how content it made me. But the press didn't want to believe that we were happy and that I had moved on with my life. There were stories that I had pushed Alex into marrying me just because he had won *Celebrity Big Brother*; that I saw it as a way of boosting my own popularity. There was even a story that he wanted a divorce. I thought, 'What more can they make up? Will they end up writing that I'm dead?'

There were stories as well about how I wanted to control Alex and stop him from speaking to the media. But all I wanted to do was protect him. For instance, when he came out of the Big Brother house he did a shoot for a tabloid and the money was shit. I went along with him and there was no make-up artist. There was a stylist, though, and funnily enough it happened to be one Maddy Ford. A couple of months later it was revealed in the press that she'd had a brief fling with Pete. It's a small world, isn't it?

The photographer wanted Alex to lie on the bed with his shirt off in some really tacky-looking poses, and Alex didn't have copy control which meant the tabloid could pretty much say what they liked and it would look as if he had come out with those comments. When the article came out, sure enough the journalists had twisted what he had said. So, yes, that did piss me off, because I could see that Alex was being taken advantage of. I wanted him to have the same management as me, who could protect him from these situations, and I wanted our diaries to be worked together. But in no way do I want the life I had with Pete, where we worked together all the time. I also felt that if Alex and I did interviews on our own, it would be best if neither of us went into details about our relationship.

Then a story came out claiming our marriage wasn't legal because the minister who had conducted the ceremony wasn't properly licensed. We immediately contacted the Wynn Hotel and they confirmed that the press story was complete rubbish and the minister was fully licensed. They also said that they'd had many other people calling them up who had got married at the Wynn by the same minister, and who had seen the story and been upset. It wasn't just our dreams that the press were trying to shatter. Journalists should realise that there are innocent parties affected by the rubbish they try and whip up.

I had been strong so far and put up with the treatment I had received from the press since Pete walked out on me, and I was still trying hard not to let their stories get to me. I held on to the fact that I knew the truth about my relationship with Alex, I knew how in love we were. But when I saw that the press were still writing negative and untrue stories about me after my wedding, I did get really upset. I had moved on and remarried. What was wrong with that? Why couldn't it be seen in a positive way? I felt as if I was being bullied; that I had been bullied for the last year. It was like a form of mental torture where every single thing I did was ripped apart, where nothing but lies were written about me, where I was constantly made out to be a bad person. I didn't know how much more I could take. It was a feeling which was to get worse over the months which followed.

*　*　*

After my wedding I had only one thing on my mind – and that was having another baby. I had made it public knowledge that I wanted children with Alex. And now we were married, the time felt right. In fact, we had been trying for months to conceive and I felt concerned that I hadn't got pregnant – usually I am very fertile. By April

2010 I became so worried about this that we contacted my obstetrician, Dr Gibb, who put us in touch with a fertility doctor.

I know Alex felt upset too that I hadn't got pregnant. As I already had three children, he must have felt as if he was the one with the problem. We had a really emotional phone call one time, when he was away filming, where things had caught up with him.

'Do you still think of me as a man when I haven't got you pregnant? Do you love me any less?' he asked, sounding very low. My heart went out to him then and I longed to reassure him.

'Get this one thing straight, Alex, don't *ever* think like that,' I told him. 'I love you, and I'm with you whatever happens. We will have a baby one day; we'll do whatever it takes. We're in this together.'

When we went to see the doctor he carried out a full series of tests on each of us. I had an HIV test, I was checked for cervical cancer, my breasts were checked for any suspicious lumps and I had various blood tests. Afterwards Alex and I were each given a clean bill of health – my only problem was low blood pressure, which I've always had. The tests revealed that neither of us had a fertility problem, it was simply that the sperm weren't connecting with the egg for some reason. The doctor said that we should continue to try for a baby naturally for another year before seeking any intervention. But I wasn't convinced. By now I knew my body very well. I knew how quickly I usually fell pregnant, and Alex and I had been trying for the last eight months. I felt we needed to help things along. Neither of us was getting any younger.

We were then put in touch with another doctor, who specialises in fertility treatment. 'I'm the girl who wants everything yesterday,' I told her, only half joking. I really did want a baby. Of course, we would have to pay for the fertility treatment, but at least we could start it straight away. I think it's very tough on couples who can't afford to pay; who have tried for several years for a baby then have to go on a waiting list for fertility treatment which could take several years more. Plus they have the added pressure of meeting all the criteria: of being the right age, the right weight. It must be so stressful that I can completely understand why some couples split up. The strain all that places on your relationship must be enormous.

The doctor booked us in to start treatment. We were having something called ICSI (Intra-cytoplasmic Sperm Injection). We had yet more tests, the results of which were all OK, and then I had to have a scan to check my ovaries were functioning healthily. According to the doctor I had some lovely eggs there, which sounded promising. She explained that ICSI has a 65 per cent success rate. While I was anxious about the treatment, given that it didn't have a 100 per cent success rate, I thought, 'Surely this will work as I've already had three children?'

There were other serious issues we needed to discuss

now we were having fertility treatment. We had to go through a detailed information pack with the doctor and to sign various documents giving our consent to various procedures. One of the issues was what would happen to the embryos created by us if anything happened to me or Alex – to put it bluntly, what would happen if either of us died? Would the remaining partner be able to use those embryos by themself? I didn't hesitate. I knew what I would want and told Alex, 'If anything happens to me, then of course you can use the embryos. That way there can be lots of Mini-Mes after I've gone! The more the merrier!'

And Alex said the same.

ICSI would involve me taking hormones to stimulate egg production, the goal being to produce a good number of eggs so as to help increase the chances of having several viable embryos. For my doctor a 'good number' of eggs meant me producing around twelve or thirteen. The stimulation of egg production takes around two weeks and during this time I would be monitored closely using ultrasound and blood tests. Then, once the eggs were ready, the doctor would retrieve them using a needle that goes through the vaginal wall and into each follicle. This would be done under anaesthetic – which was just as well as it sounded painful! Just before my procedure took place Alex would have to provide a sperm sample. Once the eggs and sperm are ready ICSI is performed – this is when an individual sperm is selected and injected into each egg.

When the embryos are formed and have started to grow, it's time to put them back into the uterus.

For some reason I imagined that I would be taking hormone tablets to stimulate egg production, but then the doctor showed me an injection pen and the realisation dawned that I was going to have to inject the drugs. Despite all my experience of surgery, I am still needle-phobic . . . and what made this worse was that I would have to inject myself in my stomach! The doctor demonstrated the technique to Alex and all I could think was, 'How the hell am I going to get that needle into me?' We were going to be in Egypt on holiday during the time I would be doing the injections. The doctor told that us that it was perfect timing we were going away because that way I would be nicely relaxed. Of course, what none of us knew then was that a certain Icelandic volcano was about to erupt . . .

The doctor gave us the drugs, saying I had to inject myself at the same time every day, so we chose 6 in the evening as by then we would have come back from the pool and be chilling out in our villa before dinner . . . or panicking about doing the injection, as it turned out. After seven days I would have to introduce another sort of injection. The doctor explained that I would look bloated because my ovaries would be swelling up. That wasn't great news. I've got such a small frame that anything like that would really show up on me – and I could just imagine what the press would make of it. Then I thought, 'Stuff it! I am going to go topless on holiday. I don't care if the paps get a shot of me. If I look as if I've put on weight, so what? I know why I look the way I do. And I'm at the stage in my life when I'm over thirty with three children, so of course I'm not going to look perfect. But I'm happily married and I want to have a baby. I don't have to justify to anyone why I look the way I do.'

The doctor also gave me progesterone suppositories. These would help keep the progesterone levels high and strengthen the lining of the womb, increasing the chance of a pregnancy. I would have to take them for twelve weeks, morning and evening, along with 75 mg of aspirin.

* * *

We went away to Egypt with Harvey, and Polly and Andrew and their two boys as it was the school Easter holidays. It wasn't a honeymoon, just a break with friends and kids. I'd wanted to take all the children, but Pete was taking Princess and Junior to Dubai. We stayed at the Hilton Sharm Dreams Resort at Sharm el-Sheikh. Until the volcano struck, it was a very relaxed holiday where we chilled by the pool and ate out. We all got on well together. I didn't take a nanny and quickly realised that it was a good thing we had gone on holiday with another family as Alex kept up his intensive training programme and would go off and train every day. He is incredibly disciplined and focussed and trains seven days a week. I was a bit annoyed that he carried on with his usual routine, I know how committed he is to his sport but I did think he could have eased off a bit as this was supposed to be a holiday . . . But the good outweighed any negatives. Harvey had a great time – he loved swimming in the pool, and quickly got used to the new routine. One day I arranged for him to have a massage, which he absolutely loved. Alex also got to spend more time with him as there was no nanny, and grew to understand more about Harvey's special needs and how to interact with him.

Then it was time for my first injection. Alex said that he would do it. 'I'll dart it in,' he told me. 'Let's get it over and done quickly.'

'You can't do that!' I exclaimed. 'I know it will hurt. I'll have to do it myself.' So I lay on the bed, holding the needle above my stomach, trying to psych myself up. I got the tip of the needle just above my belly button. I decided that when I breathed out I would simply let the needle pierce the skin. But as I lay there, I thought, 'Oh, God, I can't do it!' I felt weak and sick because I hate needles so much. I screwed my eyes shut and could feel the needle pierce my skin. I had to get on with it! So I pushed it in and then clicked the top to release the drug. Then I had to pull the needle out. I had to do everything really, really slowly. Alex told me I should do it quickly, but I said, 'How can I do that? It will be like I'm stabbing myself!' And I thought if I allowed him to do it to me and it hurt, I would end up having a go at him and I didn't want to do that. It would be best if I did it myself.

The doctor had been right when she said I would get bloated – my belly blew up. When I looked in the mirror, I really didn't like what I saw. My body seemed to have transformed itself into a weird bloated shape. I kept telling myself that this was how it had to be if I was to get pregnant. The suppositories gave me the most terrible wind as well. One night I looked at the website to see if this was normal, and thank God for websites because it seemed I was not alone. 'Listen to this, Alex,' I said. 'There's a woman here who says that usually her husband's the main farter in the house, but now it's her!' Lots of other women had made comments about feeling bloated and full of wind. As I was very ladylike and didn't fart in front of Alex, the bloating felt worse!

Then came the news of the volcanic eruption that caused a huge ash cloud and all flights were cancelled. We were due to fly back on Tuesday as I was supposed to be having a scan on Thursday. This was so the doctor could assess my ovaries and see if she needed to adjust the medication. She would be able to check how many eggs were forming and whether she needed to increase the dose of hormones I was on. As soon as I knew I couldn't get back, I called her. She told me that the latest I could have it done would be Sunday. If I didn't manage to fly back by then, we would have to stop the treatment and then start again in two months' time.

Immediately I started worrying, thinking I could be going through all the stress of the injections for nothing. And, to top things off, I was also running out of medication for Harvey. But I got in touch with Great Ormond Street and a doctor there said he could go for a week without his medication and be OK. That was the absolute maximum, though, and it shouldn't happen again, but obviously this was an emergency. I was very relieved about Harvey, but I still had the stress of not knowing whether my fertility treatment would work at all because we were stuck in Egypt and I was worrying about being able to get back in time for the scan. I was beginning to feel pessimistic, that it was fate, it wasn't meant for me to get pregnant this time. So much for a holiday where I would be relaxed about the fertility treatment . . .

We managed to get on a flight back on Friday, 23 April, and I saw the doctor the following day. The scan revealed that I had nine eggs and the doctor said that ideally she wanted to see a few more grow. I felt disappointed. If only I had been able to fly back on time, she could have adjusted the medication and I would have been able to produce more eggs. The doctor increased the hormone dose and when I went to see her again on the Monday she adjusted it again. By now I was on two injections and the second really hurt. It was a much thinner needle and it stung.

At this point, Alex and I were still debating about whether to put in two embryos or one. The doctor had recommended we put two in, but we had been worried that might mean twins. And while I knew I wanted more children – I'd love to have another four, in fact – having twins would be difficult to manage with three other children, especially with Harvey's special needs. But, as it turned out, I didn't really have a choice. The doctor examined the lining of my womb and told me that how many children I could have would really depend on the strength of this. The two Caesareans I've had have already weakened the lining – the same would be true of any woman, not just me. The doctor explained that she could just implant one embryo and I could go on to have the baby, but that might be the last baby I could ever have. And, of course, with two embryos there was a greater chance of a successful pregnancy. It was a lot to take on board, but Alex and I ended up deciding that we would have two embryos implanted.

So on Wednesday we returned to the clinic – I was having the eggs removed under anaesthetic, Alex producing a sperm sample. I had my usual panic about needles but before I was given the anaesthetic we all had a giggle because, just as Alex was about to go into the room next door to do what was required of him, all these moans and groans started coming from his phone. He had accessed some porn to assist with the sample business but couldn't work out how to turn down the volume on his phone. He was really embarrassed. Everyone one else thought it was funny – I guess there's not much that fazes doctors and nurses who work with couples trying for a baby . . . But then it was my turn to be embarrassed when the nurse told me that I had to lie back and put my legs into the stirrups at the side of the bed – this in a room with three other people in it. 'This is so degrading.' I exclaimed, 'I didn't even give birth like this! You're going to have to give me the anaesthetic and then put my legs in that position while I'm out of it. I really can't do it in front of you!'

Three days later I was due back at the clinic, this time for the doctor to put the embryos back into my uterus. 'If you want me to come with you, I'll come,' Alex told me. 'If not, I'll go training.' Deep down, of course I wanted him to come with me; I wanted him by my side for every single stage of the fertility treatment as we were doing this to have a baby together. But I replied, 'It's up to you. Everyone is different. But I know that if I was a man in this situation, I would be there for my partner. But if you don't want to come, you don't have to.'

Sometimes I think I am my own worst enemy because I should have been open with him about how I felt. I should have told him that I wanted him to be with me. Instead, because I had seemed so casual, Alex said that he would go training. I tried to tell myself that this was OK, that I would be fine on my own, but I was a bit gutted. This hopefully was the start of a new life, one we had created together.

As I drove to the clinic on my own I tried to tell myself not to get pissed off that Alex wasn't with me, but I was upset and hurt. He shouldn't have had to ask if I wanted him to come with me, it should have been obvious. I often do little tests on men. I don't know why but it's something I've always done, and then I remember how they reacted and store it up for future use. This had been a little test for Alex, to see if he would support me. Because of his reaction, I thought, 'If he's not going to come with me to watch our embryos being implanted, which is a big deal, imagine what he will be like when I have the baby. Will he be there for me? Will he give me the support I need?'

At the clinic I was able to see the embryos magnified on the screen – they were like two little bubbles as the doctor sucked them into a syringe – an incredible sight. Then the doctor put the embryos into me via a catheter, which was painless. The doctor jokingly said that I could sneeze, I could do anything, the embryos were not going to fall out. As I left the clinic I felt a surge of excitement as I thought, 'I'm pregnant!' And in a way I was, because now I had the embryos inside me all they had to do was grow.

Alex called me soon afterwards and told me that his mum had just had a go at him for not being with me at the clinic, and that she had told him that he should have been with me every step of the treatment. 'I didn't realise that I should have been there with you, I'm sorry,' he said.

'Your mum's right,' I thought, 'she's got heart.' 'Yes, I would have liked you with me Alex, but you weren't.' I played it cool again, telling him the procedure had gone well and that I had seen the two embryos. I don't think Alex had realised how vulnerable I felt or what I'd expected of him. I already knew men and women had different feelings about pregnancy from my past experiences. I don't think the reality of having a child actually hits men until the baby is born, because it hasn't been them who have carried the baby for nine months. Maybe having fertility treatment was the same. Because the treatment mainly involved things happening to me and my body, it wasn't such an emotional process for Alex.

I definitely felt this was a time when I needed my partner by my side to support me, but I also knew that I was bad at letting people in and telling them how I really felt. Even when I was doing the injections, I wouldn't let on to Alex what a big deal it was. Though the truth is, it was! I really wanted a baby, and I was injecting myself, which is one of my worst nightmares. But I would try to appear casual about it, and so I would do the injection while he was in the bath or relaxing on the bed and checking his messages. And all along I wished he had been more supportive, had asked me if I was OK, had cuddled me to make me feel better. I suppose I was testing him, thinking that it was a good chance to see how he really felt about me. I had told him just before we started the fertility treatment that this was a new journey for me, and that although I'd had children, I'd never had this treatment before with anyone. I suppose I was telling him that he didn't have anyone else to compare himself with. But I did wish I could have expressed my feelings more fully so that Alex would have seen I needed more support. I didn't like what I was having to do to myself; I didn't like the fact that my body was changing and knowing that I wasn't yet pregnant, knowing that I might not even get pregnant this time. I'm the kind of person who, even when something is really bothering me, will make out that I am fine when I'm not. So I probably have to take the blame for Alex not knowing how vulnerable I felt – because I didn't show him.

For now we just had to wait. I couldn't have a bath for five days or have sex for a week. In twelve days' time I would do a test and we would know if the pregnancy had taken. I felt quite optimistic for the first seven days. I convinced myself that I would be pregnant and that most likely I would be having twins. Because of that I didn't care about feeling so bloated, uncomfortable and unattractive. If I was pregnant then none of those things mattered. I was dying to do the clearblue test to find out.

For the first days I held on to the feeling of optimism, but then the waiting really got to me. And on top of being anxious about whether I was pregnant or not, throughout this time negative stories about me continued to appear. Our lovely holiday in Egypt was described as 'the honeymoon from hell'. As it was coming up to a year since Pete and I split up, comparisons were made between how his life was after our break-up and how mine was. And Pete always came out better, that he was happy and successful in his new life while I was pining for my old one, which wasn't true.

And the press had also been saying that I was having fertility treatment. I was really upset that they had got hold of this – it was so personal, so private. What right did they have to keep digging away at Alex and me?

I have no idea how the story came out. I can only assume that the paps had seen us coming out of the fertility clinic. I had stopped getting the papers, but every now and then I would see the headlines or someone would tell what had been written and it really got to me. What had I done to deserve this? Celebrities who've been caught taking drugs haven't received the treatment I've had in the press; footballers who've cheated on their wives haven't been portrayed in the negative way I constantly seem to be. Pete walked out on me and I was destroyed by the press for an entire year. Why couldn't they accept that I was happy and settled in my new life with Alex? I felt so drained by it all, I started to feel the weight of all the past year's bad press crushing down on me. And now, waiting to find out whether I was pregnant or not, I felt incredibly vulnerable, didn't know how much more of it I could take.

I broke down in front of Alex and my mum one morning in early May. I had tried so hard to stay strong. I was worried that if I didn't appear to be strong, that if I did break down and need to see a therapist, it could be said that I was unstable and my children might be taken away from me. I knew I had to do something, knew I had to take a stand against those parts of the press that had written such lies about me. And with that in mind, I decided I would instruct a solicitor to start building a case against those publications that had blatantly done so.

But as the emotions caught up with me, I started experiencing stomach cramps. A few hours later I discovered I was bleeding. A wave of shock and disappointment went through me. I phoned the doctor and she told me that it didn't look like good news, but that I should have an early night and bed rest. Alex was really supportive then and I felt he was there for me. That night we looked on the website and read about other women's experiences. There were some reassuring stories from women who'd had bleeding early on in their pregnancy and feared they had lost the baby, then gone on to give birth successfully. I wanted to feel hopeful but as the bleeding continued I knew that the chances were not good. The following day the bleeding seemed to get heavier, then it stopped. Maybe I was still pregnant? But the day after that it started up again. I did a pregnancy test, feeling in my heart that I already knew the outcome, and sure enough it was negative.

Alex and I were both very upset. We had been so hopeful, so excited about the prospect of having a baby, and now all our dreams were dashed. We went back to see the doctor, to discuss what might have happened and what the way forward was. She thought it likely that the pregnancy hadn't gone ahead because we were stranded abroad and I couldn't get back in time for her to increase the medication, combined with the stress that being stranded had caused. We would have to wait two more months before we could start another course of treatment. But before that the doctor was going to scan me and give me hormone boosters, to see if I could get pregnant naturally. She felt that there was no reason why we shouldn't manage that for ourselves. So, upset as we were, I did feel that there was hope. Once again I read about other women's experiences. They had all been through so much; some of them were on their fourth or fifth cycle of fertility treatment and hadn't given up, they were still being positive. I really admired their courage and sympathised with anyone who was trying for a baby. I knew how lucky I was already to have three beautiful children. While Alex didn't yet have a biological child, he was still part of a family with kids, and I was sure we would have a baby together one day. If we weren't successful in our attempts then we would adopt.

* * *

A few weeks later, at the end of May, the KP Baby range was launched. I had long wanted to bring out a range of babywear, adding my own unique touch of sparkle and glamour to baby garments. It was very important to me that it was all of high quality while also remaining affordable. I had been offered the chance to sell it from a major department store but that would have meant charging more for the items as the store would want their cut. So I decided to sell the products exclusively online at more reasonable prices.

I didn't find it hard being around babies since I had found out that I was not pregnant. And if I saw a pregnant woman I wasn't going to wish that it was me. It was their happy moment, I wanted them to enjoy it. I'm always broody anyway! Even though I hate being pregnant because I feel so physically uncomfortable, the feeling of excitement outweighs anything bad because I am so excited about the imminent arrival of my new baby. I absolutely love newborns: love their smell, their skin, love bathing them and dressing them in their sleep suits. But when I appeared at the Baby Show in Birmingham to promote my baby range, being around all those infants made me remember just what hard work caring for them can be. I think you forget once your children are past the baby stage how difficult those early years are – the crying, the feeding, the sleepless nights. But I love the baby stage, and if my body can handle having four more children, I will definitely have them.

Besides the launch I had our wedding blessing to look forward to on 3 July. I'd had offers from celebrity magazines. They had contacted my management, wanting to know what the theme was and which celebrities I was inviting. I'd told my management to go back to the magazines and tell them that this was a simple wedding blessing. It was not a celebrity event geared towards the press. It was what a wedding blessing should be – it would be about Alex and me and our families and friends celebrating. We were not going to live our lives purely for the benefit of celebrity magazines, end of.

Alex and I were filming the run-up to the blessing, the ceremony itself and our honeymoon in Thailand for a three-part special for ITV called *Katie and Alex: For Better, For Worse*. As we both enjoyed the filming and got on so well with my production company crew, it really didn't feel like work and wasn't stressful at all – it was fun. I had said all along that I didn't want to work with Alex, didn't want us to film a reality show together – I don't want any repetition of the Katie and Peter experience – but because this was about our wedding, of course we both had to be filmed. They could hardly just film the bride! But apart from the wedding special, I was determined that I would have my own reality show, which Alex would be in from time to time, just as the kids are if they're around, and he would have his own TV show on fighting, but it would never be the full-time Katie and Alex Show. Alex is very like me when it comes to filming. He can only be himself, and I like that about him.

Even though we only had six weeks to plan the blessing ceremony, that wasn't stressful either. Looking back, I cannot understand why my first wedding became so difficult to plan, though I guess it didn't help that I was suffering from post-natal depression and everything seemed overwhelming at the time. By the end of May I still didn't have a wedding dress, nor had we settled on a theme. But it didn't matter; I knew it would all come together. In fact, this time the planning was enjoyable because we were just doing it for ourselves and the people closest to us. My mum was brilliant. She sorted out the budget and did all the negotiating with the caterers, the people involved in designing and putting up the marquee, and the ones in charge of the entertainment. And Alex's mum Carol was also involved in the planning meetings, and in helping to decide what food to go for.

We decided to have the wedding at our house in Woldingham in Surrey, in a marquee in our back garden. That meant we would have to keep the number of guests down to around 150 so straight away the wedding would have an intimate feel, which was what we wanted. We had planned to have the blessing service there as well, but because space was limited and it would involve rearranging the inside of the marquee, I thought it might be better to have it at my local church a short distance away. Alex and I were getting on brilliantly in the run-up to the big day. There was only a minor disagreement about my bridesmaids, because I thought two didn't seem like enough and wanted to involve more of my friends. I did end up getting my own way on that, but as for Alex saying that he was under the thumb in the TV show . . . believe me, he gives as good as he gets! If he doesn't want to do something then he won't do it, no matter how much I stomp my feet and demand that he does! And, like any girl, I do try and push my luck occasionally. But I like the fact that he doesn't pussyfoot around me, and respect him for it.

With just weeks to go to the wedding I was still undecided about what kind of dress I wanted, and then a good friend sent me a picture of some wedding dresses she thought I would like, made by Dizzie Lizzie Couture. Typical me – the dress I especially liked was called a Wow! dress and it looked perfect, very fairy tale. I called up a boutique which stocked the dresses and asked if they would be able to bring over a selection for me to have a look at. I was so busy with work that I didn't have time to go to them. Very kindly, they drove the dresses over to the studio where I was recording the title sequences for our wedding special. The very first one I tried on was the Wow! dress, and I absolutely loved it. It was of white silk, with a corset top embellished with Swarovski crystal love hearts and a massive skirt with layers and layers of tulle underneath. As soon as I put it on I felt I looked exactly how a bride should look. I was pretty sure that Alex would feel the same as I had already shown him a selection of wedding dresses to get an idea of what he liked and he seemed to like the full-on white numbers as much as I did.

With just a few days to go before our big event, Alex and I had our stag and hen nights. Mine was organised by my best friends Gary, Phil and Melodie at the Mayfair Hotel. But unlike most hens on their night out, I didn't drink at all. Everyone else was knocking back champagne and cocktails but I stuck to orange juice. I didn't want to drink because now that I'm getting older it takes me two days to recover from a hangover, and I wanted to feel fantastic in the run-up to the wedding. And yet again I proved to myself that I can enjoy myself without having a drink. It was a brilliant night, such a laugh, my friends even arranging for three male strippers to give us a show. Saucy . . . But I was such a good girl, I drove everyone back home at the end of the night and woke up the next day feeling fresh as a daisy.

Alex went a bit more wild than me, I think it's fair to say. Things started off in a restrained fashion when he and his friends went clay-pigeon shooting for the afternoon, then they went to a casino and strip club and were treated to a pole-dancing display. Afterwards Alex, who'd had quite a bit to drink, stripped down to his pants, climbed to the top of the pole and gave a display of his own which was given scores out of ten by the dancers. It seems I might have met my match when it comes to being an exhibitionist . . . But I love the fact that he's got that touch of showmanship to him. I have too, and it means we can have fun together.

There was such a great atmosphere and buzz around the house as it drew closer to the day of the ceremony, so many people coming in and out to set up the marquee, the lights, sound system, flowers, security . . . I loved it all, and having the marquee in our back garden made it seem even more exciting. It was a bit like counting down to Christmas! I thought it would be a good thing if Alex and I spent the night before the blessing apart. I wanted the big day to feel extra-special. Plus I had all my bridesmaids staying over and it would be fun if we could all sleep in my bedroom and have a girlie laugh. In fact, I woke up to find Alex in the en suite bathroom. 'How long are you going to be?' I asked, wanting to get in myself. So much for not seeing each other until we met at the church. But I made sure he didn't see me in my dress until the moment I walked up the aisle.

I had to have a quick sunbed session before I could start getting ready, and my friend Melodie drove me to a salon in nearby Caterham. I lay on the back seat under a blanket to stop the paps outside the house from getting a shot. Back home, the feeling of anticipation was even more exciting. It was great to have so many of my family and friends with us; everyone was rushing around, frantically getting ready, and there was such a happy, party atmosphere. The caterers were on hand, offering everyone drinks. It sort of reminded me of that scene from the movie *Home Alone*, just as the family are packing up to leave for the Christmas holidays. On the landing guests were having their make-up done by a team of make-up artists, and Junior's bedroom had been given over to guests having their hair done. Wherever you walked in the house there was something going on.

Junior and Princess were caught up in the excitement as well. I'd wanted them both to be as involved as possible in the blessing. Princess was one of my bridesmaids and Junior was going to read out a poem in church, which he had been rehearsing with my friend Michelle Heaton. At one point the alarms in the house went off, triggered we think by the low-flying helicopters chartered by the paps. And did I know the code to turn the alarm off? No. Unfortunately the fire brigade turned up, but thankfully Marcus, our event manager, eventually managed to track down the code and switch it off.

While we were getting ready, our guests were assembling at the local golf club for drinks before a Routemaster bus took them to the church. Because we wanted to keep the location secret from the press, none of our guests knew where the ceremony was actually going to take place. They had simply been asked to arrive at the golf club. However, there were paps outside the house and I knew that they would track us down to the church. As Gary did my make-up and Nick and Royston worked on my hair, arranging it into an elegant bun with a tiara, and we were all chatting and laughing away, I had no idea how vicious the paps would become once I arrived at the church . . .

It was something of a military operation getting the guests to the church from the house as there were so many of them. But I was actually ready on time, believe it or not! And then I had to wait nearly an hour to be picked up. I loved the way I looked for the ceremony. The dress was stunning, and although it had such a full skirt, the silk was so light I didn't feel weighed down. I felt I looked exactly how a bride should look and how I wanted to look.

I was supposed to travel to the church with Paul, my step-dad, as he was going to be giving me away, but in the rush to get people to the church he ended up going ahead of me, which was a shame as it would have been nice to make the journey with him. I travelled to the church in an 80s-style A-Team van, as we thought that would be fun and also we could cover up all the windows. We had security patrolling the grounds of the house and around the church to prevent the paps getting any pictures, and I thought they had everything in hand.

Nothing could have prepared me for what happened when the van arrived at St Paul's. It's a beautiful church in a sleepy village and should have been the perfect setting for our wedding blessing. But the paparazzi didn't care that this was a blessing ceremony; all they cared about was getting a shot of me that they could sell. I know that I have chosen to be in the public eye and have to expect paps to follow me closely, but I swear that I suffer their attentions on a more extreme level than anyone else. All those paps knew perfectly well that I hadn't signed an exclusive magazine deal, and they knew I didn't want photographs in the press, but they didn't care. It's like a game to them where they are going to do whatever it takes to get their photograph. But I won't play by their rules. My game is, 'No, you're not ruining my day by getting a picture of me.'

So the van pulled up outside the church. I had Gary

and Hannah, my new PA, with me, along with the two guys who had made the wedding suits, and straight away we could hear shouting and swearing from the paps as they struggled with the security guards to get close to the van. It was a scorching summer day outside and I was getting really hot and flustered inside the van. And then all hell seemed to break loose as the paps started rocking the van, ripping off the boards we'd put over the windows to try and get a picture of me. One man managed to wrench open the back door and shove his camera in, trying to get a shot; someone else tried to open the front door. Hannah got whacked with a camera, and all the while they were shouting. It was so frightening.

I ducked down in my seat, desperate to keep myself from being photographed. I seriously felt that if the paps could have tipped over the van in order to get a shot of me, then they would. I've thought this for a long time but that day confirmed it: the paparazzi have absolutely no respect for me as a human being, they treat me like an animal. To them I just represent the chance to make money, they don't give a shit about anything else. The fact that our marriage was to be blessed, that my children were in the church and must have been able to hear the shouting and screaming that was going on outside . . . neither of those bothered them for a second. I felt so overwhelmed with anger and frustration that they were doing this to me I started to cry.

After about ten minutes – which, believe me, felt

much longer – my security guys thought it was safe for me to get out of the van. They had put up a screen to keep the paps at bay – but the flimsy material was never going to stop them. As my security team hurried me into the church, some paps charged at the screen, ripping it down. Desperate to make it into the church without being photographed, I stumbled and tripped on the steps. Then I was inside. The heavy wooden door was shut behind me. We had made it without the paps getting a shot of me. But just as we were safely in, some of the paps forced open the door at the opposite entrance, nearly knocking down one of the church wardens as once again they tried to barge in and take a photograph.

I felt so shaken and angry that I was still crying as Paul walked me up the aisle to where Alex was waiting. He looked gorgeous in his blue suit and I tried to forget about the ugly scenes with the paps, but it was hard. I managed to smile and blow kisses to Harvey, Junior and Princess who were being so good as they sat at the front of the church. I tried to focus on Alex as we exchanged our vows and wedding rings. I did feel so happy that we were having this blessing and that our families and friends were there to see it. And then Junior read out a poem. He loves performing usually but I think in this instance he did come over as a bit shy – understandably. Not everyone got to hear it, but I was so proud of him. He ended his poem by saying, 'I love you, Mummy, and big Alex.' My lovely son looked so smart in his suit, though as soon as we arrived back at the house he raced upstairs, took it off and put on his pyjama bottoms. I didn't mind at all, so long as he was relaxed and happy. Princess looked sweet in her bridesmaid's dress, but after the ceremony she fell asleep and when she woke up decided to change into a floaty pink dress. My children are like me . . . they like to be comfortable and chilled out at home! But I kept my wedding dress on for the entire event.

Back at the house we had drinks and canapés and the chance to mingle with our guests, then the entertainment began with a very unusual performance of 'Nessun Dorma', from one of the balconies, which I think got everyone in the mood for what was to follow. Then a curtain went back to reveal the dining area of the marquee, and Chris, who was in charge of entertainments and acting as Master of Ceremonies, got all the guests to take their seats for the wedding breakfast. We'd kept everything simple, stylish and classic with arrangements of white flowers and a huge glittering crystal chandelier. It looked beautiful. Before dinner was served there was a lovely surprise for Alex and me when a soldier who had just returned from serving in Afghanistan marched in and presented us with a ceremonial sword to cut our wedding cake. Alex's dad was in the Paras and Alex himself was in the TA so there's a strong army connection running through his family.

The wedding breakfast started off with lovely dips

and bread followed by a hog roast for the meat eaters and an aubergine and goat's cheese tart for the veggies, rounded off by a trio of yummy desserts. In true wedding tradition, speeches followed dinner. But just before the speeches began I had a surprise of my own when a farmer came in with a very special present for me . . . well, me and the children really . . . a micro-piglet! It was from my great friend Jane who was one of my bridesmaids. I've known her since I was sixteen. The children were thrilled, and when I asked Princess what she would like the piglet to be called, she said, 'Bingle', so 'Bingle' it was. I've wanted a micro-piglet for ages. I just hope he wasn't alarmed by the smell of the hog roast . . .

My step-dad Paul's speech was short and sweet. I know he doesn't really like standing up and speaking but it was lovely the way he welcomed Alex into the family and said he could see that Alex truly loves me. Alex's speech too was heartfelt. He said he was like an oyster: rugged on the outside, but inside there was a pearl in his heart and I was his pearl. He said he couldn't live without me. I feel the same about him . . .

As the speeches went on I could feel myself getting more and more tearful. When it came to my turn, I had to brush away the tears and almost broke down, though typically for me I tried to joke about not wanting to ruin my lashes. But it was an emotional moment for me because I was surrounded by all my family and friends and the people I'd really wanted to be there. We simply couldn't invite everyone because of the space, so the guests were those who were most important to Alex and me. It was a great chance for me to say thank you to all the people who'd helped put this great day together, from my mum and Alex's, to my nannies, who are just brilliant, and of course my best friends Gary and Phil. In fact, it was talking about them that really set me off. They are such special people in my life, have both been through so much with me and always been so good to me. I really don't know what I would have done without them.

After dinner it was time for the entertainments, and the night club part of the marquee was unveiled, complete with a stage, bar and dance floor. Alex and I had really gone for it and chosen all the things that we loved. So it kicked off with a West End cabaret performance, followed by violinists playing 80s hits on Swarovski crystal-studded violins. And then the disco began and our guests hit the dance floor and I was there too in my wedding dress, throwing some moves. It was such a brilliant laugh. The whole day had been perfect, exactly what we had wanted. Alex went to bed before me, but because we had so many people staying over at the house, I felt I couldn't disappear so I stayed up as well. It was just a cuddle and a kiss that night, but I knew we would make up for it another time . . .

In the morning there was more rushing around as we got packed to go to Thailand. I wouldn't describe the trip as our honeymoon as we were taking the film crew with us; it was more like a fun holiday. We intended to have a third proper long honeymoon, just the two of us, away from the cameras at a later date. As we drove away from the house I commented that I was sure I had forgotten something. We were halfway to the airport and stuck in traffic when I realised what that something was – I had left my fertility drugs behind. I was supposed to be starting a new cycle of treatment while we were away. But I wasn't upset. It was probably for the best as we had been so busy recently with the ceremony that it would be better to wait a little longer until I felt more relaxed.

Our trip to Thailand was fantastic. We spent two very entertaining and eye-opening days in Bangkok, seeing some of the shows; then we flew to the tropical island of Koh Phangan and stayed at the luxury Rasananda Resort. It was a beautiful setting and reminded me of the Maldives because it felt so remote . . . that was until the paps tracked us down again and photographed us sunbathing on our private balcony. I tried not to let it get to me, but sometimes I felt as if I could never escape from them.

* * *

Right now, as I finish this book, I'm getting ready to move into a new house in West Sussex. It will be our retreat, somewhere completely private, where my family and I can enjoy life without the paparazzi trying to take pictures of us all the time. It had got to the stage where I didn't even feel I could take Junior to ride his pony any more around the last house because we would be photographed.

The new house is much smaller than my one in Woldingham but it is set in 52 acres, and to me that land is more important than the size of the house. I'm moving all my horses there and we're going to build a gym and a swimming pool. It will be a much more relaxed way of life for the children; they can play outside on their bikes, and ride their ponies, and we won't have to worry that anyone can take a photo of them there.

Lately I have felt so hounded, that I can't escape being photographed wherever I go, that I've reached the point now where I hate the paparazzi. To me they are nothing but scum. They proved it yet again on the day of our blessing ceremony and they prove it every time they follow me when I drive anywhere. They play this cat and mouse game with me where one of their cars will go in front of me and one will go behind, so I am stuck in the middle. It is unbelievably dangerous. I have told the police more than once about what the paps do, but they haven't done anything about it so far. I keep saying that if I die in a car crash because of this, the police will be to blame for not helping me. I know that sounds extreme, but it's how I feel.

I am looking forward to finalising the divorce settlement with Pete – it seems to have dragged on a very long time. I still feel I need to see him and talk about why we broke up. It sounds crazy but it's been well over a year since we split up and I've only seen him twice, once when I dropped the children off and once when Harvey was in hospital. We've never discussed the argument that led to him walking out and it feels like unfinished business in my head. I would like to be able to put my side across then close that chapter, though I also know that nothing is going to change. But Pete was once my best friend as well as my husband, and to find myself in a situation where we weren't even talking was a huge shock to me. I advise all women, however happy their marriage seems and however much in love they are, to be on their guard because they never know what could happen next.

Looking back, I do regret making my relationship with Pete so public. With us it seemed that work took over and our marriage became a business relationship, which was not what I wanted. Though Pete and I were in love and similar in so many ways, I think we cut ourselves off from other people too much. It was hard on me not being able to socialise because of Pete's problem with me having a drink when we went out. Basically I don't think any couple should be together 24/7.

I would like to be friends again with Pete but he seems to be surrounded by people who would be dead set against that. Some of them have sold hurtful stories about me, including my former best friend, and I couldn't associate with anyone who had gone out of their way to hurt me.

This last year since I split with Pete has been tough. My children, my family, Alex and my friends have all helped me through what has been one of the worst times of my life. It has been a year in which I've been battered by the press, misjudged and lied about. I always bear in mind the saying that you cannot judge a book by its cover, and I've certainly never said that I am perfect. I'm not trying to be. I'm just trying to live my life, to be a good mum and a good wife, to enjoy myself. And I definitely want to have more children and get back on track to a place where I'm happy with my work.

Alex has been there through thick and thin with me, which makes me love him all the more and want to be there for him too. When the media turned on me and such cruel lies were being written about me, he stuck by me and helped me through. Alex accepts me for who I am. He's like my knight in shining armour. He has made me realise what's truly important in life. He's so grounded. Fame doesn't faze him at all, and in our relationship it's not about which of us is the most famous. Our jobs don't mean anything compared to the way we connect, our chemistry and the strong bond between us. Fame doesn't last forever anyway. If I stop being famous it won't matter because I'll still have my children and a husband who loves me. Hopefully, everything's in place for Alex and me to have our happy ever after . . .

And I've said this in my last two books so I'll say it again: never underestimate the Pricey! (Oops, it should be Reidy! I'll get my wrists slapped.) You only live once. And I intend to make the most of every minute.

Angel

Katie Price

A sparkling and sexy tale of glamour modelling, romance and the treacherous promises of fame.

When Angel is discovered by a model agent, her life changes for ever. Young, beautiful and sexy, she seems destined for a successful career and, very quickly, the glitzy world of celebrity fame and riches becomes her new home.

But then she meets Mickey, the lead singer of a boy band, who is as irresistible as he is dangerous, and Angel realises that a rising star can just as quickly fall . . .

'The perfect sexy summer read' *heat*

'A page-turner . . . it is brilliant. Genuinely amusing and readable. This summer, every beach will be polka-dotted with its neon pink covers' *Evening Standard*

'The perfect post-modern fairy tale' *Glamour*

arrow books

Angel Uncovered

By Katie Price

Angel Summer looks as if she has found her happy ever after. She's married to the love of her life, sexy footballer Cal, they have a beautiful baby girl and Angel is Britain's top glamour model. But all is not as it seems and there is heartache in store.

When Cal is transferred to AC Milan, Angel feels isolated being so far away from her family and friends instead of embracing the WAG lifestyle of designer shopping and pampering. Surrounded by beautiful people, will Angel and Cal pull together or will they turn elsewhere to seek comfort? Angel's worst nightmares come to life when an old flame of Cal's comes back on the scene and suddenly Angel is fighting to save her marriage, and herself . . .

'Glam, glitz, gorgeous people . . . so Jordan!' *Woman*

'A real insight into the celebrity world' *OK!*

'Brilliantly bitchy' *New!*

arrow books

Paradise

Katie Price

It's six months since beautiful model Angel Summer found herself having to choose between a life with Ethan Turner, the laid-back Californian baseball player, or giving her marriage to football star Cal Bailey another go. Her friends and family were stunned when she picked Ethan, but it looks like Angel made the right decision: Ethan loves her and she loves him.

But nothing is perfect. Ethan has secrets in his past that could threaten their relationship and when he faces financial ruin the couple are forced to star in a reality TV show about their life together. Despite everything, though, Angel is convinced that Ethan is the man for her. So why can't she stop thinking about Cal?

As the tabloids have always been quick to point out, the path of true love has never run smoothly for our sexy celebrity, and when her dad falls dangerously ill Angel rushes back to England to be by his bedside, throwing her and Cal back together. But Ethan loves her, Cal has a girlfriend, and Angel has made her choice. It's too late to go back now . . . isn't it?

'A fabulous guilty holiday pleasure' *Heat*

'Peppered with cutting asides and a directness you can only imagine coming from Katie Price, it's a fun, blisteringly paced yet fluffy novel.' *Cosmopolitan*

arrow books